A Commentary on the Charter of the United Nations

First published in 1950, *A Commentary on the Charter of the United Nations* presents a collection of documentary material detailing various aspects of the UN Charter. It discusses themes like the evolution of the Charter; purposes and principles; Pacific settlements of disputes; the General Assembly; the Security Council; International Economic and Social Co-Operation; the Economic and Social Council; the International Court of Justice; transitional security arrangements etc. to show how, during the first three years of the existence the organs of the United Nations have applied and interpreted the provisions of the Charter. This is an important historical reference work for scholars and researchers of international law, international relations and international politics and diplomacy.

A Commentary on the Charter of the United Nations

Norman Bentwich and Andrew Martin

Routledge
Taylor & Francis Group

First published in 1950
by Routledge & Kegan Paul Ltd.

This edition first published in 2024 by Routledge
4 Park Square, Milton Park, Abingdon, Oxon, OX14 4RN

and by Routledge
605 Third Avenue, New York, NY 10017

Routledge is an imprint of the Taylor & Francis Group, an informa business

© Norman Bentwich and Andrew Martin, 1950

Publisher's Note
The publisher has gone to great lengths to ensure the quality of this reprint but points out that some imperfections in the original copies may be apparent.

Disclaimer
The publisher has made every effort to trace copyright holders and welcomes correspondence from those they have been unable to contact.

A Library of Congress record exists under LCCN:

ISBN: 978-1-032-76165-7 (hbk)
ISBN: 978-1-003-47735-8 (ebk)
ISBN: 978-1-032-76167-1 (pbk)

Book DOI 10.4324/9781003477358

A Commentary on the

CHARTER

OF THE

UNITED NATIONS

by

NORMAN BENTWICH, LL.D. (Hon.)

barrister-at-law

and

ANDREW MARTIN, Ph.D.

barrister-at-law

LONDON

ROUTLEDGE & KEGAN PAUL LTD.

BROADWAY HOUSE: 66-74 CARTER LANE EC4

First Published 1950

PRINTED IN GREAT BRITAIN BY
KNIGHT & FORSTER, LTD.
LEEDS

CONTENTS

CHAPTER

COMMENTARY ON ARTICLES :

CONTENTS

PREFACE

It is a primary condition of the establishment of peace, law and order between States that the individual citizen should understand the organization of the international community and gain some sense of world-citizenship. This consideration has been uppermost in our minds when writing this short Commentary on the Charter of the United Nations. It addresses itself not to the specialist in international law but, in the first place, to the general public interested in international affairs which, in newspaper reports of the proceedings of the United Nations, is constantly faced with references to Articles of the Charter. At the same time, we have tried to meet the needs of university students of International Law and International Relations and of members of adult educational classes in Current Affairs. Finally, we have borne in mind the requirements of the many delegates, civil servants and experts who attend the General Assembly of the United Nations and the manifold conferences of its different organs and specialized agencies.

The understanding of the Charter requires some knowledge of the fundamental institutions and principles of international law. We have written on the assumption that not all our readers would have that knowledge ; and wherever necessary, have included in the Commentary a brief explanation of technical terms. On the other hand, considerations of space have made it imperative to restrict to a minimum references to official documents and to the literature of the subject. Where we say that a point is controversial, the reader must take our word for it.

Throughout the Commentary we have tried to show how, during the first three years of their existence, the organs of the United Nations have applied and interpreted the provisions of the Charter. To that extent we have abandoned the canon of legal science that, at the early stages of the practical application of a constitution, a commentary should be based exclusively on the text of the instrument and on the *travaux préparatoires*. We have set ourselves the objective of showing, not how the Charter ought to be interpreted by strictly legal standards, but how it is being applied in actual practice. In other words, we have considered the Charter as the constitution of a living organism and the basis of a constant and manifold activity.

A commentary should be objective ; nevertheless, we have not concealed our dissatisfaction with certain features of the Charter and disappointment at the relative political failure of the United Nations during its early career. The first treatises on the subject tended to be too hopeful ; and to see nothing but progress from the Covenant of the League. Since then the high hopes which were formed at San Francisco have given place to considerable disappointment. What was to be an instrument of world peace has proved to be a forum of world conflict. The General Assembly as well as the Security Council has been freely used not to solve disputes, but to stimulate and exacerbate them. It would be foolish to suggest that the gradual division of the United Nations into two *blocs* engaged in a cold war should, or could, be ascribed to defects in the Charter. At the same time, it is clear that the unfortunate voting procedure prescribed for the Security Council has greatly contributed to preventing this most important organ of the United Nations from serving as an effective instrument of conciliation in major disputes ; and that, by leaving the precise definition of the Member States' military obligations to separate agreements (none of which has in fact been concluded), the Charter has created an illusory system of collective security. The result has been, inevitably, a widening gap between what the Organization was meant to achieve and what it can be expected to achieve in the foreseeable future.

In the collection of documentary material we have had valuable help from Mrs. Joan Brown and Miss Barbara Keeley, Reference Librarians of the United Nations Information Centre in London ; and we are much indebted to Miss Antonia Gerard and Mrs. Anna Martin for their generous and competent secretarial assistance.

London, May 1949   NORMAN BENTWICH
                                ANDREW MARTIN

THE EVOLUTION OF THE CHARTER

The succession from the League of Nations. One of the major tasks of the peace-making at the end of the First World War was to devise a permanent form for the habit of using international conferences as a means of settling disputes between States and organizing inter-State co-operation. That habit had been steadily gaining ground since the end of the Napoleonic wars ; but only one serious attempt had been made to create permanent machinery for the peaceful solution of conflicts. Before the Hague Conferences of 1899 and 1907, the movement for the judicial settlement of inter-State disputes had advanced by single instances and bilateral treaties. By setting up a Permanent Court of Arbitration, the Hague Conventions demonstrated both the feasibility and the desirability of standing institutions for the elimination of war.

The architects of the peace settlement of 1919 set out to supplement the existing judicial organization by " a general association of nations under specific covenants for the purpose of affording mutual guarantees of political and territorial integrity to great and small States alike ". There was no question of setting up any form of supra-national government or, indeed, of seriously limiting the sovereignty of national States. The League of Nations was to be, essentially, a continuously functioning international conference with an annual Assembly of Government representatives, a Council holding periodic meetings, and a permanent Secretariat.

During the first ten years of its activity, from 1920 to 1930, the League realized some of the hopes of its founders. Although from the beginning it suffered from a fatal weakness owing to the non-adherence of the United States and the exclusion of the Soviet Union, which was feared as a subversive power, it served to maintain general peace. Particularly during the period 1924-1930, disputes were referred to it from many quarters of the world and settled by methods of conciliation. The system of mandates functioned satisfactorily. Post-war financial reconstruction was greatly speeded up by loans issued under the auspices of the League. Efficient organizations were built up for the abolition of slavery, the control of traffic in dangerous drugs and the traffic

A*

in women, for the protection of children, the relief and settlement of refugees, and the study of health and disease in their international aspects.

The second decade of the League's history was a period of steady decline and disillusion. In the 1930's, the Organization had to meet a double challenge, and it failed doubly. In 1931, Japan, a permanent member of the Council, embarked on a war of aggression against China, a Member of the League, and prosecuted the campaign in defiance of both the Council and the Assembly. In the same year, the economic slump, which had started in 1929, reached the proportions of a world-wide economic crisis ; and, although it was clear that only a combined effort could avert catastrophe, the Members of the League, instead of creating a mechanism of co-operation, resorted to a mechanism of commercial warfare. The World Economic Conference which was convened in London in 1933 was a complete futility.

There followed a series of direct blows against the system of collective security. First, in 1933, Germany withdrew from the Disarmament Conference and gave notice of withdrawal from the League. In 1935, Italy started on a wanton aggression against Ethiopia, a Member of the League, and was met by a half-hearted application of economic sanctions, which were calculated to cause enough inconvenience to rouse the passions of the Italian people, but not enough economic pressure to be effective against aggression. In 1936, Germany re-occupied the Rhineland in defiance of the Versailles Treaty and the Locarno Pact. In the same year, Italy and Germany together intervened to help the Fascists in the Spanish Civil War ; and all the League could do was to make verbal protests. There followed, in 1938, the forcible incorporation of Austria in the German Reich ; and in March 1939, the German occupation of Czechoslovakia. In the face of these portents of an approaching general war, the League as an organization proved to be wholly impotent. During the fateful summer of 1939, not a single country called for a meeting of the League Council or the Assembly, either before or after the invasion of Poland by the German armies.

The second World War began just twenty-five years after the outbreak of the first. The League of Nations was not dissolved, but it was an empty shell. It was a bitter irony that the Assembly, which met in December 1939, had to vote, because of the aggression on Finland, for the expulsion of the Soviet Union which had been admitted only five years before. The memory of that expulsion has remained a factor in Russia's international relations and in her attitude to the new world order of the United Nations.

The utter failure of the League to avert a new world war has given rise to a notion that the legal organization of the international community collapsed altogether at the outbreak of hostilities in September 1939. Constitutionally, that view is unfounded. The war did not destroy the legal existence of the League ; the Covenant continued in force until the formal winding-up of the organization by a resolution passed at its last Assembly in April, 1946. The political functions of the League ceased with the expulsion of the U.S.S.R. in December, 1939. But though the Assembly and the Council were not convened for the rest of the war, under emergency resolutions passed by the 1939 Assembly, the Secretary-General, acting under the authority of the Supervisory Commission (the League's permanent financial organ), was invested with powers sufficient to maintain not only the legal framework of the organization, but, at a reduced scale and in a decentralized form, some of its non-political functions. Economic and financial research, particularly into the problems of post-war reconstruction, and the work of the Health Section and the Opium Section of the Secretariat continued. The International Labour Organization established temporary headquarters at Montreal, Canada, and continued its activities throughout the war. The third principal organization of the League system, the Permanent Court of International Justice at The Hague, also continued in being.

Thus the nucleus, and with it the idea, of a world organization survived the catastrophe of 1939 ; and at no time during the war was the re-establishment of a general political organization of States seriously in doubt. As the war progressed, however, it became more and more certain that the resuscitation of the League would be firmly opposed by the U.S.S.R., which was not prepared to rejoin an organization from whose ranks it had once been expelled ; and that it would find little support in the U.S.A. By 1943, the Great Powers among the Allies were agreed that these political considerations, and the hardly less important psychological factor, that any post-war world organization had better be dissociated from the memories of the League's political failure, required a new departure.

The Moscow Declaration. On October 30, 1943, the Governments of the United States of America, the United Kingdom, the Soviet

Union and China issued from Moscow a " Declaration of Four Nations on General Security ". In Article 4, they stated

" That they recognize the necessity of establishing at the earliest practicable date a general international organization based on the principle of the sovereign equality of all peace-loving States, and open to membership by all such States, large and small, for the maintenance of international peace and security."

This Article — the first among the war-time statements of policy directly referring to the post-war organization of the international community — affirmed three important principles :

(1) The general organization of States was to be newly established. The idea of reviving the League in its original or in an amended form was discarded.

(2) The organisation was to be based on the principle of the sovereign equality of its Members. The proposals, widely canvassed during the war, for a more organic association of States on a federal basis were not to be implemented. The political atmosphere made it unlikely that, at the end of hostilities, the Allies would be more ready than they had been in 1919, to accept serious inroads on their national sovereignty.

(3) The organization was to be open to all peace-loving States, large and small, regardless of their participation in the wartime coalition against the Axis Powers.

Of the purposes of the new international organization, Article 4 of the Declaration mentioned only the maintenance of international peace and security. Article 7 of the Declaration referred to another objective :

" They (the Four Powers) will confer and co-operate with one another and with other Members of the United Nations to bring about a practicable general agreement with respect to the regulation of armaments in the post-war period."

This statement should be read in conjunction with a passage in the Preamble to the Declaration, which spoke of the necessity of maintaining international peace and security " with the least diversion of the world's human and economic resources for armaments ". That phrase, which was eventually embodied in Article 26 of the Charter, indicated an approach to the problem of disarmament fundamentally different from the ideas of 1919. In Article 8 of the Covenant, the members of the League recorded their conviction that the reduction of national armaments was an essential guarantee of the maintenance of peace, and that the private manufacture of armaments was open to grave objections.

In the Moscow Declaration, the emphasis lay on the economic wastage involved in competitive armaments, not on their threat to the peace of the world ; and no stand was taken against the continuation of a system in which the manufacture of armaments is left to private enterprise.

The Declaration by United Nations. Article 7 of the Moscow Declaration referred expressly to " Members of the United Nations " ; and the Preamble of the Declaration reaffirmed the determination of the signatories to prosecute the war until the unconditional surrender of the enemy, " in accordance with the Declaration by United Nations of January 1, 1942". This document is linked with the Charter not only historically, but organically by Article 3 of the Charter ; all States which had signed the Declaration became eligible for original membership in the United Nations Organization.

The Declaration by United Nations was first signed in Washington on January 1, 1942, by the representatives of 26 belligerents; 21 more nations adhered to it between June 5, 1942 and March 1, 1945. In the operative part of the document the signatories pledged themselves fully to employ their military and economic resources, in co-operation with each other, for the prosecution of the war and not to make a separate armistice or peace with the enemies. These provisions were, by their nature, irrelevant to the formulation of the Charter. But in the Preamble to the Declaration, the United Nations declared, first, that they supported the "common programme of purposes and principles" embodied in the Atlantic Charter ; and, secondly, that complete victory was essential " to defend life, liberty, independence and religious freedom and to preserve human rights and justice in their own lands as well as in other lands ". That was the first occasion on which the international protection of human rights, which in 1945 came to be enshrined in several Articles of the Charter, was stated to be among the specific peace-aims of the Allies.

The Atlantic Charter. The " common programme of purposes and principles ", to which the Declaration referred, had been embodied in a " Joint Declaration of the President of the United States of America and the Prime Minister of the United Kingdom ", signed on August 14, 1941, and known as the Atlantic Charter.

It consisted of a set of eight principles. Five were relevant to the peace settlement rather than to the constitution of the United Nations. They were concerned with (*a*) the renunciation by all belligerents of any claim to territorial or other aggrandizement ; (*b*) a territorial settlement in accordance with the freely expressed wishes of peoples ; (*c*) the right of all peoples to choose their form of government ; (*d*) the access of all States, on equal terms, to trade and to the raw materials of the world ; and (*e*) the freedom of the high seas.

The remaining three principles, on the other hand, had a strong formative influence on the San Francisco Charter. The " hope to see established a peace which will afford to all nations the means of dwelling in safety within their own boundaries " was sought to be fulfilled in Chapter VII of the Charter, which is designed to lay the foundations of a more effective system of collective security than that of the League. The belief that " all the nations of the world, for realistic as well as spiritual reasons, must come to the abandonment of the use of force " has become the keynote of Chapter VI, and generally, of all those provisions in the Charter dealing with the pacific settlement of disputes. Finally, the desire " to bring about the fullest collaboration between all nations in the economic field, with the object of securing for all improved labour standards, economic adjustment and social security ", has found ample expression in Chapters IX and X, which set out to organize the economic and social co-operation of the United Nations on a wider plane and in greater detail than the Covenant of the League had attempted.

The Dumbarton Oaks Proposals. Through the Moscow Declaration of October 1943, which linked the Atlantic Charter and the Declaration by United Nations with the proposals for the establishment of a new general international organization, the four principal Allies assumed responsibility for the elaboration of a constitutional plan. By the late summer of 1944, the Foreign Offices of the four Governments had completed their preliminary studies and were ready for exploratory conversations. These were held at Dumbarton Oaks, near Washington, in two phases : from August 21 to September 28, 1944, between the representatives of the United States, the United Kingdom and the Soviet Union ; and from September 29 to October 7, 1944, between the United States, the United Kingdom and China. The agreements were embodied in a document entitled " Proposals for the Establishment of a General International Organization ". With the exception of the voting procedure in the Security Council, on which the conversations yielded no agreement, these Proposals covered all subjects which the four delegations then considered to be the essential contents of a constitution for a new world organization. But the language was not, technically, the language of an international treaty. Obligations and functions were merely suggested, not formulated ; and on many points e.g. the qualifications for membership only the basic ideas were laid down, without details.

The organizational plan was, in its outlines, similar to that of the League. The action of the new organization was to be effected, as before, through an Assembly and a Council. The latter was to be called " Security Council ", to distinguish it from a second council, at that time envisaged as a subsidiary organ of the Assembly, which was to take charge of economic and social affairs. The idea of splitting up the work of what, in the system of the League, had been a single Council, was not new ; a reform of this kind had been strongly urged in 1939 by the Bruce Committee of the League.

In addition to the General Assembly and the Security Council, the Organization was to have two principal organs : the Secretariat (which had ranked as a subsidiary organ in the hierarchy of the League) and an International Court of Justice. The Proposals did not specify whether this Court was to be the continuation of the already existing Permanent Court of International Justice at The Hague (closely related to, but not constitutionally an organ of, the League) or a new judicial body.

Under the Covenant, the Assembly and the Council of the League were each competent to deal with any matter within the sphere of action of the Organization. Constitutionally, there was no delimitation of functions. The Dumbarton Oaks Proposals advocated a radical change. The Security Council was to carry " primary responsibility " for the maintenance of peace and security ; and the functions of the General Assembly were, in that sphere, to be reduced to discussion and, within certain limits, to recommendations.

With regard to the new Assembly, another important departure from precedent was suggested. In the League, the Assembly had to decide by unanimous vote, except in procedural matters. Legally, the risk of the action of the Assembly being vetoed by a single dissentient member was ever-present ; in practice, it had been considerably reduced by procedural rules and understandings. At Dumbarton Oaks it seemed advisable to banish the risk once and for all ; and the Proposals were drafted on the basis that unanimity would not be required on any occasion, and that, apart from certain important questions to be decided by a qualified majority, the General Assembly would proceed by simple majority vote.

The proposals for the composition of the Security Council were modelled on the Covenant to the extent that they affirmed the right of the Great Powers to permanent representation. But while the total number of seats on the Council of the League was variable—with the approval of the majority of the Assembly, the Council had power to create additional permanent and elective seats — it was now suggested that there should be a fixed total of eleven members, of whom six were to be elected by the General Assembly.

These departures from the League model were of secondary importance compared with the proposed definition of the Security Council's powers in the matter of sanctions. The Council of the League never possessed the right to compel Member States to take enforcement action. It could recommend them to do so, but without prejudice to the ultimate discretion of Members to decide whether a case for sanctions had arisen. If it did arise, they were under a direct and immediate obligation to each other, but not to the League as such, to apply economic sanctions; they were not, however, under any circumstances obliged actively to join in military operations. Under the Dumbarton Oaks Proposals, the right to determine the existence of an imminent or actual act of aggression was to be withdrawn from the Members and to be vested in the Security Council. It was for the Council to determine whether and when, and in what order, economic, diplomatic and military sanctions should be taken. Members were to be required to join in these sanctions in the manner and to the extent decided, and not merely recommended, by the Council. Moreover, in the case of military sanctions, the armed forces contributed by Members were to act under the strategic direction of the Council and its own Military Staff Committee.

These provisions involved a radical change in the status of Members and of the Organization itself. Nominally, Members were to retain their full sovereignty. Constitutionally, the Security Council was not a supra-national authority, only an agent acting for and on behalf of sovereign States. But the incidents of this particular relationship between principals and agent were so formulated as to amount to a delegation of authority, irrevocable for the duration of the Organization, and involving a duty for the principals to give effect to the decisions of the agent in all matters relating to sanctions.

This new conception of the relationship between sovereign States and the executive organ of a public international organization went to the root of the legal character of the Organization itself. The League, no organ of which wielded compulsory powers over Member States, could be properly classified as an " association " of sovereign units. But the new world organization conceived at Dumbarton Oaks did not conform with this or any other previous type of inter-State relationship. The United Nations is more " organic " than an association of States, but less organic than a composite State. The absence of legislative powers in the General Assembly and the tacit admission of the right of withdrawal suggest an analogy with confederations. But the analogy is far from being complete. The Security Council has compulsory powers which are not unlike the powers of a federal government in the field of defence ; and in the matter of the protection of human rights, the right of petition by individuals and groups, which is inherent in the Charter, establishes a close parallel to that direct relationship between federal organs and the nationals of component States which is an essential characteristic of federal constitutions.

The primary concern of the Proposals was with matters of peace and security. The responsibilities of Members and of the Security Council with regard to the pacific settlement of disputes and to sanctions were defined in considerable detail. Economic and social co-operation, on the other hand, was treated with conspicuous brevity. Apart from providing a separate Council to direct this co-operation, the Proposals followed the conception of the Covenant. They were drafted on the assumption that considerations of efficiency militated against excessive centralization. The new organization was not to absorb the specialized agencies which were already in operation, or about to be established ; it was to co-ordinate their activities and prevent overlapping efforts.

The system of mandates maintained by the League was not mentioned in the Proposals. Although its continuation, in a modified form, had been considered at Dumbarton Oaks, no final agreement could be reached in time for its inclusion in the document.

The Chinese Proposals. In the second phase of the Dumbarton Oaks conversations the Chinese Government put forward certain suggestions which were approved by the United Kingdom and the United States, but, pending their formal acceptance by the

Government of the U.S.S.R., could not be included in the published text of the Proposals.

These suggestions were concerned with (1) a clear expression in the Charter of the principle that, in discharging its responsibilities for the pacific settlement of disputes, the Organization should act with due regard for justice and international law and not merely in furtherance of what may seem politically expedient ; (2) the inclusion among the responsibilities of the Assembly of the development and codification of international law ; and (3) the extension of the activities of the Economic and Social Council to the field of educational and other forms of cultural co-operation.

In due course, the Government of the U.S.S.R. agreed to join in sponsoring these proposals ; and at San Francisco, they were included in the final text of the Charter.

The Yalta Agreement. A conference held in February 1945 at Yalta in the Crimea, between Mr. Churchill, President Roosevelt and Marshal Stalin, made further important contributions to the development of the Charter.

In the first place, it was able to resolve the difficulty encountered at Dumbarton Oaks in reaching agreement on the voting procedure in the Security Council. The formula (Article 27 in the final text of the Charter) provided that, apart from procedural matters, which were to be decided by any seven votes out of a total of eleven, all decisions of the Security Council required the affirmative vote of seven members, including the concurring votes of the five permanent members. But a member who was a party to a dispute was to abstain from voting on motions concerned with the peaceful settlement of that dispute.

Secondly, the Charter of the new world organization was to include provisions for the administration, under international supervision, of (a) the existing mandates of the League of Nations, (b) territories to be detached from the Axis Powers, and (c) any other territory that might voluntarily be placed under trusteeship.

Finally, a " Conference of United Nations " was to be called at San Francisco on April 25, 1945, to prepare the Charter of the new world organization along the lines of the Dumbarton Oaks Proposals. The Governments qualifying for invitation were those which had declared war on Germany or Japan by March 1, 1945, and had signed the Declaration by United Nations.

The invitations were issued on March 5, 1945 by the Government of the United States, on behalf of itself and the three other sponsors of the Conference, i.e. the Governments of the United Kingdom, the U.S.S.R. and China. France, who had not taken part in the conversations at Dumbarton Oaks, agreed to attend the Conference, but declined to act as a sponsor.

Preliminary Conferences. Immediately after the publication of the Dumbarton Oaks Proposals, the British and United States Governments issued explanatory commentaries ; and, throughout the Allied countries, great efforts were made by the written and spoken word to make the Proposals known to the mass of the people.

The world-wide discussion of the Proposals received a fresh impetus from the publication of the voting formula agreed upon at Yalta, and from the invitation extended to all Governments participating in the San Francisco Conference to state their views and comments in advance, if they so wished.

Apart from the preparations of individual Governments, groups of States arranged collective discussions both before and after receiving formal invitations to San Francisco. An Inter-American Conference on Problems of War and Peace met in Mexico City from February 21 to March 8, and placed on record (1) the claim of Latin America to adequate representation on the Security Council, (2) the desirability of solving inter-American disputes by regional methods, (3) the need for creating an international agency to promote intellectual and moral co-operation among nations, and (4) the support of Latin America for the principle of universality as an ideal towards which the new world organization should tend.

Talks were held in London, in April 1945, between representatives of Australia, Canada, India, New Zealand, the Union of South Africa and the United Kingdom, and resulted in the British Commonwealth accepting the Dumbarton Oaks Proposals as the basis of the United Nations Charter. But the final communiqué emphasized that in certain respects the Proposals required " clarification, improvement and expansion ".

A Committee of Jurists, representative of 44 Governments, met at Washington, from April 9 to 20, 1945, at the invitation of the United States Government, which was acting also for the other sponsoring Governments. The purpose of the meeting was the drafting of recommendations for the Statute of the principal judicial organ of the United Nations.

Without pronouncing on the preliminary question whether this judicial organ should be a continuation of the Permanent Court at The Hague or a new tribunal, the Committee addressed itself to the task of producing a draft Statute suitable for adoption either as an amended constitution for the old Court or as the constitution of a new Court. The result was a document which — apart from the textual adaptations required by the replacement of the League by the United Nations and from provisions, altogether lacking in the old Statute, for constitutional amendments — was identical with the old Statute. It included, however, alternative texts on two important subjects. The first concerned the nomination of judges, and offered to the San Francisco Conference a choice between retaining the old system of nomination by the national groups in the Permanent Court of Arbitration, and a new system of nomination directly by Governments. The second alternative text dealt with the vital question whether the jurisdiction of the Court should continue to be optional or should be obligatory. Eventually, the San Francisco Conference rejected both of the proposed changes.

The Dumbarton Oaks Proposals contained no provision for the enforcement of the Court's judgments. The Committee strongly urged the filling of this gap : and its recommendations led to the incorporation, in Article 94(2) of the Charter, of a clause investing the Security Council with a wider and more specific authority than the League Council had enjoyed, for giving effect to the judgments of the Court.

The San Francisco Conference. The Conference assembled at San Francisco on April 25, 1945. Of the 47 signatories of the Declaration by United Nations, 46 were represented at the inaugural session. Poland, pending the recognition of her Provisional Government by the Western Allies, had not been invited, but provision was made for her to sign the Charter at a later date, as an original Member. On April 30, the Conference approved the admission of Argentina, the Byelorussian S.S.R. and the Ukrainian S.S.R. ; and on June 5, the admission of Denmark which had just been liberated.

At a meeting of the Heads of Delegations it was agreed that the material to be considered by the Conference should be
" the Dumbarton Oaks Proposals, as supplemented by the Crimea Conference, and by the Chinese proposals agreed to by the sponsoring Governments, and the comments thereon submitted by the participating countries ".

The work of the Conference was divided among (*a*) four General Committees (Steering, Executive, Co-ordination and Credentials) ; (*b*) four Commissions to deal, respectively, with General Provisions, the General Assembly, the Security Council, and Judicial

Organization ; (c) twelve Technical Committees, set up within the Commissions, for the detailed examination of the chapters assigned to them.

The work of the Technical Committees extended over a period of six weeks and involved the study of an immense volume of documents. Their recommendations were submitted (1) for approval, to the appropriate Commissions, and (2) for textual revision, to the Co-ordination Committee assisted by an Advisory Committee of Jurists. The comprehensive draft was then approved, first, by the Steering Committee and, on June 25, by the Conference in plenary session. On the following day, the Charter was signed by the delegates of 50 nations. The modifications which the Dumbarton Oaks Proposals underwent, in the course of the Conference, fall under two headings : changes and additions.

(A) *Changes.* Without altering the essential character of the organization contemplated in the Proposals, the Conference re-arranged the text in nineteen Chapters instead of the original twelve, substituted comparatively short Articles for the longer Sections of the original draft and removed many obscurities. The Purposes and Principles of the Organization were textually amplified, partly to make room for those considerations of " justice and international law " which had been stressed in the Chinese proposals, and partly to introduce the principle of non-intervention in domestic affairs, in a wide formulation which was advocated by many delegations, in particular the Australian. The qualifications for membership, left open in the Proposals, were strictly defined. In the organizational structure, the Economic and Social Council was raised to the rank of a principal organ, and a Trusteeship Council was added. The functions of the General Assembly were extended to cover all matters affecting the peace of the world or the general welfare of nations, and a specific duty was laid upon the Assembly to assist in the attainment of human rights and fundamental freedoms. Special qualifications were laid down for election to non-permanent seats in the Security Council, and the Council's jurisdiction in the pacific settlement of disputes was extended so as to cover disputes voluntarily submitted to it by the parties, even in cases where international peace and security are not endangered. To the authority of the Council to suppress acts of aggression, the important power was added to apply preventive measures ; at the same time, the inherent right of Member States to take individual or collective measures of self-defence was recognized. The purposes of the Organization in the economic and social field were re-defined and amplified ; health and the promotion of educational and cultural co-operation were specifically included. The Economic and Social Council was given a free hand to set up Commissions; it was authorized to make recommendations not only to the General Assembly and the specialized agencies, but also direct to Member Governments ; and it was given power to arrange consultations with non-governmental organizations.

In the Chapter dealing with the International Court of Justice, it was made clear that Members were not precluded from referring their disputes to other tribunals. The right to request the Court for advisory opinions was granted, in addition to the Security Council, to the General Assembly and to such other organs and specialized agencies as the Assembly may authorize to do so. To the Chapter on the Secretariat Articles were added to stress and safeguard its character of an International Civil Service immune from the influence of national Governments. Finally, the procedure laid down in the Proposals for the amendment of the Charter was completed by provisions for a General Conference to review the Charter as a whole.

(B) *Additions.* The most thorny question on the agenda of the Conference was the voting formula for the Security Council which had emerged from the Three-Power meeting at Yalta. The smaller Powers apprehended, as events have shown with good reason, that if one of the Big Five, or one of their protégés, menaced the peace, the Security Council would be powerless to act ; and they therefore struggled to reduce the right of veto. But the Great Powers held out on this vital provision, and sought to justify it on the ground that they were to carry the main burden of maintaining world peace. The war was still being waged ; and the wartime alliance still kept the Powers together, though there were already serious, but unrevealed, rifts between them.

In addition to embodying in the Charter the voting formula agreed at Yalta, the Conference added three new Chapters on non-self-governing territories. Chapter XI has been described as " the first comprehensive statement of colonial policy to be included in an international instrument " ; its formulation and inclusion were due largely to the initiative of the United Kingdom and Australia. Chapter XII established an international trusteeship system for the administration of the three categories of territories mentioned in the Yalta decisions. The functions of the Organization in relation to these territories were assigned partly to the Security Council and partly to a Trusteeship Council, whose composition and powers were described in detail in Chapter XIII.

The Dumbarton Oaks Proposals provided that the Statute of the International Court " should be annexed to and be part of the Charter ". The Conference considered the draft submitted by the Committee of Jurists and approved the final text of the Statute.

Finally, the Conference added four Articles, grouped together as Chapter XIV under the heading of " Miscellaneous Provisions". The two Articles dealing with (a) the compulsory registration and publication of international treaties, and (b) the resolution of conflicts between obligations under the Charter and obligations under other instruments, had precedents in the Covenant of the League. The other two, which provide for the legal capacity of the Organization and for privileges and immunities, were designed to prevent the repetition of legal difficulties which the League had encountered because of the absence of provisions in the Covenant. *Ratification.* The Charter came into force on October 24, 1945, when the number of ratifications deposited with the Government of the United States reached the minimum required by Article 110. In order to bring the Organization into effective operation, it was still necessary, however, to complete certain preparations of a legal-technical character.

The Preparatory Commission. On June 26, 1945, the signatories of the Charter, by an agreement on Interim Arrangements, established a " Preparatory Commission of the United Nations " for the purpose of making provisional arrangements for the first sessions of the General Assembly and the three Councils ; for the establishment of the Secretariat ; and for the convening of the International Court of Justice. The Commission was to consist of one representative of each Member Government ; and its functions were to be exercised, between sessions, by an Executive Committee of 14 members. The Preparatory Commission held its first session on June 27, 1945, at San Francisco and agreed that the Executive Committee should carry on the work of the Commission in London.

The Executive Committee met on August 16, 1945, and worked until November 24, when the full Preparatory Commission re-assembled for its second session. By December 23, 1945, the Commission and its eight Technical Committees produced a final Report on the subjects covered by its terms of reference.

The documents drafted by the Commission, which formed the essential contents of the Report, included (1) Provisional Agenda for the first sessions of the General Assembly, the Security Council and the Economic and Social Council, (2) Provisional Rules of Procedure for the General Assembly and the three Councils, (3) recommendations on the committee structure of the General Assembly and the organization of the Economic and Social Council, (4) a Draft Resolution for the General Assembly, calling on the States administering territories under League mandates to take practical steps for placing these territories under trusteeship, (5) recommendations concerning the registration and publication of treaties, (6) recommendations concerning privileges and immunities, including a Draft General Convention and a Draft Treaty with the United States for the location of the Headquarters of the United Nations, (7) Provisional Staff Regulations and Provisional Staff Rules for the Secretariat, (8) Provisional Financial Regulations for the United Nations, (9) recommendations concerning the location of the Headquarters of the United Nations in the United States of America, and (10) Draft Resolutions for the General Assembly concerning the assumption by the United Nations of certain functions, powers and activities of the League of Nations.

Several of these documents, notably the Rules of Procedure, the Staff Regulations, Staff Rules and the Financial Regulations, have proved to be instruments of more than ephemeral value. They interpreted and developed the rudimentary procedural provisions of the Charter and became an integral part of the constitutional framework of the United Nations.

Among the many recommendations of the Preparatory Commission, great political importance attached to the one concerning the permanent headquarters of the Organization. The Palace of the League at Geneva, although destined to become the property of the United Nations and to be used for its purposes, was not to be the home of the new Councils and the Secretariat. The Preparatory Commission recommended, and the First General Assembly decided, that the home of the Organization should be in the United States. That was a token of the passing of the primacy from Europe. In fact, the principal *bloc* of States within the Organization is composed of 22 American nations. Nevertheless, the first part of the First General Assembly, to which fell the task of considering and adopting the recommendations of the Preparatory Commission and setting up the organs provided for in the Charter, was held in London from January 10 to February 14, 1946.

The winding-up of the League. In December 1945, the Preparatory Commission set up a Committee to negotiate with the Supervisory Commission of the League a " Common Plan " for the transfer of the League's assets. This " Common Plan " was, on February 12, 1946, approved by the General Assembly of the United Nations which, at the same time, declared that the Organization was willing to take over from the League the custody of the original signed texts of international agreements deposited with the League Secretariat, and to continue the performance of certain technical functions arising under the instruments in question. Thenceforth, these arrangements only required the formal assent of the League Assembly to become effective. That assent was given in a series of resolutions passed by the last Assembly of the League held at Geneva from April 8 to April 18, 1946 ; and from April 19, 1946, the League of Nations ceased to exist.

There was yet to be determined, however, the extent to which the United Nations was to take over the technical services and non-political functions of the League, other than those concerned with the custody of international agreements or arising under them. Pending a survey of these functions by the Economic and Social Council, the General Assembly decided in February 1946 to continue, provisionally, the work of the following League departments : the Economic, Financial and Transit Department, particularly the research and statistical work ; the Health Section, particularly the epidemiological service : and the Opium Section and the secretariats of the Permanent Central Opium Board and Supervisory Body. Eventually, in December 1946, the General Assembly passed a resolution approving, in general terms, the continuation of the non-political functions and activities previously performed by the League Secretariat and the various committees and commissions of the League, excepting the functions and activities entrusted direct to specialized agencies. This resolution was, however, without prejudice to the right of the General Assembly to decline the assumption of specific, non-routine functions arising under international agreements concluded during the existence of the League.

Instruments complementary to the Charter. Neither the machinery nor the functions of the United Nations are governed exclusively by the provisions of the Charter. It is not a comprehensive code. Its procedural provisions must be read in conjunction with the

Rules of Procedure adopted by the various principal and subsidiary organs, with Staff Regulations, Financial Regulations and many other instruments of a technical character. There is an even greater abundance of international agreements relevant to the functions of the Organization. In the field of security, the part that can be effectively played by the United Nations is determined not only by the rules of the Charter, but by the various international treaties which have brought, and are still bringing, into life regional agencies for security or self-defence, such as the Inter-American system, the Brussels Pact, the North Atlantic Pact, the network of East-European alliances. Again, in the economic and social field, the functions of the Organization are limited, partly by the basic documents of the many specialized agencies and the agreements which these agencies have concluded with the United Nations, partly by regional arrangements, of which the Organization for European Economic Co-operation is an important example. Finally, various political, technical, administrative, arbitral and other functions have been, and are still being, entrusted to the United Nations by bilateral and multilateral treaties, including the Peace Treaties of 1947 with Italy, Roumania, Bulgaria, Hungary and Finland. [1]

Thus, to speak of the Charter as " the Constitution " of the United Nations is a simplification. The reader of the Charter must constantly bear in mind the existence of a host of other instruments, all of which are, in varying degrees, relevant to the functioning of the new world organization. It is equally important that he should remember that, in comparison with the inter-war period, the scope of the international order is now considerably enlarged. The United Nations is a more comprehensive organization than the League; although it does not yet comprise the enemy States of the second World War, it has included from the beginning the Soviet Union, the United States and all the American countries. In the second place, its organs, particularly the Security Council, have been designed to be more continuously in action than the organs of the League. Again, the Organization is directly concerned to assure the fundamental rights of the individual person. Finally, by the creation of many international functional

---

[1] The chief responsibilities of the United Nations under the Peace Treaties are (i) to assure the integrity and independence of the Free Territory of Trieste, (ii) to decide on the final disposal of the former Italian Colonies if the Big Four-Powers are unable to reach an agreed solution, and (iii) to appoint chairmen for the arbitral Commissions having ultimate jurisdiction over disputes concerning the interpretation and execution of the five Peace Treaties.

bodies, the objects of international co-operation have been widely extended.

In the original conception of this new system, the emphasis lay on the central political organization and, consequently, the Charter was regarded as the most important constitutional instrument of the post-war period. That conception rested on the assumption that the unanimity between the Great Powers, which had made the winning of the war possible, would remain a permanent feature of international relations. This assumption has been stultified. Since San Francisco, the historical record has been one of steadily growing estrangement and tension between the Soviet Union and its former allies. This tension has affected, in the first place, the capacity of the United Nations to safeguard international peace. The emphasis has shifted, gradually, from collective security as envisaged in Chapter VII of the Charter, to regional arrangements for security and self-defence, such as the Inter-American system, the East European alliances, the Brussels Pact and the North-Atlantic Treaty. The world is driven to regard pacts between groups of Powers as more important guarantees of security than the Charter itself.

In the economic and social field, the development has been similar, although less marked. The Soviet Union has kept aloof from some of the most important functional organizations, including the International Labour Organization, the Food and Agriculture Organization and the International Trade Organization; and while it would be an exaggeration to say that the functional agencies show, as yet, a tendency to become regional, the hope that they would soon become universal has been disappointed. Moreover, certain fundamental problems of post-war reconstruction, particularly in Western Europe, have had to be solved outside the United Nations system altogether, through group-arrangements such as the Organization for European Economic Co-operation which has been established to administer the Marshall Plan at the receiving end.

Constitutionally, these developments have not yet found expression. The Charter stands as it stood on the day it came into force. Time and again, the need for its amendment has been urged in the General Assembly and elsewhere. These suggestions have been consistently resisted by the Soviet Union and have no chance of being adopted while the struggle between East and West continues. As a result, some of the fundamental provisions of the Charter and, in particular, the Articles dealing with collective security, are out of accord with political realities; although legally binding, they are the goal of future endeavour rather than the landmarks of present achievement.

COMMENTARY ON ARTICLES

PREAMBLE

We, the peoples of the United Nations, determined—
- to save succeeding generations from the scourge of war, which twice in our lifetime has brought untold sorrow to mankind, and
- to reaffirm faith in fundamental human rights, in the dignity and worth of the human person, in the equal rights of men and women and of nations large and small, and
- to establish conditions under which justice and respect for the obligations arising from treaties and other sources of international law can be maintained, and
- to promote social progress and better standards of life in larger freedom,

and for these ends—
- to practise tolerance and live together in peace with one another as good neighbours, and
- to unite our strength to maintain international peace and security, and
- to ensure, by the acceptance of principles and the institution of methods, that armed force shall not be used, save in the common interest, and
- to employ international machinery for the promotion of the economic and social advancement of all peoples,

have resolved to combine our efforts to accomplish these aims.

Accordingly, our respective Governments, through representatives assembled in the city of San Francisco, who have exhibited their full powers found to be in good and due form, have agreed to the present Charter of the United Nations and do hereby establish an international organization to be known as the United Nations.

Purpose of the Preamble. There are no definite rules of international law concerning the form of treaties, but it is usual to preface their operative provisions by a statement of the motives for the conclusion of the treaty. This statement, which normally is followed by the names of the Heads of the contracting States and of their duly authorized representatives, is called the *Preamble*.

The Preamble of the League Covenant summarized in a single paragraph both the fundamental objectives of the League and the means of achieving them. It declared that the purpose of the

1

League was to promote international co-operation and to achieve international peace and security. It went on to state that the means towards these ends were the acceptance of obligations not to resort to war, the prescription of open, just and honourable relations between nations, a firm establishment of the under-standings of international law as the actual rule of conduct among Governments, the maintenance of justice, and a scrupulous respect for all treaty obligations in the dealings of organized peoples with one another.

The Purposes and Principles of the United Nations are set forth in detail in Articles 1 and 2 of the Charter. The Preamble is, in essence, an abridged version of those two articles, cast in more general terms.

It is based on a draft prepared by Field-Marshal Smuts after the British Commonwealth conversations held in London in April 1945. Compared with the Preamble of the League Covenant, its most distinctive feature is the stress laid on the concern of the new Organization not only with the rights of States large and small, but also with the position of the individual, his fundamental freedoms, the equal rights of men and women, and the dignity and worth of the human person.

The Preamble of the Covenant operated with legal concepts : obligations, prescriptions, rules of conduct. The Preamble of the Charter strikes a more political note with its emphasis on tolerance, social progress, better standards of life and larger freedom. Stress is laid on the democratic character of the Organization by the use of the phrase " We the peoples of the United Nations "; while the Preamble of the Covenant still talked in terms of " The High Contracting Parties ". This de-parture from precedent was calculated to satisfy the popular demand that the new Organization should be primarily concerned with the welfare of peoples rather than the formal authority of Governments. But this change in the customary phraseology has no legal relevance. Peoples cannot enter into valid agreements except through their respective Governments ; and the last paragraph of the Preamble does, in fact, recognize that the authority of the Charter derives from the agreement of the Governments represented at San Francisco, and that Govern-ments, and not the peoples, are — in the legal sense — " Members of the United Nations ".

Binding Force. The authorities on international law are divided on the question whether the preamble of an international instrument is as binding on the parties as any other part. But even those who hold that a preamble has not the same effect as the operative provisions of a treaty admit that it constitutes valid evidence, for purposes of interpretation, of the common intention of the parties at the time of making the treaty. For the Charter, the distinction is not in any case of practical importance ; there is nothing in the Preamble that would add to or subtract from the operative provisions of the main text.

Name of the Organization. The title " The United Nations " had been suggested by President Roosevelt and by Field-Marshal Smuts. The suggestion was supported by the British Government on the ground that the name fittingly indicated that the Organization resulted from the common effort of nations which had saved civilization from Fascism, and whose close union would continue in the future. The proposed name did not, however, go unchallenged at San Francisco. Several delegations felt that it might be unwise to perpetuate the title of what was in effect a military coalition formed during the Second World War, and through that title, certain implications of hostility against a group of States. Eventually the title[1] was adopted unanimously, as a tribute to the memory of its first sponsor, President Roosevelt. It has the slight disadvantage that the words " United Nations " now denote both the Organization as such and the nations which are its Members. This leads to considerable confusion in usage, even in official documents.

---

[1] By a resolution of December 7, 1946, the General Assembly recommended that the Members of the United Nations " should take such legislative or other appropriate measures as are necessary to prevent the use, without authorization by the Secretary-General, of the emblem, the official seal and the name of the United Nations ".

CHAPTER I

PURPOSES AND PRINCIPLES

ARTICLE 1

The Purposes of the United Nations are :—

1. To maintain international peace and security, and to that end : to take effective collective measures for the prevention and removal of threats to the peace, and for the suppression of acts of aggression or other breaches of the peace, and to bring about by peaceful means, and in conformity with the principles of justice and international law, adjustment or settlement of international disputes or situations which might lead to a breach of the peace ;

2. To develop friendly relations among nations based on respect for the principle of equal rights and self-determination of peoples, and to take other appropriate measures to strengthen universal peace ;

3. To achieve international co-operation in solving international problems of an economic, social, cultural, or humanitarian character, and in promoting and encouraging respect for human rights and for fundamental freedoms for all, without distinction as to race, sex, language, or religion ; and

4. To be a centre for harmonizing the actions of nations in the attainment of these common ends.

Binding Force. The objectives of the United Nations which were summarized in the Preamble are, in the present article, restated in fuller detail. These " Purposes " are not pious declarations of intention. They create legal rights in favour of the Organization as such, in favour of all Member States and, within certain limits, in favour of non-members. This legally binding force is expressly recognized in Article 14, which provides for the peaceful adjustment of situations arising, *inter alia*, from the violation of the Purposes (Article 1) and Principles (Article 2) of the United Nations. Paradoxically there is no provision in the Charter for the expulsion of Members who may render themselves guilty of the persistent violation of the Purposes, whereas under Article 5 a persistent infringement of the Principles is a ground (indeed, the only ground) for applying that penalty.

1. *Maintenance of peace and security.* This is rightly placed at the head of the list of the Organization's objectives, for none of its

B

other aims can be achieved if there is no peace. Universal peace —
peace between and within States — is the ultimate objective; but
the primary objective is international peace. The Organization
does not claim authority to intervene in internal conflicts as
long as their repercussions do not endanger international peace.

The first task of the Organization is to preserve peace. In the
face of a threat to peace or of a breach of it, the organs of the
United Nations are not entitled in the first instance to inquire
whether the *status quo* was in conformity with the principles of
justice and international law. An attempt to adjust the *status quo*
to those principles must wait until the threat or use of force has
been stopped. At San Francisco it was urged that this conception
of the Organization's attitude to the moral and legal foundation
of peace was too rigid, and might lead to the United Nations
becoming the guardian of forced and morally unjustifiable settlements on the Munich pattern. That argument was overruled on
the principle that " order comes before the law ". Faced with an
imminent threat of war, the United Nations must be prepared
to act as policemen before they will act as arbitrators.

In maintaining international peace the Organization relies on a
system of collective security, i.e. on arrangements — set out
partly in the Charter, partly in special agreements to be concluded under Article 43 — whereby all Members must co-operate
in the prevention and suppression of threats to the peace and
acts of aggression. For fuller details the reader is referred to
Chapter VII.

Breaches of the peace are usually preceded by open disputes or,
at least, by situations pregnant with disputes. It is one of the main
tasks of the United Nations to bring about without resort to
force the settlement of such disputes and the adjustment of dangerous situations. The methods of adjustment and settlement are
set out in detail in Chapter VI.

2. *Development of friendly relations.* It is obviously more difficult
to maintain peace in an atmosphere of suspicion, fear, resentment
and jealousy than in a community of friendly nations. But when
the Charter declares the development of friendly relations to be
one of the chief purposes of the United Nations, it gives no
pointer to any definite line of action. The text does not go beyond
enabling the Organization to sponsor any scheme for the better-
ment of international understanding.

The reference to the " equal rights and self-determination of
peoples " does not involve a guarantee that the United Nations

will alter the *status quo* in accordance with these principles. The text is cautious : " respect " for those principles will have to be the " basis " of the proposed development of friendly relations.

The postulate of equal rights is a legal principle. It is universally admitted by international law, but in relation to sovereign States,[1] not in relation to " peoples ".

Self-determination was one of the basic political concepts of the peace settlement of 1919, and was reaffirmed in passages of the Atlantic Charter which expressed a desire " to see no territorial changes that do not accord with the freely expressed wishes of the peoples concerned ", and proclaimed respect for " the right of all peoples to choose the form of government under which they will live ".

In essence, Article 1(2) is a declaration of good-will towards peoples which have not yet achieved self-determination in either the legal or the political sense ; and at the same time a notice of opposition to what are usually called the methods of power politics. But it would be unwarranted to argue that the paragraph is a sufficient basis for immediate claims by not fully self-governing peoples for a change in their status.[2]

The phrase authorizing the Organization " to take other appropriate measures to strengthen universal peace " is indefinite. Organs of the United Nations may rely on this general clause when they propose to take measures which are not specifically authorized in the Charter, and yet seem suitable to promote the cause of peace. It is noteworthy that, whereas paragraph 1 speaks of " international " peace, paragraph 2 refers to " universal " peace — a wider concept which seems to embrace the stability of internal relations. Article 2(7) prohibits intervention by the United Nations in essentially domestic matters, but under the present clause the Organization has authority to take due account of domestic situations when formulating any programme which does not involve "intervention" in the technical sense of the word.[3]

3. *International co-operation.* The first two paragraphs of this Article have dealt with the chief political purposes of the Organization. Paragraph 3, dealing with the non-political activities of the United Nations is not — as is sometimes suggested — purely ancillary to the definition of the Organization's responsi-

---

[1] See comment on Article 2(1).
[2] See comment on Article 73.
[3] See comment on Article 2(7).

bility for the maintenance of peace and security. The solution of economic, social, cultural and humanitarian problems is essential to creating conditions which are favourable to peace. Besides, the League experiment has shown that a world organization may fail to maintain peace and yet achieve lasting results in other fields. To create greater economic stability, wider prosperity, more complete social justice, to raise educational standards and relieve distress in any part of the world : these are aims which in themselves are worthy of the efforts of a universal international organization. This idea has found practical application in the setting up of an Economic and Social Council, a principal organ of the United Nations specifically charged with the furtherance of international co-operation in the non-political field.

The promotion of, and the encouragement of respect for, human rights and fundamental freedoms have received specific mention among the Organization's principal objectives. Before the First World War international law tended to concern itself almost exclusively with relationships between Governments, without claiming authority to protect the citizen against his own Government. The experiences of the inter-war period, the world-wide tensions arising from the discrimination practised by certain Governments against racial, religious, social and political groups, have added impetus to the movement for the international pro-tection of human rights. The term had never before been authori-tatively defined ; the working out of a definition has become one of the responsibilities of the United Nations.[1] But it is generally accepted that " human rights and fundamental free-doms " mean those minimum rights of the individual which at any given stage of civilization are deemed to be inseparable attributes of the human person. They are by no means confined to the " Four Freedoms " listed by President Roosevelt in one of his memorable speeches. Freedom of speech, freedom of religion, freedom from fear and freedom from want stand, each of them, for a group of rights in the political, social, economic and spiritual sphere of human life. The Charter does not specify them ; it only postulates that, whatever these freedoms may be in their ultimate definition, they must be available to all without dis-tinction as to race, sex, language or religion.

A word of warning, however, is necessary. Article 1(3) does not amount to a guarantee that the United Nations will presently enforce the undisturbed enjoyment of human rights and funda-

[1] See comment on Article 62.

mental freedoms. That is the ultimate purpose ; but the Charter only asserts that the Organization will strive to promote, and encourage respect for, human rights, e.g. by studying the state of these rights in the various countries, by trying to find a common denominator acceptable to all, or at least to the majority of States, and by endeavouring to secure the adoption of suitable international conventions.

4. *Co-ordination.* It is not envisaged that all international action in the political, economic, social, cultural and humanitarian field shall necessarily flow through the United Nations, still less that all existing international organizations shall be absorbed by the Secretariat. The text speaks of " *a* centre " — not of " *the* centre ". The idea is of co-ordination rather than of strict centralization ; the Organization is to provide a forum for discussion and a clearing-house for information in all matters of international relevance.[1]

ARTICLE 2

The Organization and its Members, in pursuit of the Purposes stated in Article 1, shall act in accordance with the following Principles :—

1. The Organization is based on the principle of the sovereign equality of all its Members.

2. All Members, in order to ensure to all of them the rights and benefits resulting from membership, shall fulfil in good faith the obligations assumed by them in accordance with the present Charter.

3. All Members shall settle their international disputes by peaceful means in such a manner that international peace and security, and justice, are not endangered.

4. All Members shall refrain in their international relations from the threat or use of force against the territorial integrity or political independence of any State, or in any other manner inconsistent with the Purposes of the United Nations.

5. All Members shall give the United Nations every assistance in any action it takes in accordance with the present Charter, and shall refrain from giving assistance to any State against which the United Nations is taking preventive or enforcement action.

6. The Organization shall ensure that States which are not Members of the United Nations act in accordance with these Principles so far as may be necessary for the maintenance of international peace and security.

[1] For a fuller treatment of the subject, see Chapter X, and particularly the comment on Article 55.

7. Nothing contained in the present Charter shall authorize the United Nations to intervene in matters which are essentially within the domestic jurisdiction of any State, or shall require the Members to submit such matters to settlement under the present Charter ; but this principle shall not prejudice the application of enforcement measures under Chapter VII.

Binding force. In the pursuit of the Purposes set out in Article 1. the Member States and the Organization (which has a legal existence separate from that of its Members) are bound by fundamental Principles. These Principles are set out in the form of definite obligations, the persistent violation of which may, under Article 6 of the Charter, lead to the expulsion of the offending Member.

1. *Sovereign equality.* The term " sovereign equality " combines two different concepts. Neither of them means exactly what the words imply in ordinary usage.

" Sovereignty ", in its generally accepted sense, implies that the State reigns supreme over its territory and over all persons and things therein ; and also that the State will not accept orders from any outside authority or be bound by any rule not of its own making.

No State — and in particular, no Member of the United Nations — is in effect sovereign to such an unlimited extent. All are bound by international law. They are bound not only by those rules of international law which they have expressly accepted in treaties and conventions. These could still be called " rules of their own making ". States are bound also by that part of international law which is not set out in treaties, but has evolved from the customs and practices of civilized States in their mutual relationships. Moreover, Members of the United Nations are also bound by the provisions of the Charter, many of which impose strict limitations on the State's freedom of action in relation to its own territory, citizens and resources. The most striking are those which require each Member to take part in " sanctions ". In the face of a threat to, or of an actual breach of, the peace, the Security Council, (which, when viewed from the angle of a sovereign State, is an " outside authority "), may call upon the military and economic resources of any Member of the United Nations ; it has a claim on its manpower and, within certain limits, to the use of its territory ; it can order any Member State to do certain things, and refrain from doing others.

The sovereignty of a Member State of the United Nations is therefore of a limited kind. By signing the Charter, it delegates to the Organization powers which it could previously wield without any limitations, other than those which follow from specific treaty obligations and the customary rules of international law. Moreover, not even that residue of sovereignty which remains unaffected by specific provisions in the Charter is safe from curtailment. Article 2(7) purports to prohibit the Organization from intervention in matters which are " essentially domestic " ; but the limits of the " essentially domestic " jurisdiction of a State are fluid. Matters which today may, by universal agreement, be still within those limits, might tomorrow be lifted from the sphere of domestic jurisdiction — not so much by a change in the principles of international law as by the Organization's own interpretation of its responsibilities.

The concept of " equality " is linked with the theory of sovereignty. If no sovereign State, however small, is legally bound to accept orders from any other State or outside authority, however powerful, it follows logically that, as members of the international community, all States are equal. None can be bound except by its consent ; and no decisions in which they have not concurred can be enforced against them.

Members of the United Nations are not equal in this sense. Some Members have special privileges. The five Great Powers have permanent seats in the Security Council and the Trusteeship Council ; others have not. In the Security Council the negative vote of one of the Great Powers has the weight of the negative vote of five smaller Powers taken in the aggregate. When it comes to amending or revising the Charter, the Great Powers' concurrence is essential ; other Members must submit to the will of the majority, unless they prefer to withdraw from the Organization altogether.[1]

Moreover the conception that States, being equals, cannot be bound by majority decisions is incompatible with the Charter. In the League, apart from exceptional cases, all decisions of the Assembly and the Council had to be unanimous. Not so in the United Nations. All its organs decide by a majority vote in all matters ; subject to the veto of the Great Powers, even the Security Council so decides. As a rule the simple majority of those present and voting is sufficient. No qualified majority is required except in the Security Council (Article 27), in the case of certain matters

[1] See comment on Article 6.

of importance dealt with by the General Assembly (Article 18), and for the amendment and revision of the Charter (Articles 108-109).

As applied to a Member of the United Nations, " equality " therefore has a specific meaning. It means that all States are equal before the law : the violation of the rights of the smallest State must be taken as seriously as the violation of the rights of the mightiest. It follows that, in deciding on disputes between its Members, the Organization must act impartially, unmoved by considerations of power. Equality also means that each Member is entitled to immunity from interference with those affairs which are essentially its own concern ; that the " personality ", territorial integrity and political independence of small States must be respected ; and that might and wealth do not relieve any State of the duty to comply faithfully with its international obligations.

2. *Good faith.* Treaty obligations must be fulfilled. That hardly needed saying. The emphasis of the text lies elsewhere. First, in the reminder that the Organization can only live up to its full potentialities if all Members, not only some of them, fulfil their obligations. Secondly, that obligations must be fulfilled in good faith. Whether obligations are so fulfilled is a matter on which the various organs of the United Nations will form their own opinion and act accordingly. " Good faith " is undoubtedly a flexible term. But so is malice ; and yet, in the common law of many countries malice has proved to be capable of definite interpretation.

3. *Pacific settlement of disputes.* The procedure for the peaceful settlement of disputes is set out in detail in Chapters VI and XIV. To ensure that Members avail themselves of that procedure is one of the fundamental objects of the Organization. The corresponding duty of Members, through its inclusion among the Principles, becomes a fundamental obligation.

This obligation has important limitations. In the first place, it only relates to international disputes — not to disputes of a domestic character. In the second place, the Organization is not concerned with all kinds of international disputes — only with those which may endanger international peace and security. Nevertheless, Members are not at liberty to settle minor disputes by force or the threat of force ; unless they are prepared to settle these disputes peacefully, they must leave them in abeyance.

On the other hand, it is contrary to the intentions of the Charter that major disputes shall remain unsettled for any length of time.

The obligation of Members is not negative, a mere abstention from the use of force. It is a positive duty, designed to clear the atmosphere from the dangers inherent in unsettled disputes. Once a potentially dangerous conflict has arisen, Members must set in motion the procedure of settlement without undue delay, whether or not the other party is a Member.

The term " peaceful means " has no definite meaning. Article 33 enumerates some of them, but the list is not exhaustive ; the General Assembly and the Security Council have power to add to it, either by the combination of existing methods of settlement or by creating precedents for new procedures.

4. *Threat or use of force.* The Charter does not eliminate the threat or use of force from international relations. On the contrary, Members are required to join in the use of force whenever they are called upon by the Security Council. That obligation is the very foundation of the Charter's system of collective security. But Members must refrain from the threat or use of force in any manner that is inconsistent with the Purposes of the United Nations ; and that prohibition covers everything except self-defence (Article 51) and participation in collective sanctions. The text singles out two specific groups of cases. No threat or use of force is permissible against (1) the territorial integrity or (2) the political independence of any State. It does not matter whether that State is a Member or not. Whether any action is in effect directed against territorial integrity or political independence is a question of fact which will be determined by the appropriate organs of the United Nations.

Where the League Covenant forbade " resort to war ", the Charter prohibits " the threat or use of force ". The different terminology is justified by the experience of the inter-war period. The use of force without an actual declaration of war has developed to a fine art. By prohibiting what is of the essence of war (i.e. the use of force), the Charter intends to cut short the unending squabble which attends a decision as to the existence of a state of war. Unfortunately, " force " itself is a flexible term. Under modern conditions the threat or use of economic retaliation may be as effective against a weaker State as the threat or use of armed force. But it appears that the prohibition of Article 2(4) is directed exclusively at force in the sense of " armed force ".

5. *Assistance.* Every Member must join, if called upon, in sanctions applied by the United Nations. None of them can lawfully ignore or

resist that call on the ground that it wishes to pursue a policy of neutrality, or has by treaty pledged neutrality to the State against which sanctions are applied. Nor is a Member entitled to render any assistance whatsoever to such a State, though it may have promised it by treaty.

Sanctions are not the only actions to which the fifth paragraph of the Article relates. The actions of the Organization cover wide sectors of economic, social, cultural and humanitarian co-operation ; and all Members are in duty bound to support them with every means in their power.

The duties of Members of the Organization may in certain cases clash with their obligations under other international treaties, particularly those concluded before the Charter came into force. This conflict is formally resolved by Article 103, which provides that in such cases the obligations under the Charter must prevail.

6. *Non-members*. Whether international treaties can validly impose obligations on States which are not parties to them is a highly controversial problem. In any case the Charter does not purport to impose legal obligations on non-members. It does, however, impose upon the Organization itself an obligation to ensure—by persuasion, if possible, but by the application of force, if necessary—the compliance of non-members with the Principles of the United Nations. The former will have to obey not as a matter of law, but as the result of the realities of power. However, the authority claimed by the Organization is strictly limited. There must be no interference with non-members, except so far as it may be necessary for the maintenance of international peace and security. Secondly, the only demand that can be made on outsiders is that they act in accordance with the Principles of the Charter. For practical purposes these can be reduced to one fundamental proposition : disputes must be settled peacefully, and the threat or use of force for selfish ends is outlawed. There is nothing in this to which any outsider could legitimately object. It is a different question whether, by its record so far, the United Nations has made good its claim to be accepted by the whole world as the arbiter of a new international order based on the rule of law.

As a corollary to the limited authority it claims over them, the Organization holds itself at the disposal of non-members who may wish to avail themselves of its services. The terms are set out in Articles 35 and 93.

7. *Domestic jurisdiction.* It is a recognized principle of international law that, over a wide range of their responsibilities, national States are immune from outside interference. The way in which a nation frames its political constitution ; the division of powers between the executive, legislative and judicial organs of the State ; the principles and methods of public administration ; the regulation of the relationship between the citizen and his Government ; questions of economic, social and cultural policy — all these are commonly regarded as matters of national, not of international concern. Freedom of action in these spheres has always been jealously guarded by national governments and consistently admitted by international law. But the limits of this " domestic jurisdiction " have not been closely defined. It is clear that a matter ceases to be within exclusive domestic jurisdiction as soon as it is regulated by international treaty. The converse of that rule does not operate with equal force. Many matters may not be regulated by international treaties, and yet the action of national governments in these matters may have tangible, and indeed violent, international repercussions. The way in which national, racial or cultural minorities are treated in one State may cause the gravest resentment in another State where members of the same national, racial, cultural or political group are in the majority or have considerable influence. The immigration laws of one country may create difficult problems for others which are forced by the lack of national resources to encourage the emigration of their surplus population. The customs and tariff policy of an importing State is of the utmost concern to States with large exports to sell. It is not a matter of indifference to countries in search of raw materials if certain Powers bar access to them through a restrictive colonial policy. The practice of regulating by international treaties a great variety of matters which transcend the interests of a single State has been steadily growing in modern times. As a result the borderline between domestic jurisdiction and international regulation has become fluid, and the field which international law can properly recognize as being solely within the jurisdiction of a national State is steadily narrowing.

The existence of a borderline is recognized by the Charter ; but no attempt is, or could be, made to define the two fields it separates. With constant pressure for the international regulation of more and more incidents of government, a dogmatic definition is no longer possible. At the same time the absence of a definition has already created, and must continue to create, increasing tension within the Organization. Naturally every attempt to project its authority into fields previously reserved to national governments provokes resistance. The success or failure of the United Nations experiment depends to a considerable extent on the manner in which the reservation of the Charter in regard to domestic jurisdiction will be interpreted.

At this stage it is difficult to predict the probable trend of interpretation. It will be determined by the relative strength, within each organ of the United Nations, of the groups of States favouring or resisting the restriction of national sovereignty. The Security Council (in which the Soviet Union, with its unconcealed opposition to any surrender of sovereignty, wields a power of veto) is likely to apply the Seventh Principle in a more restrictive manner than any of the other principal organs. The General Assembly has already proved that it is ready to overrule objections to its competence if it is satisfied that friendly relations between nations had, in fact, been impaired by actions which are *ex hypothesi* essentially domestic.[1]

From the legal point of view, the following considerations are relevant to the interpretation of the text :

(a) *Matters " essentially domestic "*. The Dumbarton Oaks Proposals suggested that " matters which by *international law* are *solely* within the domestic jurisdiction of the State concerned " should be exempt from the jurisdiction of the Security Council. At San Francisco it was decided that the exemption should apply not only to the Security Council, but to the Organization as a whole ; and further, that it should be applicable to all activities of the Organization (e.g. social and economic co-operation), and not only to disputes and situations relevant to the maintenance of peace. Moreover, the reference to international law as a measuring rod was dropped ; and the phrase " *solely* within the domestic jurisdiction " was replaced by the term " *essentially* within the domestic jurisdiction ", on the ground that, under modern conditions, there are few things in which one State is alone interested.

The deletion of the reference to international law seems to indicate that, from the point of view of the United Nations, it is a question of fact and not of law whether a given matter justifies intervention by the Organization. The only reliable theoretical standard—that of international law—has been discarded. Political theory is an unworkable measuring rod for the purposes of an

[1] See comment on Article 10 and Article 14.

organization whose members conduct their respective national lives on the most contradictory principles of political science. Whether an issue is essentially domestic must, therefore, be decided by practical standards ; and no other is conceivable than the reaction of the outside world to a given situation arising in, or to an action taken by, a national State. Clamour in the outside world is not sufficient justification for the United Nations to intervene. But the Seventh Principle must not be allowed to bar the way if, after proper and impartial investigation, the competent organ of the United Nations has come to the conclusion that, though domestic in appearance, an issue calls for international action.

(b) *Intervention.* The Charter does not say that the Organization must take no notice of essentially domestic issues, but only declares that it must refrain from two specific lines of action.

First, it must not require its Members to submit for settlement disputes or situations arising from essentially domestic matters. If they submit them of their own volition, neither the Security Council nor the General Assembly are entitled to object.

Secondly, the Organization's activities must stop short of intervention. " Intervention " has a technical meaning in international law. It means " dictatorial interference by a State in the affairs of another State for the purpose of maintaining or altering the actual condition of things "[1] — a direct pressure exercised through force or the threat of force or, at least, through a demand purporting to be made by right. The discussion or study of a problem, or an inquiry into it, by any organ of the United Nations is not " intervention "; not even a formal recommendation is intervention if it does not purport to decide the issue against one or several of the parties. Recommendations not addressed to an individual State but disposing of a problem in general terms cannot, as a rule, be regarded as intervention.

(c) *Enforcement measures.* The essentially domestic character of an issue does not bar intervention by the United Nations when the conflict has resulted in a threat to the peace, a breach of the peace, or an act of aggression. The Charter is built on the overriding principle that the importance of averting or stopping breaches of the peace transcends all considerations of sovereignty.

(d) *The position of non-members.* The prohibition of intervention in domestic matters is so formulated that it protects Members and non-members equally. Conversely, when it comes to threats

---

[1] Oppenheim-Lauterpacht *op. cit.* Vol. I., p. 272.

to the peace, breaches of the peace or acts of aggression, the Security Council is as free to act against non-members as it is against Members.

(e) *The role of the International Court.* Since in the final formulation of the Seventh Principle the criterion of international law has been abandoned, neither Members nor any organ of the United Nations have any obligation to refer to the International Court of Justice the question whether, in a disputed case, the issue is essentially domestic. Members can do so by agreement, and, under Article 96, organs of the United Nations and specialized agencies may ask the Court for an advisory opinion.

CHAPTER II

MEMBERSHIP

ARTICLE 3

The original Members of the United Nations shall be the States which, having participated in the United Nations Conference on International Organization at San Francisco, or having previously signed the Declaration by United Nations 1st January, 1942, sign the present Charter and ratify it in accordance with Article 110.

Classes of Members. The Charter provides for two classes of Members : (a) original and (b) those admitted later.

There is no discrimination in favour of the original as against later Members. They all enjoy the same privileges and share the same burdens. The distinction, however, is important, in that, as regards original Members, their participation in the Organization is considered as acquired by right, while that of future Members is dependent on the fulfilment of certain conditions.

Qualifications for original membership. These were (a) ratification of the Charter (b) participation in the San Francisco Conference, or previous adherence to the United Nations Declaration of January 1, 1942.

All the signatories to the Declaration attended the Conference with the exception of Poland, who could not be invited pending the establishment of a Government of national unity, as stipulated in the decisions of the Yalta Conference of February, 1945. There are 51 original Members of the United Nations.

Difference from the League system. The regulation of original membership by the Charter differs from the regulation in the Covenant on two points:

(a) The Allied and Associated Powers of the First World War which ratified the Treaty of Versailles, or any other Peace Treaty incorporating the Covenant, were automatically entitled to original membership of the League. Original membership of the United Nations depended on ratification of the Charter itself.

(b) Under the Covenant, 13 States which remained neutral during the First World War were declared eligible for original membership subject to their adherence to the Covenant. Under the Charter no neutral of the Second World War could become an original Member of the United Nations.

The five sponsoring Great Powers and the majority of the signatories of the Charter ratified it by October 24, 1945, and became Members on that date. The remainder became Members on the day when they deposited their instruments of ratification with the Government of the U.S.A.[1]

ARTICLE 4

1. Membership in the United Nations is open to all other peace-loving States which accept the obligations contained in the present Charter and, in the judgement of the Organization, are able and willing to carry out these obligations.

2. The admission of any such State to membership in the United Nations will be effected by a decision of the General Assembly upon the recommendation of the Security Council.

Conditions of admission. Five conditions must be fulfilled :
(1) *The applicant must be a State.* The Charter does not define the attributes of statehood. Normally, a community becomes a State when — *de facto* or *de jure,* expressly or by implication — it is recognized as such by the Family of Nations. But the United Nations is not bound to regard previous general recognition as a necessary criterion. The mere fact that one or more Members of the Organization have refused to give recognition to a State does not prevent the General Assembly and the Security Council from admitting it to membership, if, from the circumstances of the case, they conclude that the community in question has passed the stage of being merely " a State in the making ". On the other hand, once a State has been admitted, it would seem that no Member of the United Nations is entitled to withhold individual recognition — at any rate, *de facto.*

Full sovereignty is not an essential condition. The Byelorussian S.S.R. and the Ukranian S.S.R. are original Members of the Organisation although, as parts of the U.S.S.R. they are not fully sovereign. It does not, however, follow that the constituent States of a federal unit are normally eligible for membership. The case of the two Soviet Republics was exceptional in that, under the recently amended constitution of the U.S.S.R., they had been authorized, in theory at least, to conduct their external

---

[1] See List of Signatory States on p. 217.

affairs independently. Without that constitutional amendment they could not have become Members of the Organization.

Membership is not confined to States having a democratic system any more than it was in the League of Nations. As, however, Article 1(3) proclaims as one of the fundamental purposes of the Organization the promotion of human rights and fundamental freedoms, it is arguable that States in which fundamental political freedoms are lacking are not eligible for membership.[1] Moreover, an interpretative commentary approved by the San Francisco Conference with regard to the admission of new Members made it clear that this Article

" cannot be applied to the States whose régimes have been established with the help of military forces belonging to the countries which have waged war against the United Nations, as long as those régimes are in power ".

That interpretation was directed against General Franco's Government in Spain. Later, in the Potsdam Declaration of August 2, 1945, the United Kingdom, the U.S.A. and the U.S.S.R. expressly declared that " they for their part would not favour any application for membership put forward by the present Spanish Government ".

(2) *The applicant must accept the obligations contained in the Charter.*

It is not clear that acceptance must be unconditional in all cases. Under the Covenant, neutrals of the First World War were eligible for membership of the League on condition that they acceded to the covenant " without reservation ". All the same, in 1920, the Council of the League approved the admission of Switzerland, notwithstanding its reservations in regard to military sanctions.

It is questionable whether any reservations of neutrality will be permissible under the Charter. In the League, no Member was under any legal obligation to take part in military sanctions, apart from affording passage through its territory. Article 2(5) of the Charter, on the other hand, imposes on Members an unqualified obligation to " give the United Nations every assistance in any action it takes in accordance with the present Charter " : and Article 43 provides that " all Members undertake to make available to the Security Council, on its call and in accordance with a special agreement or agreements, armed forces, assistance

---

[1] It was on these grounds that the British, United States and French delegations to the Security Council have so far opposed the admission of Roumania, Bulgaria and Hungary.

and facilities, including rights of passage, necessary for the purpose of maintaining international peace and security ".

(3) *The applicant must be a peace-loving State.* To quote the records of the San Francisco Conference

" to declare oneself peace-loving does not suffice. What nation has ever professed any other sentiments ? "

The condition of " peace-lovingness " is therefore a question of fact, to be determined by the Security Council and the General Assembly after careful scrutiny of the historical and political record.

(4) *The applicant must be willing to carry out the obligations of the Charter.* A mere declaration of intention is obviously not sufficient, but the Charter makes no mention of the right of the Security Council and the General Assembly to call for specific undertakings. In the League, the position was different. Under Article 1 of the Covenant, the admission of new Members was dependent on their providing effective guarantees of a sincere intention to meet their international obligations. The first League Assembly (1920), when considering the applications of the Baltic States and Albania, required them to grant national minorities a status similar to those guaranteed in the " Minorities Treaties " drawn up in 1919 ; and in 1923, Ethiopia had to guarantee the abolition of slavery as a condition of admission.

The Security Council and the General Assembly have not, so far, defined their position to the question whether they had power to call for proof, in the form of specific undertakings, of an applicant's willingness to carry out the obligations of the Charter.[1]

(5) *The applicant must be able to carry out the obligations of the Charter.* This condition, which had no precedent in the Covenant, affords an opportunity for a general survey of political, economic and social conditions in the applicant State and, particularly, for an expression of opinion on the stability of its régime. Unpopular dictatorships are unstable *ex hypothesi;* they are unsuitable applicants for membership of an Organization which must be able to rely on the staying power of Member Governments in emergency situations which may easily arise from a call to arms under Article 42.

---

[1] Opportunity has not been lacking. The admission of Roumania, Bulgaria and Hungary has been opposed in the Security Council on the basis that their régimes showed no respect for human rights and fundamental freedoms. The applications have been rejected on the formal ground that they failed to secure the necessary number of votes. In the view of the present writers, it would have been permissible for the Council to say that it was not prepared to recommend these States for admission until they had given specific undertakings for the protection of human rights and fundamental freedoms in a manner acceptable to the United Nations.

Extraneous conditions. In October 1947 the Soviet delegation to the Security Council vetoed the admission of Italy and Finland on the grounds that the five European allies of Germany must be deemed to form, for the purposes of Article 4, an inseparable group; no member of the group could be admitted without the simultaneous admission of all the others ; if the applications of Roumania, Bulgaria and Hungary failed owing to the opposition of the Western Powers, those of Italy and Finland must also fail. Likewise, the Soviet delegation resisted the applications of Transjordan, Eire and Portugal ; it contended that it was an implied condition of admission that the attitude and behaviour of applicant States towards the aggressors of the Second World War must have been impeccable. The Soviet Union also opposed the admission of Austria, on the ground that the proposed State Treaty between that country and the Allied Powers was still in abeyance.

Faced with the deadlock in the Security Council, the General Assembly, in November, 1947, requested the International Court of Justice for an advisory opinion. In its Opinion delivered on May 28, 1948, the Court by a majority declared that :

(a) a Member of the United Nations which is called upon, in virtue of Article 4 of the Charter, to pronounce itself by its vote, either in the Security Council or in the General Assembly, on the admission of a State to membership in the United Nations, is not juridically entitled to make its consent to the admission dependent on conditions not expressly provided by paragraph (1) of the said Article ; and

(b) in particular, a Member of the Organization cannot, while it recognizes the conditions set forth in that provision to be fulfilled by the State concerned, subject its affirmative vote to the additional condition that other States be admitted to membership in the United Nations together with that State.

On the basis of this Advisory Opinion, the General Assembly, in December, 1948, requested the Security Council to reconsider the applications of Italy, Finland, Transjordan, Portugal, Eire and Austria.[1]

Procedure. Under the Rules of Procedure of the Security Council and the General Assembly, a State which desires to become a Member must submit a formal application to the Secretary-General. The latter sends a copy of the application to the General Assembly or, if it is not in session, to all Members. The original

---

[1] These applications were still in abeyance in May 1949.

application is placed before the Security Council ; and the Council is expected to make a recommendation at the next session (regular or special) following the receipt of the application. Normally the case is first examined by a committee of the Council on which all its members are represented. If the Council makes a positive recommendation (and this requires a majority of seven votes, including the concurring votes of the five permanent members), the recommendation is forwarded to the Assembly with a complete record of the discussion. The Assembly then re-examines the application on its merits, and decides by a two-thirds majority of those present and voting. If the application is approved, membership becomes effective as from the date of the Assembly Resolution.

If the Security Council rejects the application or postpones its consideration, it must submit a special report to the Assembly with a complete record of the discussion. The rejection is not final. Reconsideration may at any time be requested by the applicant or any Member of the Organization or the General Assembly.[1]

New Members admitted under Article 4. Afghanistan, Iceland, and Sweden became Members with effect from November 9, 1946 ; Siam with effect from December 15, 1946 ; Yemen and Pakistan with effect from September 30, 1947; the Union of Burma with effect from April 19, 1948; and Israel with effect from May 11, 1949.

ARTICLE 5

A Member of the United Nations against which preventive or enforcement action has been taken by the Security Council may be suspended from the exercise of the rights and privileges of membership by the General Assembly upon the recommendation of the Security Council. The exercise of these rights and privileges may be restored by the Security Council.

Conditions of suspension. Only Member States against which preventive or enforcement action has been taken (Chapter VII) may be suspended from the rights and privileges of membership. The main purpose is to prevent States guilty of a threat to the peace, a breach of the peace or an act of aggression (Article 39) from obstructing the Organization in the discharge of its functions.

[1] In the League, the admission of new Members was within the jurisdiction of the Assembly ; no recommendation from the Council was necessary.

There is no guarantee that this purpose can be achieved if the offending State is a permanent member of the Security Council and, as such, entitled to veto any recommendation under this Article.

The powers of the Security Council and the General Assembly are permissive. They may, but they need not, suspend an offending Member.

Procedure. The Assembly decides by a two-thirds majority of the members present and voting, but it cannot act without a positive recommendation from the Security Council. The voting procedure in the Council is governed by Article 27(3), but the proviso that a party to a dispute shall abstain from voting does not apply to decisions under the present Article.

Whereas the concurrent action of the Council and the Assembly is necessary to suspend the rights and privileges of a Member, these may be restored by the Council acting alone.

Effects of suspension. Suspension does not in any way affect the obligations of the Member ; it only affects its rights and privileges. As a rule, suspension and restoration must operate on the totality of these rights.[1] Whether the application of the Article has any effect on the rights and privileges of the Member in specialized agencies (Article 57) depends on the constitution of the agency concerned.[2]

ARTICLE 6

A Member of the United Nations which has persistently violated the Principles contained in the present Charter may be expelled from the Organization by the General Assembly upon the recommendation of the Security Council.

Termination of membership. There are three ways in which a State may cease to be a Member of the Organization : (1) the termination of its sovereign statehood ; (2) withdrawal ; (3) expulsion.

Termination of statehood. This case required no express regulation in the Charter, as it follows from Article 2(1) and Articles 3-4 that membership of the Organization is inseparable from sovereign

---

[1] A partial suspension of rights is, however, possible under Article 19.

[2] Article (3) of the Constitution of UNESCO provides that a Member which has been suspended from the exercise of its rights and privileges in the United Nations must be suspended from its rights of membership in UNESCO, if the United Nations so requests.

statehood. It comes to an end *ipso facto* with the loss of that status, e.g. when a Member becomes part of a federal State.

Withdrawal. Under the Covenant[1] any Member of the League could withdraw after giving two years' notice, provided that its international obligations, and particularly those under the Covenant, were fulfilled. Members could also withdraw if they dissented from an amendment to the Covenant.[2]

The Charter contains no provision admitting the right to withdraw from the Organization. The San Francisco Conference took the view that, if such a right were expressly granted, some Members might use it as a means of escape from long-term obligations, or as a weapon with which to extort concessions from the Organization. But the appropriate committee of the Conference included in its report a declaration that, notwithstanding the absence of specific provisions in the Charter, withdrawals would be admissible if (1) exceptional circumstances compelled a Member to " leave the burden of maintaining international peace and security on the other Members " ; (2) if, " deceiving the hopes of humanity, the Organization was revealed to be unable to maintain peace, or could do so only at the expense of law and justice " ; and (3) if the rights and obligations of a Member were, without his concurrence, changed by amendment of the Charter or, conversely, if an amendment accepted by the majorities prescribed in Articles 108-109 failed to secure the requisite number of ratifications.[3]

Expulsion. No Member of the Organization can be expelled for an isolated breach of its obligations under the Charter, however grave it may be. Expulsion is applicable only in the case of a " persistent " violation of the Principles set forth in Article 2. Particular importance attaches to the Second Principle which prescribes the fulfilment in good faith of all obligations assumed " in accordance " with the Charter. This phrase would seem to cover, in addition to obligations " under " the Charter, all treaty obligations accepted under the auspices of the Organization. *A fortiori*, repeated threats to, or violations of, the peace (Article 39) may entail expulsion, whether or not Article 5 had been previously applied against the offending State.

Expulsion terminates both the rights and the obligations attached to membership, but does not altogether withdraw the

---

[1] *Covenant*, Article 1.
[2] *Covenant*, Article 26.
[3] See comment on Articles 108 and 109.

expelled Member from the jurisdiction of the Organization. As a non-member, the State concerned may still be compelled by the Organization to act in accordance with the Principles of the Charter so far as may be necessary for the maintenance of peace and security,[1] and in the conditions of Article 32 and Article 35(2) it may still claim access to the Security Council and the General Assembly.

Moreover, expulsion is no bar to a subsequent application for re-admission, provided the conditions of Article 4 are fulfilled.

Expulsion requires the concurrent action of the Security Council and the General Assembly in the same way as suspension under Article 5.[2] This makes a permanent member of the Security Council virtually immune from expulsion, except in the highly improbable case that it had been previously suspended under Article 5 from the rights and privileges of membership.

[1] Article 2(6).
[2] See p. 25.

CHAPTER III

ORGANS

ARTICLE 7

1. There are established as the principal organs of the United Nations : a General Assembly, a Security Council, an Economic and Social Council, a Trusteeship Council, an International Court of Justice, and a Secretariat.

2. Such subsidiary organs as may be found necessary may be established in accordance with the present Charter.

" Principal " and " subsidiary " organs. The division into principal and subsidiary organs applies only to the central organization and not the United Nations system as a whole. The manifold functional organizations (Article 57) are not organs of the United Nations but " specialized agencies ". Again, the regional agencies referred to in Chapter VIII are not organs of the United Nations, even in those cases where all the constituent States are Members of the United Nations.

The distinction between principal and subsidiary organs does not imply a hierarchy of functions in the sense that subsidiary organs only deal with ancillary tasks. The Military Staff Committee (Article 47) or the Interim Committee of the General Assembly (established under Article 22) are entrusted with functions of the utmost importance. Again, subordination to a principal organ is not an essential feature of subsidiary organs. The Secretariat is a principal organ, and yet it is subordinated to instructions from other bodies, some of which may be subsidiary organs (e.g. the Human Rights Commission). Nor is it an essential element of the definition that the subsidiary organ shall have been set up by a principal organ. The Military Staff Committee derives its existence direct from Article 47 of the Charter; and none of the principal organs has authority to abolish it or change its composition or curtail its responsibilities.

Thus the essential difference between principal and subsidiary organs lies elsewhere. The number and designation of the principal organs having been established by the Charter, none of them can be abolished, and no further organs set up without amendment of the Charter. In contrast, any number of subsidiary organs can

be set up, and (save for the Military Staff Committee) abolished
or reorganized, without recourse to the complicated procedure
of constitutional amendment. In this respect, the discretionary
powers of the competent principal organs are limited only by
Article 68, which provides that the Economic and Social Council
must set up commissions " in economic and social fields and for
the promotion of human rights ".

Relations between principal organs. The character of these relations
is more complicated than it was in the League, if only because the
number of principal organs has increased from two to six. The
Covenant (Article 2) provided that " the action of the League . . .
shall be effected through the instrumentality of an Assembly and
of a Council, with a permanent Secretariat ". If we compare that
with Article 7 of the Charter, we find that (1) the functions of
what used to be one Council are now divided between three co-
ordinated bodies : the Security Council, the Economic and Social
Council and the Trusteeship Council ; (2) the Secretariat has
become a principal organ ; and (3) the Court, which was not an
organ of the League, but a separate body closely connected with
it, is now an integral part of the Organization.

Interdependence. The Charter establishes no hierarchy among
the principal organs. None of them can operate independently
of one or more of the others. In some cases this interdependence
takes the form of subordination ; but the same organ, which is
subordinated for some purposes, appears as the superior organ
in other matters.

Thus the three Councils are subordinated to the Assembly,
inasmuch as (1) their members (excepting the permanent members
of the Security Council and of the Trusteeship Council) are
elected by the Assembly ; (2) the finance required for their
activities is voted by the Assembly (Article 17) ; (3) they have to
report to the Assembly (Article 15) ; (4) any agreements between
the Economic and Social Council and the specialized agencies are
subject to approval by the Assembly (Article 63(1)) ; (5) the
Economic and Social Council has to perform any functions that
may, from time to time, be assigned to it by the Assembly (Article
66(3)) ; (6) the Economic and Social Council must not perform
services at the request of Members or specialized agencies, except
with the approval of the Assembly ; and (7) generally, the
Economic and Social Council and the Trusteeship Council
operate " under the authority " of the Assembly (Article 60 and
Article 85).

On the other hand, the Assembly is subordinated to the Security Council, in that, under Article 12, while the Council is seised of any dispute or situation affecting peace and security, the Assembly must not make any recommendation on the matter, except by request of the Council.

Several important activities require joint action by the Security Council and the General Assembly, such as (1) the admission of new Members (Article 4) ; (2) the suspension of the rights and privileges of Members[1] (Article 5) ; (3) the expulsion of Members (Article 6) ; (4) the determination of conditions on which non-members may become parties to the Statute of the International Court of Justice (Article 93) ; (5) the appointment of the Secretary-General (Article 97) ; and (6) revision of the Charter (Article 109).

The Charter contains express provisions for " assistance " by one principal organ to another, i.e. (1) by the Economic and Social Council to the Security Council (Article 65) ; (2) by the Trusteeship Council to the Assembly (Article 85) ; (3) by the Economic and Social Council to the Trusteeship Council (Article 91) ; and (4) by the International Court of Justice, in the form of advisory opinions, to the Assembly and the Security Council (Article 96).[2]

The maintenance of international peace and security is, under Article 24, the "primary" responsibility of the Security Council. Primary responsibility, however, does not mean exclusive jurisdiction. In fact, with the exception of enforcement measures, all questions relating to international peace and security (including disarmament and the regulation of armaments) are within the concurrent jurisdiction of the Security Council and the Assembly. *Functions entrusted to subsidiary organs.* See comment on Articles 22, 29, 47 and 68.

ARTICLE 8

The United Nations shall place no restrictions on the eligibility of men and women to participate in any capacity and under conditions of equality in its principal and subsidiary organs.

---

[1] But suspended rights and privileges may be restored by the Security Council without reference to the Assembly.

[2] Since the entry into force of the Charter, general authority to request the Court for advisory opinions has been given to the Economic and Social Council, to the Trusteeship Council and to specialized agencies (see comment on Article 96).

The mere ratification of the Charter involves no obligation for Member States to abolish such discrimination against women as may exist under their respective national laws. It is one of the basic assumptions of the Charter[1] that in time the equal rights of men and women will be admitted all over the world. The achievement of that objective is, however, left to national action and to international conventions concluded under the auspices of the Organization and of the appropriate specialized agencies.

The Article, therefore, has a limited application. It guarantees that the Organization, as such, will place no restrictions on the eligibility of women, on an equal footing with men, for participation in its principal and subsidiary organs. As far as posts in the Secretariat are concerned, the Organization has it in its power to give full effect to this principle of equality ; and in that respect its record is exemplary. But it is for the Member Governments alone to decide whether and to what extent they will respect the equality of women in appointing representatives to the General Assembly, the three Councils and the various subsidiary organs.

[1] See the Preamble, Article 1(3), Article 55(c) and Article 76.

CHAPTER IV

THE GENERAL ASSEMBLY

Composition

ARTICLE 9

1. The General Assembly shall consist of all the Members of the United Nations.
2. Each Members shall have not more than five representatives in the General Assembly.

Character of the Assembly. The General Assembly is the only principal organ in which all Member States are directly and continuously represented. Full effect is given in its organization to the principle of sovereign equality proclaimed in Article 2(1). Whereas in the Security Council and the Trusteeship Council the Great Powers have privileged representation, and in the former also privileged voting rights, in the General Assembly the equality of Members is unqualified.

It is a fallacy to talk of the General Assembly as a World Parliament. Parliament connotes legislative powers : and the General Assembly has not those powers. If an analogy is wanted, it would be more accurate to say that the General Assembly, similarly to the Assembly of the League, is a standing conference of the States of the world, great and small. We have come to take for granted such a standing conference and to expect it to develop a consciousness and tradition of its own. But we may remember that in 1920 it was something new.

In the earlier system of the Concert of Europe no permanent organization of any kind was available to the smaller European Powers for co-operation in solving issues of general policy. The position was much the same in the Americas. Admittedly, many diplomatic congresses, with the participation of the lesser Powers, were held in the decades preceding the First World War ; but they dealt with specialized problems of a technical character, not with political problems of universal interest. The permanent association of the smaller Powers with political decisions on world issues dates from the Covenant of the League.

Thus, in the wider framework of the Family of Nations, the General Assembly is destined to play the same part as the

Assembly of the League. But within the framework of the Organization itself, the characteristics of the two assemblies are different. Under the Covenant, the " action " of the League was to be effected " through the instrumentality of an Assembly and of a Council ": the powers of the two organs were undifferentiated, and each of them had both deliberative and executive functions.[1] In contrast, the Charter prescribes a clear-cut differentiation of competence. The General Assembly is debarred from taking any " action " in the sphere of security; all decisions relating to provisional measures and sanctions (Chapter VII) are reserved for the Security Council exclusively. The powers of the General Assembly do not go beyond " recommendations " in any field of international activity. Its main functions are the consideration of general principles, the discussion of particular questions, the initiation of studies. It is a deliberative assembly whose impact on Member States and the outside world depends on the cogency of its arguments and the moral authority of its recommendations. Such administrative powers as it has only operate *within* the Organization. Some of them, notably the election of the non-permanent members of the Councils, the adoption of the budget and the approval of trusteeship agreements, may have a considerable influence on the policy of the executive organs and on the financial and military strength of the Organization as a whole ; but this influence is indirect.

Composition. The Dumbarton Oaks proposals did not specify the number of representatives allowed to each Member State. Even at San Francisco, several delegations felt that Members should be free to decide on the size of their delegations, provided no delegation had more than one vote. Eventually, they yielded to the concern expressed by some of the small States lest the Great Powers should send delegations of an overwhelming size ; and finally the maximum number of representatives was fixed at five.[2]

Under the *Rules of Procedure*, in addition to its principal representatives, each Member is entitled to send to the Assembly not more than five " alternate representatives " and an unlimited number of advisers, experts and persons of similar status. The reasons for this are technical. Apart from the fact that the principal

[1] Article 15 of the Covenant enabled the Council to refer to the Assembly any disputes between Members, and made it compulsory for the Council so to do if either party, within fourteen days after the submission of the dispute to the Council. requested that it should be referred to the Assembly.

[2] In the Assembly of the League the maximum number was three.

delegates need expert advice on many items of the agenda, five delegates are not, as a rule, sufficient to assure the adequate representation of Members in the numerous committees and sub-committees which transact most of the business of the Assembly. The advisers, experts and persons of similar status may act as members of committees, but not of the Assembly in plenary session, and they are not eligible for appointment as chairmen, vice-chairmen or rapporteurs of committees. These posts, and seats in the General Assembly in the place of principal representatives, are reserved for the alternate representatives.

The Charter does not recognize any hierarchy within the national delegations, but in consequence of the rule (Article 18) whereby each Member State can only cast one vote, the Organization must, in some form or other, take note of internal arrangements designed to regulate the use of voting power. The Rules of Procedure are formulated on the assumption that each delegation has a chairman with power to designate alternate representatives for plenary sessions, and advisers, experts and persons of similar status as members of committees. The Rules do not specify the powers of the chairman in regard to voting rights in plenary sessions, but in practice each delegation votes through its chairman or through a member designated by him.

FUNCTIONS AND POWERS

ARTICLE 10

The General Assembly may discuss any questions or any matters within the scope of the present Charter or relating to the powers and functions of any organs provided for in the present Charter, and, except as provided in Article 12, may make recommendations to the Members of the United Nations or to the Security Council or to both on any such questions or matters.

General clause. Articles 10-17 which are grouped under the title " Functions and Powers " do not fully dispose of either subject. Further functions and powers are allotted to the Assembly in Chapters IX-X and in Chapter XII.

All these provisions are either permissive or mandatory : they either allow or require the Assembly to perform specific functions.

This Article, which belongs to the group of permissive provisions, is a " general clause ". It defines the functions of the Assembly in the widest possible terms. All the remaining permissive provisions are specific applications of this clause and do not limit its general scope.

History. Article 3 of the Covenant authorized the Assembly of the League to " deal at its meetings with any matter within the sphere of action of the League or affecting the peace of the world ". The Dumbarton Oaks Proposals sought to restrict the competence of the new Assembly in two directions. First, decisions on " action " were to be reserved for the Security Council, and the risk of the Assembly and the Council making conflicting or overlapping recommendations was to be excluded ; these restrictions are embodied in Article 11(2) and Article 12 of the Charter. Secondly, the Proposals sought to limit the field of the Assembly's discussions ; these were to be confined to the general principles of co-operation in the maintenance of peace and security (including disarmament), specific questions relating to peace and brought before the Assembly by Member States or the Security Council, situations likely to impair the general welfare, co-operation in the political, economic and social fields, and administrative matters.

The San Francisco Conference did not accept this second group of restrictions. The catalogue of subjects suggested at Dumbarton Oaks seemed to be comprehensive, but like all catalogues could not be relied upon to provide for every eventuality. It was felt, moreover, that the Assembly should be able to discuss specific questions relating to peace and security upon its own initiative, not only at the request of Members or the Security Council.

In its final form, the Article is hardly less general than Article 3 of the Covenant. It deals with two main groups of subjects : (1) matters within the scope of the Charter, and (2) the powers and functions of the organs of the United Nations.

Matters within the scope of the Charter. For practical purposes, this phrase covers the whole field of international relations. The Charter is applicable not only to the international action of Member States, but, in the field of security, also to the action of non-members (Article 2(6)). It deals with the co-operation of Members not only within the Organization, but also outside it : " regional arrangements " (Article 52) are not permissible unless they are consistent with the Purposes and Principles of the United Nations. Again, the Assembly is not debarred from discussing the domestic affairs of States. First, discussion and recommendation are not " intervention " in the sense prohibited by Article 2(7) : and secondly, the responsibilities assumed by the Organization for the promotion of respect for human rights have narrowed considerably the field of essentially domestic jurisdiction.[1]

Powers and functions of organs. None of the principal organs of the United Nations can be set up, or continue after its appointed term, without the concurrence of the General Assembly. The non-permanent members of the Councils, the judges of the International Court of Justice, the Secretary-General of the United Nations are all elected by the Assembly, and re-elections are in its gift. All principal organs, except the Court, must make periodic reports to the Assembly, and for the financial means of their existence they all depend on the Assembly's budgetary powers.

Constitutionally therefore the Assembly is the supreme supervisory organ of the United Nations, and, at the same time, the final authority on the interpretation of those provisions in the Charter which define the competence of principal and subsidiary organs.[2]

ARTICLE 11

1. The General Assembly may consider the general principles of co-operation in the maintenance of international peace and security, including the principles governing disarmament and the regulation of armaments, and may make recommendations with regard to such principles to the Members or to the Security Council or to both.

2. The General Assembly may discuss any questions relating to the maintenance of international peace and security brought before it by any Member of the United Nations, or by the Security Council, or by a State which is not a Member of the United Nations in accordance with Article 35, paragraph 2, and, except as provided in Article 12, may make recommendations with regard to any such questions to the State or States concerned or to the Security Council or to both. Any such question on which action is necessary shall be referred to the

---

[1] See the discussion in the Assembly of the *Spanish Question* (1946-7) ; the *Treatment of Indians in the Union of South Africa* (1946, 1947 and 1949); the *Observance in Bulgaria and Hungary of Human Rights and Fundamental Freedoms* (1949).

[2] The question of controversial interpretations of the Charter is discussed under Article 111.

Security Council by the General Assembly either before or after discussion.

3. The General Assembly may call the attention of the Security Council to situations which are likely to endanger international peace and security.

4. The powers of the General Assembly set forth in this Article shall not limit the general scope of Article 10.

Scope. The powers set forth in this Article are all permissive, and they are all concerned with peace and security. The last paragraph of the text makes it clear that no limitation of the general scope of Article 10 is involved.

The provisions are subdivided in two main heads : paragraph 1 concerns the general principles of international co-operation in matters of security, and paragraphs 2 and 3 the responsibilities of the Assembly in regard to specific problems affecting international peace.

The text follows closely the Dumbarton Oaks Proposals, using " consider " in relation to principles and " discuss " in relation to specific questions. It has been suggested that the verbal distinction is deliberate, that " consideration " is more comprehensive than " discussion " and contemplates the making of a recommendation. That view seems to be unwarranted. The Assembly's right to make recommendations following a " discussion " is expressly admitted in Article 10 and Article 11(2). If there is any difference between the two terms, it is that " consideration " points to a broad and probably periodical review of principles, while " discussion " is concerned with immediate issues.

" *General principles* " : (1) *Co-operation in the maintenance of peace and security.* The practical purpose of referring to the Assembly the general principles relating to this subject is not clear. They are laid down with particularity in Articles 1 and 2 and Chapters VI and VII, and cannot be changed without formal amendment of the Charter. The Assembly itself felt uncertain about the way it should discharge this responsibility and, in November 1947, invited the Interim Committee to make suggestions " on methods to be adopted to give effect to that part of Article 11 (paragraph 1) which deals with the general principles of co-operation in the maintenance of international peace and security ".[1]

---

[1] For further comment, see Article 13.

" *General principles* " : (2) *Disarmament and regulation of armaments*. It is not for the Assembly, but exclusively for the Security Council (Article 26), to work out the plans of a system for the regulation of armaments, and the Charter does not say that in these plans the Council will have to be guided by principles recommended by the Assembly.

Nevertheless, the Assembly has repeatedly taken occasion to make recommendations on such principles. In conjunction with the setting up of the Atomic Energy Commission (a body whose membership and terms of reference were determined by the Assembly, but which immediately passed under the control of the Security Council) the Assembly, in January 1946, laid down that it was desirable to extend, between all nations, the exchange of basic scientific information for peaceful ends ; to control atomic energy so as to ensure its use for peaceful purposes ; to eliminate from national armaments atomic weapons and all other major weapons adaptable to mass destruction ; and to devise effective safeguards, by way of inspection and other means, to protect complying States against the hazards of violation and invasion. Again, in December 1946, the Assembly passed a formal resolution in which it recognized the need for an early general regulation and reduction of armaments and armed forces, but refrained from formulating fundamental principles apart from a few generalities: it was desirable that the general prohibition, regulation and reduction of armaments be directed towards the major weapons of modern warfare, and not merely towards the minor weapons : it was essential to provide practical and effective safeguards through inspection and other means, and to establish within the framework of the Security Council an international system operating through special organs.

On two specific points, however, the General Assembly asserted its authority. The Security Council was not to submit draft treaties or conventions to Member States without the previous approval of the Assembly. Secondly, the Assembly made a recommendation to Members, without any reference to the Security Council

" to undertake the progressive and balanced withdrawal, taking account of the needs of occupation, of their armed forces stationed in ex-enemy territories ; and the withdrawal without delay of their armed forces stationed in the territories of Members of the United Nations without their consent freely and publicly expressed in treaties or agreements consistent with the Charter and not contradicting international agreements ".

This part of the resolution was linked with the problem of general disarmament by a further recommendation to Members for

" a corresponding reduction of national armed forces and a general progressive and balanced reduction of national armed forces ".

This last recommendation manifestly went beyond the limits of the Assembly's authority to consider the " general principles " of disarmament ; it was a direct call for action.

Specific questions relating to peace and security. The second paragraph of this Article is applicable only to questions brought before the Assembly by a Member, or by the Security Council, or by a non-member acting under Article 35(2). Apart from this last category, the question need not be concerned with a controversial issue. Relevance to peace and security, and not the existence of a conflict, is the test.[1] It is not essential that the question should involve a present or potential danger to peace. That condition applies only when the Assembly, acting on its own initiative, proposes to bring a " situation " to the attention of the Council under paragraph 3.[2]

Relation to Security Council. (1) The mere fact that the Council is seised of a question does not prevent the Assembly from discussing it. But if the question before the Council is a dispute or

---

[1] In February 1946, on the proposal of Byelorussia, the Assembly made a recommendation to Members for the arrest of war criminals still at large, and for their immediate removal, for trial and punishment, to the countries in which the crimes were committed. The issue was not controversial, but it was clearly relevant to peace.

[2] Noteworthy decisions made under Article 11(2) include :

On the *Spanish Question*, a recommendation in December 1946, that the Franco Government be debarred from membership in specialized agencies, and from participation in conferences or other activities arranged by the United Nations or the specialized agencies ; and that all Member States immediately recall from Madrid their Ambassadors and Plenipotentiary Ministers.

On the *Treatment of Indians in South Africa*, a recommendation of December 1946, that such treatment " should be in conformity with the international obligations under the agreements concluded between the two Governments and the relevant provisions of the Charter ".

On the *Greek Question*, a call addressed to Albania, Bulgaria and Yugoslavia in October 1947, to discontinue aid and assistance to the guerrillas ; and specific recommendations for the settlement of the dispute, including the establishment of a Special Committee of the Assembly to assist the Governments concerned.

On the *Korean Question*, the setting up, in November 1947, of a United Nations Temporary Commission to facilitate and expedite the participation of elected representatives in re-establishing national independence ; and in December 1948, a declaration that there has been established a lawful Government of the Republic of Korea. This was coupled with a recommendation that the Occupying Powers withdraw their forces as early as practicable, and the establishment of a Commission of Korea, mainly for the purpose of bringing about the unification of the country.

situation in the meaning of Article 34, the Assembly must not make recommendations, except at the Council's request. (2) If in the view of the Assembly action is necessary on any question before it,[1] that question must be referred to the Council, either before or after discussion. In this context, "action" means action under Chapter VII[2]. (3) If the question before the Assembly is a situation in the meaning of Article 34, the Assembly may refer it to the Council, even if no action under Chapter VII seems to be necessary. The wording of paragraph 3 (" call the attention of the Council ") suggests reference without specific recommendations.

ARTICLE 12

1. While the Security Council is exercising in respect of any dispute or situation the functions assigned to it in the present Charter, the General Assembly shall not make any recommendation with regard to that dispute or situation unless the Security Council so requests.

2. The Secretary-General, with the consent of the Security Council, shall notify the General Assembly at each session of any matters relative to the maintenance of international peace and security which are being dealt with by the Security Council, and shall similarly notify the General Assembly, or the Members of the United Nations if the General Assembly is not in session, immediately the Security Council ceases to deal with such matters.

Field of application. Paragraph 1 of the Article applies only to disputes or situations, the continuance of which is likely to endanger the maintenance of peace and security. If that character of the dispute or situation is in doubt, the Article applies nevertheless, pending investigations by the Council under Article 34. It ceases to apply if the Council finds that the continuance of the dispute or situation involves no danger to peace and security.

Paragraph 2 covers the wider field of " any matters " related to peace and security ; that includes, for instance, plans for the regulation of armaments. Its provisions are administrative and

---

[1] " Questions on which action is necessary " may include not only disputes and situations, but any emergency, e.g. a sudden threat, or act, of aggression.

[2] Goodrich-Hambro, *op. cit.* p.99 take the view that, in the context of Paragraph 2, action means everything the Council has power to do under Chapters V—VIII. But the right of the Assembly to conduct its own investigations has never been challenged, and Article 14 makes it clear that the Assembly is competent to recommend measures of peaceful adjustment.

do not by themselves involve any restriction of the competence of the Assembly.

Restriction of the Assembly's competence. The Article does not limit the Assembly's right to discuss any matter within the scope of Article 10, whether or not the Security Council is seised of it. The limitation is solely on the Assembly's power to make recommendations : the Assembly must not, without a request from the Council, make recommendations on a dispute or situation in respect of which the Council is exercising the functions assigned to it in Chapters VI-VII of the Charter.

The presence of a dispute or situation on the agenda of the Council is *prima facie* evidence that the Council is in the process of exercising those functions. It is not, however, conclusive evidence. The responsibilities of the Assembly in matters of security must not be frustrated by disputes and situations being kept indefinitely on the agenda of the Council, without proper action taken. In the view of the present writers, the Assembly, by virtue of its general supervisory powers (Article 10), is entitled to find that the Council has failed to exercise its functions in relation to a particular dispute or situation. and to consider itself free from the restriction of paragraph 1.

Recommendations which had been made by the Assembly before a dispute or situation was placed on the agenda of the Council are not affected by this Article.

Recommendations at the request of the Council. Although a request from one organ of the United Nations to another would appear to be essentially procedural, it is one of the perplexities created by the Five-Power Statement on Voting Procedure that a request under this Article is a matter of substance for the purposes of Article 27, and may be vetoed by any permanent member of the Council. But it is by now established in practice that the request need not be express, and that it can be implied by the removal of the dispute or situation from the agenda of the Council ; a decision to that effect is not subject to the veto.[1]

Administrative provisions. Paragraph 2 of the Article is self-explanatory. Paradoxically, the consent of the Council, on which the action of the Secretary-General depends, seems to be a matter of substance under the Five-Power Statement and may be vetoed by any permanent member.

[1] This procedure was followed in October 1946 to enable the Assembly to make recommendations on the *Spanish Question*, and in September 1947 in the *Greek Question*. For the recommendations of the Assembly in these two cases, see comment on Article 11.

ARTICLE 13

1. The General Assembly shall initiate studies and make recommendations for the purpose of :—
    (a) promoting international co-operation in the political field and encouraging the progressive development of international law and its codification ;
    (b) promoting international co-operation in the economic, social, cultural, educational and health fields, and assisting in the realization of human rights and fundamental freedoms for all without distinction as to race, sex, language or religion.
2. The further responsibilities, functions and powers of the General Assembly with respect to matters mentioned in paragraph 1 (b) above are set forth in Chapters IX and X.

Mandatory character of Article. Whereas it is optional for the General Assembly to consider, and make recommendations on, the subjects mentioned in Articles 10-11 and Article 14, the Assembly has a positive obligation to initiate studies and make recommendations for the promotion of the objectives set out in paragraph 1 of this Article. Broadly speaking, the purposes of the United Nations are twofold : (1) the maintenance of peace and security, and (2) the promotion of international co-operation in political and non-political fields. This Article is concerned with the Assembly's responsibilities under the second heading. *Co-operation in the political field.* The meaning of the first part of sub-clause (a) is obscure. A comparison with Article 11(1) creates the impression that by " co-operation in the political field " the Charter means something different from " co-operation in the maintenance of international peace and security ". In practice, it is difficult to draw a line of demarcation or find any political subjects of international concern which are not, at the same time, relevant to peace. The Assembly itself soon became aware of the difficulty and, in November 1947, made it one of the terms of reference of the Interim Committee[1] to study suitable methods for giving effect to sub-clause (a) of this Article and to paragraph 1 of Article 11. These studies have not yet been completed, but the approach of the Interim Committee has been on the lines that the two Articles cannot be rigidly separated, except so far as under Article 11(1) the Assembly will be concerned with general principles and under sub-clause (a) of this Article

---

[1] See comment on Article 22.

with practical measures.[1] Of the vast field of political co-operation, the Interim Committee has so far explored one sector, viz. the pacific settlement of disputes. Its initial recommendations included (1) the appointment of rapporteurs and conciliators in cases brought before the Security Council; (2) the establishment of a panel for inquiry or conciliation available to Member States and non-members alike; and (3) amendments to the General Act of 1928 for the Pacific Settlement of Disputes. These recommendations were endorsed by the Third Assembly in May 1949.

Development of international law. Compared with national law, international law regulates a relatively small number of subjects. There are two principal ways in which the United Nations may bring about the steady development of the Law of Nations. First, it can encourage Member States to regulate by international treaty a growing number of relationships in the political, economic and social fields, and thereby to diminish progressively the area of domestic jurisdiction or " State discretion ". Secondly, the Organization has it in its power to create precedents. International law derives not only from treaties, but also from custom. The more States respond in individual cases to recommendations of the Assembly for the treatment in a specific manner of specific incidents of international concern, the stronger will be the precedents on which Governments can and should rely in future cases of like nature.

Codification of international law. International law is still largely uncodified. Its rules are scattered over a great many treaties and precedents. Whether codification is altogether desirable is a controversial issue between international lawyers. On the one side it is argued that codification would crystallize the law at its present stage of development, and make more difficult its adaptation to changing circumstances. On the other hand, codification would eliminate many of those controversies, now frequently encountered in practice, which revolve round the question whether a subject of international concern is covered by a legal rule at all.

The Charter manifestly favours codification, but not necessarily in the sense of reducing the whole body of international law to a single code. Less ambitious projects, e.g. the re-statement

---

[1] In addition to the recommendations mentioned in connection with Article 11(1), noteworthy decisions of the Assembly in the political field included the Resolution of November 3, 1947, condemning war-mongering propaganda, and the Resolution of November 17, 1947, on the teaching in the schools of Member States of the Purposes and Principles, the structure and activities of the United Nations.

or the formulation by international treaty of the law relating to one specific subject, are also " codification ".[1] The Charter itself is a code and so are other multilateral conventions, including the constitutions of the specialized agencies.[2]

In December 1946 the Assembly established a " Committee on Progressive Development of International Law and its Codification " to study suitable methods for giving effect to its responsibilities under the Article. On the recommendation of the Committee, in November 1947, the Assembly decided to set up a permanent International Law Commission of experts. The fifteen members of the Commission were elected in November 1948 for a three-year term and they commenced work in April 1949. The first major tasks assigned to the Commission include (1) The preparation of a Declaration on the rights and duties of States; (2) the formulation of the principles of international law recognized in the Charter of the Nuremberg Tribunal; and (3) the preparation of a code of offences against the peace and security of mankind. At its first session the Commission selected 14 more subjects for future codification and assigned tentative priorities to the international law of (i) treaties, (ii) arbitral procedure, and (3) the régime of the high seas.

One of the most effective means of furthering the development of international law is the promotion of public interest in the subject. Acting on this principle, the Assembly, in November 1947, recommended the Member States to extend the teaching of international law in their universities and higher educational institutions.

Economic and social co-operation. Sub-clause (b) of the Article is a re-statement of the objectives set out in Article 1(3). Whereas in the political field primary responsibility for the functions of the Organization rests with the Security Council, in the economic and social fields the General Assembly is the supreme authority. The Economic and Social Council, and its network of subsidiary organs,[3] are clearly subordinated by Article 60 to the directions of the Assembly. The subject will be discussed in greater detail in connection with Chapters IX-X.

---

[1] See the International Bill of Human Rights and the Convention on the Prevention of Genocide under Article 62 ; also the Conventions on the privileges and immunities of the United Nations and of the specialized agencies under Articles 104-105.

[2] See Article 57.

[3] See Article 68.

ARTICLE 14

Subject to the provisions of Article 12, the General Assembly may recommend measures for the peaceful adjustment of any situation, regardless of origin, which it deems likely to impair the general welfare or friendly relations among nations, including situations resulting from a violation of the provisions of the present Charter setting forth the Purposes and Principles of the United Nations.

" *Peaceful change* ". The United Nations is not founded on the assumption that the *status quo* is to be rigidly preserved, and that every attempt to change existing frontiers or treaty obligations must be resisted. The League was not founded on that assumption either, but in the new Organization the tendency toward change is more marked. Article 10 of the Covenant, in which the Members of the League undertook to respect and preserve against external aggression the territorial integrity of each other, had been relied upon as a solemn undertaking for the preservation of the territorial *status quo*. There is no such provision in the Charter. Again, under Article 19 of the Covenant, the League Assembly could advise only the reconsideration of treaties which had become inapplicable and the consideration of international conditions whose continuance was a potential danger to world peace. The Charter goes a long step further. The adjustments which the United Nations Assembly may recommend are confined neither to treaties nor to " dangerous " situations. The Assembly may deal with any situation, regardless of its origin in treaties or otherwise ; and the test it has to apply is not the strict one of security, but the broader test of general welfare and friendly relations. More important still, the Charter, unlike the Covenant, enables the Assembly to recommend the adjustment not only of relations between States, but also of situations within a State. This applies even where the situation is essentially within domestic jurisdiction, or is at least alleged to be so.[1] Recommendations — and the Assembly can only make recommendations under this Article — are not " intervention " in the sense prohibited by Article 2(7).

[1] In the case of *The Treatment of Indians in the Union of South Africa*, the Union Government maintained that the discriminating statutes complained of by the Indian Government were within domestic jurisdiction. The General Assembly, overruling the objection, made recommendations under Articles 11 and 14 of the Charter, including a suggestion for a round-table conference between India, Pakistan and the Union of South Africa (see Resolutions of November 17, 1947 and May 14, 1949).

c*

Field of application. " Situation", in the context of this Article, refers not only to those situations more precisely defined in Article 34, but to any state of affairs which in the judgement of the Assembly is likely to impair the general welfare or friendly relations among nations.[1]

The field which the Article was intended to cover is so wide that it would have been futile to enumerate or classify the situations to which it can be properly applied. The text gives only one example : the violation of the Purposes and Principles of the United Nations. The point is important, because recommendations under this Article are the only way in which the Organization can deal with such infringements of the Purposes (Article 1) as may fall short of actual threats to, or breaches of, the peace. The Principles (Article 2) are also protected by Article 6, which cannot, however, be invoked except in the case of " persistent " violations, and then only subject to the veto of the Great Powers. The present Article, therefore, is an additional and more easily enforced safeguard.

Binding force. The recommendations of the Assembly, if addressed direct to Members, are not binding. But recommendations addressed to organs of the United Nations must be complied with. Even the Security Council is expected to act upon them, provided the recommendation from the Assembly does not purport to dispose of a dispute or situation of the character defined in Article 34, or to prescribe specific action under Chapter VII.[2]

ARTICLE 15

1. The General Assembly shall receive and consider annual and special reports from the Security Council ; these reports shall include an account of the measures that the Security Council has decided upon or taken to maintain international peace and security.

[1] In April 1947, the United Kingdom Government as Mandatory Power for Palestine placed the question of the future government of that territory before the General Assembly. On November 29, 1947, the Assembly recommended to the United Kingdom as Mandatory Power and to all other Members of the United Nations the adoption of a " Plan of Partition with Economic Union " : and declared, in reliance on Article 14 of the Charter, that its recommendations were based on the consideration " that the present situation in Palestine is one which is likely to impair the general welfare and friendly relations among nations ".

[2] The Assembly Resolution of November 29, 1947, on the Future Government of Palestine requested the Security Council to " take the necessary measures, as provided for in the (Partition) Plan, for its implementation ". Although one permanent member of the Council (the United Kingdom) was opposed to the Plan, the duty of the Council to carry out the part assigned to it was not challenged.

2. The General Assembly shall receive and consider reports from the other organs of the United Nations.

Purpose. It is essential to the functioning of the Organization that all Members should receive periodic information on the activities of its organs and be given regular opportunities for the expression of their views. The General Assembly, the only organ on which all Members are represented, is the natural channel for the diffusion of such information and the appropriate forum for its discussion. It is this function, coupled with the budgetary powers granted in Article 17, which constitutes the Assembly the supreme supervisory organ of the United Nations.

Interpretation. The text of the Article is ambiguous. The words " shall receive " create the impression of an obligation imposed upon all other organs to supply the Assembly with such reports as it may require. In reality, the words impose an obligation on the Assembly itself : it must receive and deal with any reports the other organs may submit. The corresponding obligation of the Councils and the Secretariat is regulated elsewhere in the Charter : by Article 24(3) for the Security Council, by Article 98 for the Secretary-General, by Article 60 for the Economic and Social Council, and by Article 85 for the Trusteeship Council.[1] The point is important because, if the obligation of the Security Council were based on Article 15, the Assembly would be able to call for special reports whenever it thought fit. In effect, the supply of special reports is, under Article 24(3), at the discretion of the Council, which is entitled to disregard any request the Assembly may make for other than annual reports.

" *Consideration*" *of reports.* It is clear from the transactions of the San Francisco Conference that the Assembly has no power to record formal disapproval of any reports submitted by other organs. In the case of the Security Council such disapproval would amount to encroachment on the Council's primary responsibility (Article 24(1)) for the maintenance of peace and security.

" Consideration " implies two functions : (1) discussion, which, in view of the mandatory formulation of the text, is a positive duty of the Assembly, and (2) recommendations, at the option of the Assembly, on any subject dealt with in a report. Within the

---

[1] Article 60 and Article 85 do not expressly stipulate reports, but an obligation to supply them follows from the subordination of these two Councils to the authority of the Assembly.

limits of Article 12, recommendations may be properly made even on subjects discussed in the reports of the Security Council.

If the Assembly is dissatisfied with any report, it may express its dissatisfaction either in the form of recommendations on their subject-matter, or by " drawing the attention " of the organ concerned to critical observations made on the report while it was being debated in the full Assembly or its committees.[1]

ARTICLE 16

The General Assembly shall perform such functions with respect to the international trusteeship system as are assigned to it under Chapters XII and XIII, including the approval of the trusteeship agreements for areas not designated as strategic.

See comment on Chapters XII-XIII.

ARTICLE 17

1. The General Assembly shall consider and approve the budget of the Organization.

2. The expenses of the Organization shall be borne by the Members as apportioned by the General Assembly.

3. The General Assembly shall consider and approve any financial and budgetary arrangements with specialized agencies referred to in Article 57 and shall examine the administrative budgets of such specialized agencies with a view to making recommendations to the agencies concerned.

Importance of budgetary control. In appearance, the power conferred upon the Assembly in paragraph 1 is purely administrative. In reality it involves important supervisory and policy-making functions. When the Covenant of the League was drafted, no compromise could be reached on the controversial issue whether these functions should be entrusted to the Council or to the Assembly of the League. The question was left open, but from 1924 onwards budgetary powers were, in fact, exercised by the Assembly. The Charter confirms that practice.

Machinery. The Budget Estimates are prepared by the Secretariat, and before presentation to the General Assembly are examined

---

[1] The Assembly adopted this procedure after the examination of the first report of the Economic and Social Council ; see Assembly Resolution of December 15, 1946.

by the Advisory Committee on Administrative and Budgetary Questions.[1] The report of this committee is presented to the General Assembly at the beginning of the annual regular session, and is immediately referred to one of the Main Committees.[2] The committee stage completed, the plenary session of the Assembly decides by a two-thirds majority of those present and voting (Article 18(2)). The adoption of the Budget constitutes an authorization to the Secretary-General to incur obligations and expenditures for the purposes and up to the amounts voted. *The first four Budgets.* The General Assembly appropriated :

		U.S. Dollars
For the financial year 1946	... ...	19,390.000
For the financial year 1947	... ...	28,616.568
For the financial year 1948	... ...	34,825.195
For the financial year 1949	... ...	33,487.128

The main headings of the Budget Estimates[3] for 1949 were as follows :

		U.S. Dollars
I	Sessions of the General Assembly, the Councils, Commissions and Committees	2,516.650
II	Special Conferences, Investigations and Inquiries ...	125.690
III	New York Office...	24,335.300
IV	European Office	3,526.590
V	Information Centres (exclusive of the Information Services in Geneva)	754.490
VI	Regional Economic Commissions (other than Economic Commission for Europe)	820.610
VII	Hospitality	20.000
VIII	Advisory Social Welfare Functions	675.000
IX	International Court of Justice	695.257
	TOTAL	33,469,587

Contributions. Paragraph 2 of the Article follows the precedent of Article 6(5) of the League Covenant as amended in 1924.[4]

In apportioning the expenses among Member States, the General Assembly is assisted by an expert Committee on Contributions.[5]

---

[1] See Article 22.

[2] Committee V. (" Administrative and Budgetary ") ; see Article 22.

[3] These were slightly less than the appropriations eventually voted by the Assembly.

[4] Before the 1924 amendment the expenses of the League were not apportioned by the Assembly, but borne by the Members in accordance with the apportionment of the expenses of the International Bureau of the Universal Postal Union.

[5] See Article 22.

For the financial year 1949 the scale of assessments ranged between 39.89 per cent. of the total (U.S.A.) and 0.04 per cent. of the total (Costa Rica, Haiti, Honduras, Iceland, Liberia, Nicaragua, Paraguay and Yemen). For the same financial year the assessments of the five Great Powers were as follows :

						Per cent. of total
U.S.A.	...	...	...	...	...	39.89
United Kingdom	...	...	...	...	...	11.37
U.S.S.R.	...	...	...	...	...	6.34
France	...	...	...	...	...	6.00
China	...	...	...	...	...	6.00
						69.60

Specialized agencies The question of an integrated or consolidated budget for the United Nations and the specialized agencies was debated at the second regular session of the Assembly, and referred to the Secretary-General for further study. After consultation with the administrative heads of the specialized agencies, the Secretary-General declared in his Third Annual Report that, " apart from any question of desirability, the constitutional and political prerequisites for a consolidated budget are not capable of immediate fulfilment ". Under the agreements concluded in accordance with Article 63, with the exception of the International Bank for Reconstruction and Development and the International Monetary Fund, all specialized agencies are required to transmit their administrative budgets to the Secretary-General of the United Nations, for examination by the Secretariat and recommendations by the General Assembly.

The " financial arrangements " mentioned in paragraph 3 are concerned mainly with loans from the " Working Capital Fund " of the United Nations to the specialized agencies, particularly during the initial period of the activities of new agencies, and with the sharing of the costs of common fiscal and administrative services, including conference facilities.

VOTING

ARTICLE 18

1. Each Member of the General Assembly shall have one vote.

2. Decisions of the General Assembly on important questions shall be made by a two-thirds majority of the members present

and voting. These questions shall include : recommendations with respect to the maintenance of international peace and security, the election of the non-permanent members of the Security Council, the election of the members of the Economic and Social Council, the election of members of the Trustee-ship Council in accordance with paragraph 1(c) of Article 86, the admission of new Members to the United Nations, the suspension of the rights and privileges of membership, the expulsion of Members, questions relating to the operation of the trusteeship system, and budgetary questions.

3. Decisions on other questions, including the determination of additional categories of questions to be decided by a two-thirds majority, shall be made by a majority of the members present and voting.

Equality of votes. Each Member State has one vote in the General Assembly. To that extent, the Charter gives full effect to the principle of sovereign equality proclaimed in Article 2(1).[1]

The majority rule. Except on such " important questions " as are listed in paragraph 2, or may in future be defined, the General Assembly decides by a simple majority vote.

This is a significant departure from the Covenant of the League which, apart from exceptions specifically stated,[2] prescribed the rule of unanimity for the League Assembly, with the result that every Member of the League had a virtual right of veto.

The majority required by this Article[3] is the majority of " the members present and voting ". Abstentions do not operate as negative votes, nor can the absence from a meeting of less than half the total membership bar a valid decision.[4]

Qualified majority. There are two classes of questions on which the General Assembly decides by a two-thirds majority : (1) the " important questions " listed in paragraph 2 ; and (2) additional categories of questions to be determined under paragraph 3.

" *Important questions* ". These are :

(a) *Recommendations with respect to the maintenance of peace and security.*

---

[1] The voting rights of Members are not necessarily equal in the specialized agencies.

[2] No unanimity was required for substantive resolutions falling short of " decisions ", procedural matters, the admission of new Members to the League, the appointment of additional permanent members of the Council, and the approval of an appointment by the Council to the post of Secretary-General.

[3] A different rule applies under Articles 108-109 ; see comment on pp. 187-9.

[4] Under the *Rules of Procedure* the majority of the members of the Assembly constitutes a quorum.

These include (i) all recommendations under Article 11, (ii) any recommendations made under Article 12 upon the request of the Security Council, and (iii) recommendations under Article 14 insofar as they relate to situations which involve a danger to peace and security.

(b) *Elections to the three Councils* (Article 23(2), Article 61 and Article 86(1)).[1]

(c) *The admission of new Members and the suspension and expulsion of Members* (Articles 4-6).

(d) *Questions relating to the operation of the trusteeship system* (Chapters XII and XIII).

(e) *Budgetary questions* (Article 17).

Additional categories. By a simple majority of its members present and voting, the Assembly may determine that, in addition to those listed in paragraph 2, further categories of questions shall require a two-thirds majority vote.

This power—it has not yet been used—is limited by those provisions of the Charter and of the Statute of the International Court of Justice which expressly stipulate a majority other than of two-thirds.[2]

As a simple majority of members is entitled to create additional categories, so at any time it may abolish them by a subsequent vote. But none of the questions listed in paragraph 2 can be withdrawn from the two-thirds majority rule without amendment of the Charter.

Voting procedure. Under the Rules of Procedure, votes are normally taken by a show of hands or by standing. Any representative may request a roll-call, which is taken in the English alphabetical order of the names of members. All elections, including the appointment of the Secretary-General, are made by secret ballot.

If the voting is equally divided on matters other than elections, a second vote is taken at a meeting to be held within forty-eight hours. If there is a second tie, the motion is rejected. If a tie occurs in an election, the President draws lots, but in elections to the three Councils the balloting continues until a candidate secures the two-thirds majority required.

---

[1] Paradoxically, the appointment of Secretary-General is not listed among the "important questions", although its importance is far greater than for instance, the filling of a vacancy on the Trusteeship Council.

[2] Under Article 109(3) a simple majority vote will be sufficient at the tenth annual session of the General Assembly to call a General Conference for the purpose of reviewing the Charter. Under Article 10(1) of the Statute of the Court, an absolute majority of votes in the General Assembly is sufficient for the election of judges.

ARTICLE 19

A Member of the United Nations which is in arrears in the payment of its financial contributions to the Organization shall have no vote in the General Assembly if the amount of its arrears equals or exceeds the amount of the contributions due from it for the preceding two full years. The General Assembly may, nevertheless, permit such a Member to vote if it is satisfied that the failure to pay is due to conditions beyond the control of the Member.

In view of the unsatisfactory experience of the League with respect to the regularity of its income, the Charter prescribes the suspension of the voting rights of Members which may fall into serious arrears in the payment of their financial contributions. The suspension applies only to voting rights in the General Assembly ; voting rights in the Councils remain unaffected.

It is not intended to penalize Members for financial difficulties beyond their control. The Assembly at its discretion may grant dispensation from the suspension of voting rights, either generally or for particular sessions or meetings.

The Member's voting rights are restored immediately on payment of a sum which reduces the arrears below a figure representing the contributions due for the two full years preceding the date of suspension.

PROCEDURE

ARTICLE 20

The General Assembly shall meet in regular annual sessions and in such special sessions as occasion may require. Special sessions shall be convoked by the Secretary-General at the request of the Security Council or of a majority of the Members of the United Nations.

Regular sessions. The Covenant did not prescribe annual sessions, only sessions " at stated intervals ". It was the regular practice of the League to convene the Assembly " in general session " every year. The Charter confirms that practice.

Under the Rules of Procedure, the regular session begins on the third Tuesday in September. The session may be postponed if all Members agree : and there is at least one precedent for postponement with the consent of a simple majority.[1]

It is now established by practice that the Assembly may divide a regular session in several parts, with an interval of several months between two parts.

Special sessions. The Secretary-General must convene a special session whenever he is requested to do so by the Security Council[2] or by a majority of Members.

In such cases, the session must be held within 15 days from the receipt of the request.

Place of meetings. The General Assembly meets at the head-quarters of the Organization unless a previous session decided otherwise, or a majority of Members requests that the next session be held at another place.

ARTICLE 21

The General Assembly shall adopt its own rules of procedure. It shall elect its President for each session.

Rules of Procedure. Provisional Rules of Procedure were drawn up by the Preparatory Commission[3] and remained in force until January 1, 1948, when they were replaced by a revised set of Rules. These Rules regulate in detail the time and place of sessions, the preparation and adoption of the agenda, the composition of delegations, the presidency of the Assembly, the structure of its committees, the conduct of business and particularly of voting, the official and working languages of the Assembly, its records and the services of the Secretariat.[4]

Presidency. At the opening of each session the Assembly elects a President to hold office until its close. At the same time and for the same period it elects seven Vice-Presidents. The Assembly has a free choice, but in the case of Vice-Presidents the Rules of Procedure prescribe that due regard shall be paid to ensuring the

---

[1] The second part of the first session was postponed from September 23 to October 23, 1946, with the previous consent of 37 Members.

[2] Whether the making of such a request by the Security Council is a procedural matter in the sense of Article 27(2), is doubtful.

[3] See pp. xxiii-xxiv.

[4] It is beyond the scope of this work to give a full account of the Rules of Procedure. Brief references are included under the appropriate Articles of the Charter. For the full text of the Rules of Procedure, see United Nations Document Ref. No. A/482.

representative character of the Assembly's General Committee[1] of which all Vice-Presidents are *ex officio* members.

If there is a tie, the President has no casting vote. Indeed, neither the President nor any Vice-President who may be in the chair must vote at all. The voting rights of his country must be exercised by another member of the delegation.

ARTICLE 22

The General Assembly may establish such subsidiary organs as it deems necessary for the performance of its functions.

Terminology. This Article is a specific application of Article 7(2) which provides for the setting up of such subsidiary organs of the United Nations " as may be found necessary ". It is convenient to deal under this heading not only with *ad hoc* bodies set up for the discharge of specific functions, but with the committee structure of the Assembly in general.[2]

Classification. The committees and subsidiary organs of the General Assembly may be classified under four headings (1) Procedural Committees, (2) Main Committees, (3) Standing Committees, (4) *Ad hoc* bodies.

Procedural Committees. There are two :

(i) The *General Committee* is the " steering " organ of the Assembly. It advises on the agenda for the session as a whole and for each plenary meeting, determines the priority of items, coordinates the proceedings of other committees and revises the text, but not the substance, of the resolutions passed in full assembly. Its 14 members include the President and seven Vice-Presidents of the Assembly and the chairmen of the six Main Committees.

(ii) The *Credentials Committee* is elected at the beginning of each session to examine the credentials of delegations.

Main Committees. There are six of these and all Member States have a seat on each.

---

[1] See comment on Article 22.

[2] It is arguable that the term " subsidiary organ " should be reserved either for bodies not concerned with the routine business of the Assembly or for bodies invested with a greater degree of independence (e.g. the International Law Commission or the Board of Auditors) than its permanent committees. But it is difficult to draw a line of demarcation: and the Rules of Procedure speak of " committees and subsidiary organs " without indicating any distinguishing criteria.

Committee I. (" Political and Security ") deals with all political matters and questions of security on the agenda and with the admission, suspension and expulsion of Members.

Committee II. (" Economic and Financial "), and

Committee III. (" Social, Humanitarian and Cultural ") deal with the programmes and activities of the Economic and Social Council, its subsidiary organs, and the specialized agencies.

Committee IV. (" Trusteeship ") deals with all questions arising under Chapters XI-XIII of the Charter.

Committee V. (" Administrative and Budgetary ") deals with the responsibilities of the Assembly under Article 17, Article 19 and Chapter XV.

Committee VI. (" Legal ") examines legal problems referred by other Committees and deals with requests to the International Court of Justice for advisory opinions,[1] all matters arising under Chapter XVI and Chapter XVIII, and generally, with the development and codification of international law.

Standing Committees. There are two :

(i) The *Advisory Committee for Administrative and Budgetary Questions* is responsible for the expert examination of the budget of the United Nations and of the specialized agencies, and of financial and budgetary arrangements with the agencies. It has nine members, two of whom must be financial experts of recognized standing.

(ii) The *Committee on Contributions* advises the General Assembly on (a) the apportionment of expenses among Members ; (b) appeals for a change of assessment ; and (c) the application of Article 19. It has ten members.

The members of both Standing Committees are elected individually for a term of three years.[2]

Ad hoc bodies. These may be classified as follows :

(i) The *Interim Committee of the General Assembly*, (the " Little Assembly ") was first set up by Assembly Resolution of November 13, 1947, for the purpose of assuring the continuity of the functions of the General Assembly between the closing of the

---

[1] See Article 96.

[2] Shortly after the change of régime in February 1948, the new Czechoslovak Government terminated the appointment of Dr. Jan Papanek, until then Czechoslovakia's permanent representative at the United Nations. At the time of his dismissal, Dr. Papanek was a member of both Standing Committees. He contended that the members of these Committees were elected personally as experts and not as representatives of Governments, and that the termination of their appointment as Government representatives did not affect their membership. This point of view was supported by the Legal Department of the Secretariat, and, on October 16, 1948, it was confirmed by the General Assembly.

second and the opening of the third regular session. It was re-established in December, 1948, for the period between the closing of the first part of the third session and the opening of the fourth. The Committee's terms of reference include (a) matters specifically referred to it by the General Assembly ; (b) such disputes or situations which have been proposed for inclusion in the agenda of the General Assembly, and in the view of the Committee are important and require preliminary study ; (c) the examination of suitable methods to give effect to the responsibilities of the General Assembly under Article 11(1) and Article 13(1a) of the Charter ; (d) advice to the Secretary-General on any case for the summoning of a special session of the General Assembly ; (e) the conduct of investigations and the appointment of commissions of inquiry in matters arising within the scope of the Committee's duties.

The setting up of the Interim Committee was opposed by the Soviet *bloc* as an alleged encroachment on the exclusive competence of the Security Council to deal between regular sessions of the General Assembly with questions of peace and security. To meet that objection, the Assembly has made the Committee's terms of reference subject to a proviso which prohibits the Committee from considering any matter of which the Security Council may be seised.

Each member of the General Assembly has the right to appoint one representative to the Committee, but no such appointments have been made by the Soviet *bloc*.

(ii) *Specialized committees in charge of organizational matters*, e.g. the Permanent Headquarters Committee, the League of Nations Committee, the Committee on UNRRA, the Special Technical Committee on Post-UNRRA Relief, the Committee on Procedure and Organization, the Board of Auditors, and many others.

(iii) *Expert Committees to assist in the discharge of specialized functions of the General Assembly*, e.g. the Committee on the Progressive Development of International Law and its Codification, and the International Law Commission.

(iv) *Committees and Commissions of inquiry and conciliation*, e.g. the Special Committee on Palestine (November 1947), the Palestine Conciliation Commission (December 1948), the two United Nations Commissions on Korea (November 1947 and December 1948), and the Special Committee on the Balkans (November 1947).

CHAPTER V

THE SECURITY COUNCIL

COMPOSITION

ARTICLE 23

1. The Security Council shall consist of eleven Members of the United Nations. The Republic of China, France, the Union of Soviet Socialist Republics, the United Kingdom of Great Britain and Northern Ireland, and the United States of America shall be permanent members of the Security Council. The General Assembly shall elect six other Members of the United Nations to be non-permanent members of the Security Council, due regard being specially paid, in the first instance to the contribution of Members of the United Nations to the maintenance of international peace and security and to the other purposes of the Organization, and also to equitable geographical distribution.

2. The non-permanent members of the Security Council shall be elected for a term of two years. In the first election of the non-permanent members, however, three shall be chosen for a term of one year. A retiring member shall not be eligible for immediate re-election.

3. Each member of the Security Council shall have one representative.

Number of seats. The number of seats on the Security Council is fixed at eleven. This is a radical departure from the structure of the League Council in which the number of seats was variable.[1]

The new system has its advantages. As the number of members is rigidly laid down, the lesser Powers have no inducement, which they had in the League, to press for further seats ; they have numerical superiority in any case. Moreover a Council of eleven members is a body of manageable size. The Council of the League tended to grow too large for prompt and effective action.

---

[1] The original number was nine, including permanent seats for the five Principal Allied and Associated Powers. But the Council, with the approval of the Assembly, had power to create further permanent and non-permanent seats. By 1938 the number of elective seats had risen to eleven.

Permanent Members. The Great Powers have permanent seats for much the same reason as they had in the Council of the League. The *ultima ratio* of any proceedings of the Council is the threat of force; and no effective economic or military sanctions are conceivable without the concurrence of the Great Powers.

Unlike the Covenant, the Charter prescribes a fixed number of permanent seats. China, France, the Soviet Union, the United Kingdom and the U.S.A. remain permanent members whether or not any of them ceases to be a Great Power.[1] No other State, not even a new Great Power which might emerge from the federation of a number of lesser Powers, can obtain a permanent seat except by amendment of the Charter.

Non-permanent members. Under the Covenant, the non-permanent members of the League Council were to be selected by the Assembly " in its discretion " and " from time to time ", i.e. for periods to be determined by the Assembly.[2]

The Charter departs in two ways from the system of the Covenant. First, it withdraws from the discretion of the General Assembly the question of rotation. Secondly, it establishes positive criteria for the choice of candidates.

Term of office. Non-permanent members are elected for a term of two calendar years. This is a shorter period than the one prescribed for members of the Economic and Social Council and the Trusteeship Council. It gives the lesser Powers a speedier chance of obtaining a seat. The same purpose is served by the rule that a retiring member of the Security Council is not eligible for immediate re-election.[3]

Qualifications. In filling the six elective seats on the Council the General Assembly is faced with a delicate problem. It must be led by two considerations which do not necessarily converge. First, the distribution must be fair to the Organization, by affording representation to those Member States, or groups of them, which owing to their strategic location, manpower, or economic resources can make a valuable contribution to security.[4]

---

[1] There was an abortive suggestion at San Francisco that the permanent members should not be designated by name, and that the Organization should be free to determine from time to time which are the five Principal Powers entitled to permanent membership.

[2] From 1926, the Assembly used these discretionary powers subject to a number of self-imposed rules. Eventually these crystallized into a system based on equitable geographical distribution, rotation and the limitation of re-elections.

[3] The rule operates only against re-election immediately on retirement ; no specific " waiting period " is prescribed.

[4] The importance in this respect of Canada, Australia, Brazil and the Netherlands was strongly stressed at San Francisco.

Secondly, the distribution must be fair to the general membership : every Member State should sooner or later be given an opportunity to serve on the Council. For the lesser Powers this is an important point of prestige, and the Organization itself stands to gain by every Member State acquiring first-hand knowledge of the Council's political and technical approach to the causes and symptoms of international conflicts.

The Charter reduces these considerations to a formula which establishes two criteria for the guidance of the General Assembly without, however, making them absolutely binding. These are : (1) The contribution of the candidate to the maintenance of international peace and security and to the other purposes of the Organization.

This refers both to past and future contributions. The Assembly must take into account not only the historical record and potential contributions to economic and military sanctions, but also the record and potentialities of the candidate in regard to the objectives stated in Article 55.

(2) Equitable geographical distribution. As far as possible there should be adequate representation not only for all continents, but also for groups of States which form distinct geographical units within a continent.[1]

Number of representatives. Each Member State is entitled to one representative on the Council.

---

[1] At the first election (January, 1946) the six seats went to Egypt, Mexico and the Netherlands for one year ; and to Australia, Brazil and Poland for two years.

At the second election (November, 1946) Syria was elected in the place of Egypt ; Colombia in the place of Mexico ; and Belgium in the place of the Netherlands.

At the third election (September-November, 1947), Canada was elected in the place of Australia ; Argentina in the place of Brazil ; and the Ukraine in the place of Poland.

At the fourth election (October, 1948) Norway was elected in the place of Belgium ; Cuba in the place of Colombia ; and Egypt in the place of Syria.

As a result of these elections, the distribution of non-permanent seats among the chief geographical units may be summarized as follows in relation to the period January 1946—December 1949 :

one seat for the British Dominions ;
two seats for Latin America ;
one seat for the Near and Middle East ;
one seat for Western Europe ;
one seat for Eastern Europe.

Taking the Council as a whole the eleven seats were during the same period distributed as follows :

five seats for Europe ;
three seats for the Americas ;
one seat for the British Dominions ;
one seat for the Far East (China) ;
one seat for the Near and Middle East.

FUNCTIONS AND POWERS

ARTICLE 24

1. In order to ensure prompt and effective action by the United Nations, its Members confer on the Security Council primary responsibility for the maintenance of international peace and security, and agree that in carrying out its duties under this responsibility the Security Council acts on their behalf.

2. In discharging these duties the Security Council shall act in accordance with the Purposes and Principles of the United Nations. The specific powers granted to the Security Council for the discharge of these duties are laid down in Chapters VI, VII, VIII, and XII.

3. The Security Council shall submit annual and, when necessary, special reports to the General Assembly for its consideration.

" *Primary responsibility* ". Under the Covenant, the maintenance of peace was the responsibility of the Council and the Assembly of the League in equal measure. The Charter has conferred primary responsibility on the Security Council. The assumption was that prompt and effective action is easier for a small and continuously functioning body than for an unwieldy assembly which cannot be convened speedily enough to meet sudden emergencies. Owing to the paralysing effect of the permanent members' power of veto (Article 27(3)) that hope has been disappointed.

The responsibility of the Council is primary, but not exclusive. Articles 10-15 reserve for the General Assembly subsidiary powers which are designed, though not necessarily sufficient, to prevent a drift to war in case the Security Council should prove to be incapable of dealing with dangerous conflicts.[1]

Delegation of powers. The rule that in all matters concerning peace and security the Security Council acts " on behalf of ", i.e. as agent for, the Member States is one of the fundamental provisions of the Charter. The Members of the League retained in full measure the right to decide, each of them individually, whether the conditions in which they were severally obliged to apply sanctions, had been fulfilled.[2] In the United Nations the

---

[1] By the autumn of 1947, it became apparent that the effectiveness of the Assembly's subsidiary powers depended to a large extent on greater continuity in its work. The Assembly has sought to meet this requirement by setting up an Interim Committee (" Little Assembly ") for bridging the time-gap between full regular sessions ; see comment on Articl e 22.

[2] See comment on Article 39.

power to decide whether peace is in danger, and whether preventive or repressive action is necessary, is delegated to the Security Council. By so delegating it, and by accepting the obligation prescribed in Article 25, the Member States have yielded up a significant portion of their sovereign rights. If the League was a purely " co-operative " organisation, the United Nations, at least in the sphere of security, may be properly called an " organic " international institution. As applied to the League, the term " international government " was wholly inappropriate, for the League had no powers to wield without the consent of all its Members. In contrast, the United Nations, within the limits of the Security Council's delegated powers, was meant to become a nucleus of genuine world government.

No arbitrary powers. In discharging its duties relating to the pacific settlement of disputes, the prevention and repression of aggression and the administration of trust territories of strategic importance, the Security Council must act in accordance with the Purposes and Principles laid down in Articles 1 and 2. It has wide discretion, but no arbitrary powers. It must respect the sovereignty of Member States, especially in matters which are essentially domestic. It must respect the principle of the equal rights and self-determination of peoples. In the settlement of disputes it must be guided by justice and not by mere political expediency. When force is used, the Council must see that the territorial integrity and political independence of States do not suffer. But within the limits of these and the other fundamental Purposes and Principles, the Security Council is a free agent. In its semi-judicial functions it is not bound by any rigid rules of evidence. In framing methods of settlement it is guided by its own assessment of the chances of their success ; and when force has been unlawfully threatened or used, the Council is sole judge of the amount and kind of force that should be marshalled against it. At San Francisco these wide powers were much criticised, and it was urged that, in order to prevent possible excesses of authority, a definition of aggression should be incorporated in the Charter. Experience has proved that these anxieties were exaggerated. Throughout the first years of its existence, the Council, far from overstepping the limits of its discretion, was forced into excessive caution and passivity under the ever-present threat of the veto.

Annual and special reports. See comment on Article 15 and Article 98.

ARTICLE 25

The Members of the United Nations agree to accept and carry out the decisions of the Security Council in accordance with the present Charter.

Decisions. It is a corollary of the delegation of powers under Article 24 that Members must abide by the decisions of the Council. But the obligation is limited to " decisions " properly so-called ; mere recommendations of the Council are not legally binding. Members do not, for instance, violate the Charter if they refuse or fail to apply procedures or methods of adjustment recommended by the Council under Article 36. They cannot, however, lawfully challenge a decision under Article 39 that aggression has been threatened or committed ; and if " called upon " to comply with provisional measures under Article 40 or to join in sanctions in accordance with Articles 41 and 42, Members must obey.

Relation to Article 106. This Article applies only to the decisions of the Security Council itself. Members are not legally bound to join in sanctions which, under Article 106, the five Great Powers are authorized to take " on behalf of the Organization ".[1]

ARTICLE 26

In order to promote the establishment and maintenance of international peace and security with the least diversion for armaments of the world's human and economic resources, the Security Council shall be responsible for formulating, with the assistance of the Military Staff Committee referred to in Article 47, plans to be submitted to the Members of the United Nations for the establishment of a system for the regulation of armaments.

The approach to the problem. The Covenant of the League (Article 8) recognized (1) that the maintenance of peace required the reduction of national armaments, and (2) that the private manufacture of armaments was " open to grave objections ". On the second point the Charter is completely silent. On the first point, it seeks the reason for the reduction of armaments in the requirements not of security but of economic reconstruction. The Covenant implied that an armament race tended to precipitate

[1] See comment on pp. 184-5

conflicts. The Charter argues that such a race retards economic reconstruction by diverting from it large human and productive resources. Moreover, where the Covenant spoke of the " reduction ", the Charter speaks of the " regulation " of armaments.
The applicable standard. The Covenant prescribed the reduction of national armaments " to the lowest point consistent with national safety and the enforcement by common action of international obligations ". By 1934, the disarmament effort of the League collapsed completely, owing to the inability of Members to agree where " the lowest point " lay in practice. It has been said that the Charter has taken a retrograde step by omitting to define a specific qualitative and quantitative standard for the regulation of armaments. It would be fairer to say that it has failed to take a step forward from the Covenant. It is clear from the language of this Article, and from its reference to Article 47, that the criteria have not changed, that national safety and collective security still remain the applicable standards, and that they are left virtually undefined, in the same way as in the Covenant.

Functions of the Organization. The Charter confers no authority upon the United Nations to impose upon its Members a system for disarmament or even for the regulation of armaments. All the General Assembly can do is to consider and recommend general principles (Article 11(1)). The Security Council, however, is not only entitled, but required, to go one step further ; it must formulate plans for the regulation of armaments. The Article enables the Council to submit such plans direct to the Member States; but the General Assembly, by a Resolution of December 14, 1946, requested the Council not to do so without previous reference to the Assembly.

Planning machinery. In the discharge of its functions under this Article, the Security Council relies on three subsidiary organs :
(1) The Military Staff Committee (Article 47).
(2) The Atomic Energy Commission, established by Assembly Resolution of January 14, 1946, but placed under the direction of the Security Council. It consists of representatives of the eleven members of the Council, and includes a Canadian representative whenever Canada is not represented on the Council.
(3) The Commission for Conventional Armaments, set up by the Council on February 13, 1947, and consisting of representatives of the eleven members of the Council.

It is one of the most discouraging aspects of the early history of the Organization that, during the first three years of its existence, none of these three organs has made any real progress. It is beyond the scope of this work to analyse their disagreements on technical points. Suffice it to say that in May 1948, the Atomic Energy Commission reported to the Council that it was useless to continue its work until a political accord has been reached between the Western Powers and the Soviet Union. A resolution that the Commission should suspend its sessions was vetoed by the Soviet Union in the Security Council, and the Third Assembly (Resolution of November 4, 1948) called upon the Commission to resume its work. At the same time the Assembly expressed " deep concern at the impasse which had been reached ".

The Commission for Conventional Armaments did not, until the end of 1948, get beyond the discussion of a few general principles and the definition of those weapons of mass destruction which are the responsibility of the Atomic Energy Commission. The Third Assembly (Resolution of November 19, 1948) recorded its opinion that no agreement was attainable on any proposal for the reduction of armaments and armed forces, as long as exact information on existing armaments and forces was lacking, and recommended that the Commission should " devote its first attention to formulating proposals for the receipt, checking and publication, by an international organ of control within the framework of the Security Council, of full information to be supplied by Member States with regard to their effectives and their conventional armaments ". No recommendations were made on bacteriological or chemical weapons, although in his third Annual Report the Secretary-General had pointed out that some of these weapons were potentially as destructive of human life as atomic weapons, and expressed grave anxiety at the fact that " not a single proposal has been made by any of the Member nations for any system of preventing or controlling their manufacture, nor has there been any discussion or study of the problem in the United Nations ".

Concerning the failure of the Military Staff Committee, the reader is referred to the comment on Article 47.

VOTING

ARTICLE 27

1. Each member of the Security Council shall have one vote.
2. Decisions of the Security Council on procedural matters shall be made by an affirmative vote of seven members.

3. Decisions of the Security Council on all other matters shall be made by an affirmative vote of seven members including the concurring votes of the permanent members ; provided that, in decisions under Chapter VI, and under paragraph 3 of Article 52, a party to a dispute shall abstain from voting.

History and interpretation. The voting procedure in the Security Council was the only major subject on which the Sponsoring Governments reached no agreement at Dumbarton Oaks. At the Yalta Conference of February 1945, a formula was agreed upon between the Heads of the United Kingdom, United States and Soviet Governments. After consultations with China and France, the text of the agreed Article was included in the invitations to the San Francisco Conference. At the Conference it soon became clear that the Sponsoring Governments were not unanimous in the interpretation of the voting formula. Eventually, the appropriate technical committee submitted to the delegations of the Sponsoring Governments a set of twenty-three questions. After securing the agreement of France, on June 7, 1945 the delegations of the Sponsoring Governments issued an agreed interpretative Statement.[1] The Conference took no formal action on the Statement, which therefore is not a legally binding interpretation. It is binding in practice. The Soviet Union insists rigidly on the application of the Statement: and the other permanent Members, having joined in the Statement at the time, can raise no legal objections to the Soviet veto as long as it is used within the limits of the agreed interpretation.

Efforts to change the position have not been lacking. As far back as October 1946, the Assembly was seised of proposals to call a General Conference of Members in order to review the Charter and eliminate the veto. As, however, under Articles 108-109, no amendment or alteration of the Charter can take effect without ratification by all permanent members of the Security Council, and non-ratification by the Soviet Union was a foregone conclusion, these proposals were not proceeded with. Instead, by a resolution of December 13, 1946, the Assembly requested the permanent Members " to make every effort . . . to ensure that the use of the special voting privilege should not impede the Security Council in reaching decisions promptly ". The Council itself, in August 1947, entrusted the question to its

[1] The document will henceforth be referred to as the " Five-Power Statement on Voting Procedure ".

Committee of Experts, but no further action followed. In November 1947, the Assembly referred the whole problem to the newly-formed Interim Committee which, in March 1948, set up a Sub-Committee for the examination and analysis of past and future proposals. The Sub-Committee recommended that, in a list of 98 possible decisions of the Security Council, 36 should be regarded as procedural, and 21 more should be taken by a vote of any seven members. It further recommended that the permanent Members should consult in advance of important decisions, and that they should not exercise the veto except in questions of vital importance to the Organization as a whole. A draft resolution based on these recommendations, and embodying the further proposal that the permanent Members should forego the use of the veto where seven affirmative votes have already been cast, was introduced by China, France, the United Kingdom and the United States at the Third Assembly and was adopted on April 14, 1949, in the face of strong opposition from the Soviet *bloc*.

In view of the growing political tension between the Western Powers and the Soviet Union, the acceptance of these recommendations by the U.S.S.R. in its capacity of a permanent member of the Security Council is highly improbable and, for the time being, the work of the Council continues to be governed by the Five-Power Statement on Voting Procedure. In view of this, the Third Assembly has recommended to all Members of the Organization that in any future agreements conferring specific functions on the Council, such conditions of voting within that body should be provided as to exclude, to the greatest extent possible, the application of the rule of unanimity between the Great Powers.

The " equality " of votes. The first paragraph gives the impression that the votes of all Members have an equal weight. That is true only of procedural matters. In all other matters, the vote of the permanent Members is, in fact, a plural vote in the sense that a negative vote cast by one of them nullifies the effect of all affirmative votes, regardless of their number.

The " procedural vote ". On procedural matters, the Security Council decides by a qualified majority of at least seven votes out of a possible total of eleven.

The Charter does not define " procedural matters ", but the Five-Power Statement on Voting Procedure makes it clear that all questions falling under Articles 28-32 are procedural. They include the organizational measures necessary to enable the

Council to function continuously, the time and place of meetings, the setting-up of subsidiary organs, the adoption and variation of Rules of Procedure, and invitations to Members of the United Nations not represented on the Council and to States outside the Organization to participate in the discussions of the Council.

Moreover no single Member can prevent the consideration and discussion by the Council of a dispute or situation which has been brought to its attention under Article 35.[1]

But faced with the objection of a permanent Member, the consideration and discussion of a dispute or situation is confined to extremely narrow limits,[2] and must stop short of " investigation ", i.e. a call for reports, the examination of witnesses or the appointment of a Commission of Investigation.

The Five-Power Statement gives no exhaustive list of all decisions which can be taken by procedural vote, but declares that in controversial cases not expressly covered by it the preliminary question, whether a matter is procedural, is itself subject to the veto. At the time, the Sponsoring Governments took the view that it was " unlikely that there will arise in the future any matters of great importance on which a decision will have to be made as to whether a procedural vote would apply ". That hope has been stultified. Time and again, the Soviet Union has used the veto to turn motions which, in the view of the majority of the Council, were clearly procedural, into questions of substance.[3]

Decisions on non-procedural matters. On all matters which are not strictly procedural, the Security Council must decide by an affirmative vote of seven members including the concurring votes of the permanent Members. By casting a negative vote, any one of the permanent Members can " veto " a decision. But mere abstention from the vote, or the absence of a permanent member from the meeting, does not operate as a veto.

The rule in the third paragraph of this Article covers such a wide field of action that it is no exaggeration to say that any one of the Great Powers can prevent the effective discharge by the

---

[1] *Statement*, cl.I.(3). The rule applies even where, in the view of a permanent member, the issue is outside the competence of the Council. The United Kingdom, the U.S.A. and France, in September 1948, brought the " Berlin Blockade " to the attention of the Council. The U.S.S.R., relying on Article 107, denied the competence of the Council, but was unable to prevent the consideration and discussion of the issue and its retention on the agenda.

[2] In the words of a memorandum presented by Dr. Evatt (Australia) at San Francisco " . . . without veto the Council can only discuss whether a dispute can be discussed and can only investigate whether it should be investigated ".

[3] E.g., motions to determine whether a conflict was a dispute or a situation ; and motions to request the International Court for an advisory opinion.

Council of its responsibilities for the maintenance of peace and security. Without unanimity of the permanent Members present and voting the Council is unable (to quote only its most essential functions) :

to determine whether any given situation might lead to international friction or give rise to a dispute (Article 34) ;

to decide whether a dispute has in fact arisen, and if so, to investigate whether its continuance is likely to endanger the maintenance of international peace and security (Article 34) ;

to call upon the parties to settle their dispute by peaceful means (Article 33) ;

to recommend to the parties procedures or methods of adjustment or appropriate terms of settlement (Articles 36-37) ;

to determine whether a dispute is justiciable and, if so, to refer the dispute to the International Court of Justice (Article 36) ;

to request the International Court of Justice for an advisory opinion (Article 96) ;

to determine the existence of any threat to the peace, breach of the peace or act of aggression (Article 39) ;

to call upon the parties to comply with such provisional measures as may be necessary to prevent an aggravation of a warlike situation (Article 40) ;

to call upon Members to apply, or join in applying, diplomatic, economic or military sanctions (Articles 41-42) ;

to conclude military agreements with Member States (Article 43) ;

to formulate plans for the application of armed force (Article 46) ;

to formulate plans for the regulation of armaments (Article 26) ;

Compulsory abstention. No member of the Security Council must vote when :

(1) the motion before the Council is concerned with a dispute to which the member is a party, and

(2) the proposed decision is incidental to the pacific settlement of the dispute, with the intervention of the Council or of a regional agency.

At first sight this rule, which applies equally to permanent and non-permanent members, would appear to reduce considerably the dangers inherent in the privileged voting power of the Great Powers. In reality, its value is problematical. If a permanent Member who is alleged to be a party to a dispute denies the existence of the dispute altogether, or at least contends that it is not a party to the dispute, the rule of abstention does not come into operation until the Council has found that there is a dispute and that the Member is a party to it. But such a ruling would be a substantive decision, and, as such, subject to the veto of the permanent Members, including the Member who is alleged to be a party to the dispute.

Moreover, the rule of abstention only applies to decisions concerning the pacific settlement of the dispute, and does not apply to measures of enforcement. It follows that, even if a permanent Member were not to resist the allegation that it was a party to the dispute, it could ignore with impunity the Council's recommendations for a peaceful settlement. If it came to an imminent threat to the peace, or to an overt act of aggression, the Council would have to proceed with preventive measures or repressive sanctions under Chapter VII of the Charter. Yet all substantive decisions under Chapter VII are subject to the veto of the permanent Members, including the Member against which preventive measures or sanctions ought to be taken.

No legal principle can justify these effects of the voting formula. It is repugnant to our sense of natural justice that an interested party should be given overriding power to deny both the existence of a dispute and his interest in it ; it is even more repugnant that the aggressor — as a matter of right — should be able to frustrate any action calculated to prevent or stop his aggression. But it should be stated in fairness to the Great Powers that they have not, either before or since San Francisco, sought to justify the veto on legal grounds. They frankly admitted in the interpretative Statement that the reason for the formula was purely political :

" In view of the primary responsibility of the permanent members, they could not be expected in the present condition of the world to assume the obligation to act in so serious a matter as the maintenance of international peace and security in consequence of a decision in which they have not concurred ".

It is a logical result of the military and economic preponderance of the Great Powers that in the case of collective sanctions they would have to shoulder the major part of the risk and burden. At the end of a long and exhaustive war, none of them was prepared to sign a blank cheque ; and all insisted that they should not be committed to sanctions, or to interlocutory decisions potentially leading to sanctions, except by their express consent in each individual case.

Elections to the International Court of Justice. The voting formula of this Article does not apply when the Security Council proceeds to elect judges of the International Court of Justice.[1] Under Article 10 of the Statute of the Court, the Council decides by an absolute majority of votes, without any distinction between permanent and non-permanent members.

PROCEDURE

ARTICLE 28

1. The Security Council shall be so organized as to be able to function continuously. Each member of the Security Council shall for this purpose be represented at all times at the seat of the Organization.

2. The Security Council shall hold periodic meetings at which each of its members may, if it so desires, be represented by a member of the Government or by some other specially designated representative.

3. The Security Council may hold meetings at such places other than the seat of the Organization as in its judgement will best facilitate its work.

Continuous function. It is one of the major points of difference between the League and the United Nations that, while the Council of the League did not function continuously,[2] the Security Council does. The Charter was drafted on the assumption that the ability of the Security Council to act promptly in any emergency would greatly increase its effectiveness.

The Charter itself does not go beyond stating the general principle and prescribing the permanent representation of each member of the Council at the seat of the Organization. The detailed regulations are found in the Rules of Procedure.[3]

Meetings. The Rules of Procedure distinguish between periodic meetings and meetings held at the call of the President.

Periodic meetings are held twice a year. The Council itself decides the time.

Between periodic meetings, the President must convene the Council at intervals not exceeding fourteen days. He must call

---

[1] See comment on Article 92.

[2] The Covenant (Article 4) prescribed Council meetings " from time to time as occasion may require, and at least once a year ". Eventually, the Council's Rules of Procedure provided for four ordinary sessions every year and for extraordinary sessions in emergencies.

[3] See Article 30.

a meeting forthwith whenever (a) any member of the Council so requests ; (b) a dispute or situation or some other danger to peace is brought to the attention of the Council under Article 11(3), Article 35 or Article 99 ; (c) the General Assembly makes a recommendation or refers a question under Article 11(2).

Special representatives. Paragraph 2 of the Article may create the impression that, apart from periodic meetings, members of the Council must always act through their permanent representatives at the seat of the Organization. That is not the case. Heads of Governments and Ministers of Foreign Affairs may attend any meeting of the Council, without submitting credentials, and members may arrange for a special representative to take the place of the permanent representative at any meeting.

Place of meetings. Although each member must have a permanent representative at the seat of the Organization, the Council is free to meet at any other place. When the General Assembly is in session, it is obviously convenient for the Council to meet at the same place.

ARTICLE 29

The Security Council may establish such subsidiary organs as it deems necessary for the performance of its functions.

The subsidiary organs of the Security Council are of three kinds : permanent, semi-permanent and *ad hoc.*

Permanent bodies.

(1) The *Military Staff Committee*, the composition and functions of which are defined in Article 47 of the Charter ;

(2) the *Committee of Experts*, which advises the Council on the interpretation, amendment and revision of the Rules of Procedure ; each member of the Council has a representative on the Committee ;

(3) the *Committee on the Admission of New Members*, to which applications received under Article 4 of the Charter are referred for preliminary examination ; each member of the Council has a representative on the Committee.

Semi-permanent bodies.

(1) *The Atomic Energy Commission.*[1]

(2) *the Commission for Conventional Armaments.*[1]

---

[1] See comment on Article 26.

Ad hoc bodies. These are set up as and when the need arises in the course of proceedings under Chapters VI and VII.[1]

ARTICLE 30

The Security Council shall adopt its own rules of procedure, including the method of selecting its President.

Rules of procedure. Provisional Rules of Procedure were drafted by the Preparatory Commission. These were adopted by the Council at its first meeting, and after detailed examination by a Committee of Experts were amended in June 1946. The Rules deal in detail with the time and place of meetings, the preparation and adoption of the agenda, the representation of members, the election and functions of the President, the functions of the Secretariat, the conduct of business, the official languages, the publicity and the records of meetings, the admission of new Members, and relations with other organs of the United Nations. *Presidency.* The Presidency is held in turn by the members of the Council in the English alphabetical order of their names. Each President holds office for one calendar month. It is left to the discretion of the President whether he should occupy the chair during the consideration of a question with which his own country is " directly connected ".

ARTICLE 31

Any Member of the United Nations which is not a member of the Security Council may participate, without vote, in the discussion of any question brought before the Security Council whenever the latter considers that the interests of that Member are specially affected.

The preliminary issue. Whether the interests of a Member are " specially affected " by a question brought before the Council, is a matter for the decision of the Council at its discretion. Under the Five-Power Statement on Voting Procedure[2] the decision

[1] Notable examples were :
in 1946/47 : the Sub-Committee for the examination of the situation in Spain ; the Commission of Investigation concerning Greek Frontier Incidents ; the Sub-Committee for the examination of the *Corfu Channel Case* ;
in 1947/48 : the Truce Commission for Palestine ; the Committee of Good Offices for Indonesia ; the Commission of the Council for the investigation of, and mediation in, the dispute between India and Pakistan.
[2] See under Article 27.

can be made by any seven affirmative votes. This is somewhat paradoxical, as in most cases it will be a question of substance and not of procedure whether a State not represented on the Council has a special interest in the matter under discussion.

Procedure. If the Council gives an affirmative answer to the preliminary question, it must invite the Member concerned " to participate in the discussion ". The Member is not legally bound to respond.[1] If it does, the representative of the Government concerned will be free to argue the case before the Council, but he will have no vote.[2]

The Charter does not say whether " participation " in the discussion includes the right to make specific proposals. In practice that right is freely granted.[3]

ARTICLE 32

Any Member of the United Nations which is not a member of the Security Council or any State which is not a Member of the United Nations, if it is a party to a dispute under consideration by the Security Council, shall be invited to participate, without vote, in the discussion relating to the dispute. The Security Council shall lay down such conditions as it deems just for the participation of a State which is not a Member of the United Nations.

Field of application. This Article is applicable to disputes only. In the case of " situations " (1) non-members are not under any circumstances entitled to participation in the discussion, and (2) Members can only participate if the Council, under Article 31, decides that their interests are specially affected.

Voting procedure. According to the Five-Power statement on Voting Procedure[1] proceedings under this Article are governed by the vote of any seven members of the Council. This ruling is even more paradoxical than the one discussed under Article 31.

---

[1] In April 1948, the Czechoslovak Government declined the invitation of the Council to participate in the discussion of the situation which had arisen from the February *coup d'etat.* It contended that the issue was essentially domestic.

[2] Under Article 4(5) of the League Covenant, the Member concerned had the same voting rights as the members of the Council.

[3] In January 1946, the Ukranian S.S.R. brought the situation in Indonesia to the attention of the Council. It was invited to participate in the discussion, and eventually its representative submitted a formal resolution for setting up a Commission of Inquiry. The President of the Council raised the question whether this was in order. The point was not formally decided, but no member of the Council raised objection to " the right of proposition " being granted to the Ukranian representative.

[4] See under Article 27.

Whether a matter before the Council is technically a dispute, and who are the parties to it, is treated as a procedural question when it arises under this Article, but becomes a matter of substance if any member of the Council is alleged to be a party to the dispute.

The position of Members. Any Member State not represented on the Council is entitled, as a matter of right, to participate, without a vote, in the discussion of any dispute to which it is a party. The Council must issue an invitation, but the Member is entitled to decline.

The position of non-members. If a State which is not a Member of the Organization is a party to a dispute before the Council, it is entitled to participate, without a vote,[1] in the discussion. This right, however, is conditional upon the acceptance of such conditions as the Council may lay down for the participation of the State concerned.

These conditions are in the discretion of the Council, but the intentions of the Charter are clearly laid down in Article 35(2). Non-members should not be allowed to be in a better position than Members, and should not participate in the discussions of the Council unless they accept, in relation to the dispute under consideration, " all the obligations which a Member would have to assume in a similar case ".[2]

---

[1] In comparable cases non-members of the League were entitled to a vote (*Covenant*, Article 17).

[2] It was on this condition that the Council, in January 1947, invited Albania to participate in the discussion of her dispute with the United Kingdom, known as the *Corfu Channel Case*.

CHAPTER VI

PACIFIC SETTLEMENT OF DISPUTES

ARTICLE 33

1. The parties to any dispute, the continuance of which is likely to endanger the maintenance of international peace and security, shall, first of all, seek a solution by negotiation, inquiry, mediation, conciliation, arbitration, judicial settlement, resort to regional agencies or arrangements, or other peaceful means of their own choice.

2. The Security Council shall, when it deems necessary, call upon the parties to settle their dispute by such means.

Field of application. Throughout Chapter VI a distinction is made between two sources of danger to peace : (a) disputes ; and (b) situations which might lead to international friction or give rise to a dispute. Of the two, disputes involve a more immediate danger, for here the controversial attitudes of the parties have crystallized into definite claims and counter-claims.

The peaceful settlement of disputes is the joint responsibility of the parties and the Security Council. Their duties are concurrent, but independent. The parties are not entitled to wait for the Security Council to take the initiative ; conversely, the Security Council is not entitled to wait for the parties to take it.

This Article deals only with disputes ; it is not applicable to " situations ". Nor is it applicable to all kinds of disputes, but only to disputes of particular gravity, such as are likely to endanger the maintenance of international peace and security.

Obligations of the parties. The term " parties " refers to both Members and non-members. International peace can be endangered as much by disputes between Members as by conflicts between non-members.[1]

The first duty of the parties is to seek a solution by peaceful means. The present Article tells them how. They will have a second obligation if their quest remains unsuccessful ; in that case they will have to refer the dispute to the Security Council, in accordance with Article 37.

---

[1] See comment on Article 2(6).

Character of the dispute. There is no guarantee (indeed, experience has shown that it is most unlikely) that all parties will agree that their dispute is one which involves a danger to international peace. But if any party contends that it is, then, regardless of the different opinion of others, that party must apply or invoke methods of peaceful settlement. If the other parties do not respond, the matter will eventually come before the Security Council, with which rests the final decision on the character of the dispute.
Methods of settlement. The Charter gives no exhaustive list. It enumerates the customary methods without, however, excluding new procedures or the combination of existing ones.

" Negotiation " is a general term which covers every conceivable method of direct exchanges between the parties, both verbal and written. It may be conducted at various levels, ranging from talks between subordinate officials to conferences between Heads of States. Normally, however, negotiations are conducted through diplomatic channels.

" Inquiry " means an effort to elucidate facts which are controversial between the parties and are relevant to their respective claims. It is usually conducted by an international commission set up by the parties themselves.

" Mediation " is the intervention of an impartial Government or person whose " good offices " are made available either spontaneously or at the request of the parties.

" Conciliation " differs from mediation in that it is usually entrusted not to one Government or person, but to an international commission designated by agreement between the parties.

" Arbitration " pre-supposes a reciprocal undertaking (" submission ") by the parties to abide by the decision of one or several arbitrators. Depending on the terms of the submission, the arbitrators either decide according to law or *ex aequo et bono.*
" Judicial settlement " is applicable only to disputes of a legal, as distinct from a political, character.[1] Normally, but not necessarily, it should be entrusted to the International Court of Justice at The Hague.[2]

There is no rigid line of demarcation between arbitration and judicial settlement. As a rule, arbitral tribunals are not permanent, and are not bound by strict rules of international law. But Article 95 makes it clear that there is no objection to legal

[1] For the definition of legal disputes see comment on Article 92.
[2] See Article 36(3) and comment on Chapter XIV.

D*

disputes being referred to *ad hoc* tribunals ; and under Article 38 of its Statute, the International Court of Justice need not apply strict law if the parties agree that it should decide *ex aequo et bono*.

" Resort to regional agencies or arrangements " is not a procedure *sui generis*. The present Article refers to it by way of a reminder that, where a dispute is of a local or regional character, the parties may avail themselves with advantage of the facilities afforded by regional arrangements and agencies[1] before referring the matter to the Security Council.

The phrase " other peaceful means of their own choice " is a pointer particularly to such methods of settlement as the parties may have agreed upon before their dispute had arisen, e.g. in treaties of friendship, non-aggression, mutual assistance, and the like.

Position of the Security Council. The Council need not take official notice of all disputes that may arise in the world. The Charter admits by implication that disputes of a minor character may continue unsettled without any danger to peace. But cognizance must be taken of any dispute as soon as it is " brought to the Council's attention " in accordance with Articles 35 and 99.

Whether or not a dispute " brought to the attention " of the Council is likely to endanger peace, is for the Council to decide. This is not a procedural issue, and the decision is subject to the veto of any permanent member which is not a party.

Should the Council, without or after an investigation under Article 34, find that the continuance of the dispute is not likely to endanger peace, it can take no further action.[2] Unfortunately, the same would be true if, contrary to the sense of the majority, one of the permanent Members vetoed a resolution purporting to find that the continuance of the dispute is a danger to peace. But the veto cannot prevent the Council from " remaining seised " of the question and continuing to keep it on the agenda ; for this is a procedural matter.[3]

If the Council finds expressly or by implication that a dispute is likely to endanger peace, it need not necessarily proceed further,

---

[1] See comment on Article 52(2).
[2] Except under Article 38, at the request of all the parties.
[3] In January 1946, Iran lodged a complaint against the Soviet Union for alleged interferences in her internal affairs. Although the Soviet Union contended that a danger to international peace was not involved, and protested against the retention of the matter on the agenda, the Council remained seised of the matter until the conflict was settled by direct negotiations.

as long as it is satisfied that the parties are in the process of carrying out their obligation to seek a peaceful solution.[1] But if the Council is not so satisfied, it must choose between two alternatives :
(1) it can, under Articles 36 and 37, recommend appropriate methods or terms of settlement ; or
(2) it can, under the second paragraph of the present Article, " call upon the parties " to settle their dispute by peaceful means of their own choice.

The phrase " call upon " has no exact meaning in this particular context. It denotes something weaker than a binding decision, but stronger than a mere recommendation. Legally, the difference is immaterial. With or without a call from the Council, the failure or refusal of any party to seek a solution by peaceful means is a breach of an obligation clearly stated in Article 2(3) and Article 33(1) of the Charter.

ARTICLE 34

The Security Council may investigate any dispute, or any situation which might lead to international friction or give rise to a dispute, in order to determine whether the continuance of the dispute or situation is likely to endanger the maintenance of international peace and security.

Scope of the investigation. Apart from the exceptional case of Article 38, the Security Council is not concerned with disputes or situations which involve no danger to international peace and security. Before it can proceed with " a call " under Article 33(2), or with recommendations under Articles 36 and 37, the Council must first determine the character of the conflict. The present Article enables it to carry out such investigations as may be necessary for that limited purpose.

The Council's power to investigate is not conditional on any formal representations under Article 35 or Article 99. The existence of a dispute or of a dangerous situation is usually common knowledge, and the Council is entitled to act on its own initiative.

" *Disputes* " *and* " *situations* ". Although the Charter does not define it, the meaning of the term " dispute " is not controversial.

---

[1] In February 1946, Syria and the Lebanon brought to the attention of the Council the continued presence in their respective territories of French and British troops, contrary to " the spirit and the letter of the Charter ". A formal resolution expressing the Council's confidence that the troops would be withdrawn as soon as practicable, and that direct negotiations to that end would continue, received seven votes, but was vetoed by the Soviet Union. The Council took no further action.

It is generally taken as denoting a conflict between States in which the contesting parties have formulated definite claims, defences and, possibly, counter-claims.

In ordinary usage, the word " situation " has a less definite meaning. The Charter singles out two classes of situations in which the Security Council is expected to take an interest, if only to the extent of determining whether their continuance involves a danger to peace. The one class comprises situations which might lead to international friction. In the other class are situations which might give rise to a dispute in the technical sense of the term. When a dispute is brought to the attention of the Council, it must, and can, address itself immediately to the question whether the continuance of the dispute involves a danger to peace. But when it is confronted with a " situation ",[1] the Council must first examine a preliminary question : is it a situation which might lead to international friction or give rise to a dispute ? If the answer is negative, the Council must remove the " situation " from the agenda, as it has no competence to deal with situations which are irrelevant to international peace and security.

Procedure. It is for the Council to decide in what manner a particular dispute or situation shall be investigated under this Article. That discretion is, however, limited by the purpose of the investigation. The Council is not at this stage entitled to inquire into the rights and wrongs of the case. The sole object of its inquiry is the likelihood of a danger to international peace. In some cases it is sufficient for the Council to study the documentation submitted by the parties and listen to oral evidence and argument[2] in full session. In less clear-cut cases, it may be necessary to call for reports on current developments.[3] Where the evidence is voluminous, it is expedient to entrust a sub-committee with its examination.[4] There is, however, nothing to prevent the Council

---

[1] The terminology adopted by the parties is not, of course, binding on the Council. The " Iranian Question " and the " Syrian and Lebanese Question " (see comment on Article 33) were both described as " situations " in the first communications addressed to the Council. In effect, they were disputes and the Council treated them as such.

[2] In January 1946, the Soviet Union raised the question of the continued presence of British troops in Greece. The Council " took note " of the declarations made, and the evidence submitted, by the representatives of the Soviet Union, the United Kingdom and Greece, and " considered the matter as closed ".

[3] In May 1946, at an advanced stage of its consideration of the " Iranian Question ", (see comment on Article 33) the Council formally requested the Iranian Government to report whether all Soviet troops had been withdrawn from the whole of Iran.

[4] This was the procedure adopted in April 1946 for the investigation, at the request of Poland, of the situation arising from " the existence and activities of the Franco régime in Spain ". A similar resolution for the investigation of the situation in Czechoslovakia after the *coup* of February 1948 was vetoed by the Soviet Union.

from collecting its own evidence, or supervise its collection on the spot, through the appointment of a fact-finding commission.[1] *The position of the Great Powers.* According to the Five-Power Statement on Voting Procedure,[2] the ordering of an investigation under this Article is not a procedural matter for the purposes of Article 27, and can be vetoed by any permanent member. Legally, this is quite anomalous, for an investigation designed to establish the competence of the Council, or the lack of it, is clearly a procedural matter. The political justification of the anomaly is clearly expounded in the Five-Power Statement :

" . . . in ordering an investigation the Council has to consider whether the investigation . . . might not further aggravate the situation. After investigation the Council must determine whether the continuance of the situation or dispute would be likely to endanger international peace and security. If it so determines, the Council would be under obligation to take further steps ".

In other words, unless the Great Powers can agree in advance to see the matter through, the most convenient way of saving face is to veto the preliminary investigation and prevent the Council from establishing its competence.

ARTICLE 35

1. Any Member of the United Nations may bring any dispute or any situation of the nature referred to in Article 34, to the attention of the Security Council or of the General Assembly.

2. A State which is not a Member of the United Nations may bring to the attention of the Security Council or of the General Assembly any dispute to which it is a party if it accepts in advance, for the purposes of the dispute, the obligations of pacific settlement provided in the present Charter.

3. The proceedings of the General Assembly in respect of matters brought to its attention under this Article will be subject to the provisions of Articles 11 and 12.

Rights of Members. Any Member of the United Nations, whether represented on the Security Council or not, may set in motion the machinery of peaceful settlement by notifying the Security

---

[1] For the investigation of the dispute between India and Pakistan, the Council, in April 1948, established a Commission of five members, two of whom were chosen by the parties.

[2] See under Article 27.

Council, or the General Assembly, of any dispute or situation the continuance of which is likely to endanger the maintenance of international peace and security.

In the case of disputes, the notification normally comes from one of the parties. On the other hand, " situations " have been repeatedly reported by States which were not directly involved.[1] *Rights of non-members.* Non-members can also bring disputes (but not " situations ") to the attention of the Security Council or the General Assembly, provided the following two conditions are fulfilled : (1) the non-member State must be a party to the dispute ; and (2) it must accept in advance the obligations of pacific settlement provided in the Charter.

Legally, these requirements are justified, but the political justification of the first condition is doubtful. If international peace is indivisible—and the Organization is founded on that assumption—there seems to be no reason why outsiders should be unable to notify dangerous " situations " or a dispute in which they may not be directly involved. In practice, however, no harm is done. Information from a non-member concerning a " situation " can always be officially conveyed by a Member or, under Article 99, by the Secretary-General.[2]

The position of the Assembly. Although Members and non-members alike can choose between approaching the Council or the Assembly,[3] they must bear in mind that, so far as " action " under Chapter VII may be necessary, the Assembly will have to refer the matter to the Council, either before or after discussion (Article 11(2)). Moreover, if at the time of an approach to the Assembly the dispute or situation is already before the Council, the Assembly must refrain from making any recommendations unless it is requested by the Council to do so (Article 12).

---

[1] In January 1946, it was the Ukranian S.S.R. which brought the situation in Indonesia to the Council's attention.

In April 1946, the Polish Government requested the Council to discuss the situation in Spain.

In August 1946, the presence of British troops in Greece was raised by the Ukranian S.S.R.

In March 1948, Chile applied for an investigation of the situation in Czechoslovakia.

[2] This applies even to communications from private individuals. On March 10, 1948, the situation in Czechoslovakia was raised with the Secretary-General by Mr. Jan Papanek, the former permanent representative of Czechoslovakia accredited to the United Nations. Two days later, Chile endorsed this information under Article 35(1).

[3] In June, 1946, India requested that the treatment of Indians in South Africa be placed on the agenda of the Assembly; and eventually the matter was disposed of by Assembly resolution, without reference to the Security Council.

ARTICLE 36

1. The Security Council may, at any stage of a dispute of the nature referred to in Article 33 or of a situation of like nature, recommend appropriate procedures or methods of adjustment.

2. The Security Council should take into consideration any procedures for the settlement of the dispute which have already been adopted by the parties.

3. In making recommendations under this Article the Security Council should also take into consideration that legal disputes should as a general rule be referred by the parties to the International Court of Justice in accordance with the provisions of the Statute of the Court.

Disputes. Under this Article the Council cannot recommend " terms " for the settlement of disputes. It may only do that under Article 37 if the parties formally refer the dispute to the Council.

Acting under this Article the Council must confine its recommendations to appropriate procedures of settlement. Under Article 33, the parties to a dispute are in any case, even before the intervention of the Council, required to resort to such procedures. The purpose of paragraph 1 of the Article is to enable the Council to intervene without waiting for the parties to act under Article 37(1), or indeed for any formal notice of the dispute under Article 35. It will be recalled that, under Article 33(2) also, the Council may intervene prior to formal reference or notice. But whereas under Article 33 all the Council can do is to remind the parties, in general terms, of their obligation to seek a peaceful solution, under Article 36 it may recommend specific procedures. In the choice of these procedures the Council is not tied to the list included in Article 33(1). It may devise new methods, suggest the combination of existing procedures, or couple its recommendation of a particular procedure with advice that the parties should consider other suitable methods.[1] In legal disputes,[2] however, the Council is expected, though not bound, to recommend

---

[1] In the dispute between the Netherlands and the Republic of Indonesia, the Council on August 1, 1947, called upon the parties " to settle their disputes by arbitration *or by other peaceful means* ". This was supplemented on August 25, 1947 by an offer to assist in the settlement " through a committee of the Council consisting of three members of the Council, each party selecting one, and the third to be designated by the two so selected ".

[2] For a definition of legal disputes see comment on Article 92.

the reference of the case to the International Court of Justice.[1]

Whenever it makes recommendations under this Article, the Council should take into consideration any procedures which have already been adopted by the parties. The word " adopted " refers not only to procedures to which the parties may have actually resorted by the time the Council intervenes,[2] but also to procedures of settlement specified in any previous treaty arrangements between them which may be applicable to the dispute.[3]

Situations. Paragraph 1 of the Article applies only to situations the continuance of which is likely to endanger peace and security. The Council has no jurisdiction in situations which do not involve such a danger, and may be properly dealt with by the General Assembly under Article 14.

The parties involved in a " dangerous " situation are under no legal obligation to seek a solution by peaceful means without waiting for the Council to intervene. Article 33(1) is applicable only to disputes. Legally, therefore, Member States are free to allow such situations to drift. The purpose of the inclusion of situations in the terms of reference of the Council under paragraph 1 of this Article is to enable the Council to intervene, and prevail upon the parties to seek a peaceful solution. In the case of disputes, the Article does not allow the Council to recommend terms of settlement. When it deals with situations, its recommendations are not so restricted. The term " methods of adjustment " covers both " procedures " and " terms ". But the Council can only recommend, and not compel, the parties to follow its advice on either.

ARTICLE 37

1. Should the parties to a dispute of the nature referred to in Article 33 fail to settle it by the means indicated in that Article, they shall refer it to the Security Council.

[1] After preliminary investigation of the dispute between the United Kingdom and Albania concerning incidents in the *Corfu Channel*, the Council, on April 3 1947, recommended that the dispute be immediately referred to the International Court of Justice. Both parties complied with the recommendation, though Albania first objected to the Court hearing the case on the unilateral application of the United Kingdom. The dispute was disposed of by judgement of the Court, delivered on April 9, 1949.

[2] In the dispute between Iran and the Soviet Union, the Council, by unanimous decision of January 30, 1946, took note of past negotiations between the parties and asked to be informed of the results of further negotiations.

[3] The recommendation of August 1, 1947, calling upon the Netherlands and the Republic of Indonesia to settle their disputes by arbitration, was based on the " Linggadjati Agreement " of March 25, 1947, Article 17 of which provided for arbitration.

2. If the Security Council deems that the continuance of the dispute is in fact likely to endanger the maintenance of international peace and security, it shall decide whether to take action under Article 36 or to recommend such terms of settlement as it may consider appropriate.

Field of application. This Article applies only to disputes the continuance of which is likely to endanger peace and security. *Position of the parties.* Under Article 33 it is in the first place for the parties to decide whether their dispute amounts to a potential danger to peace. If so, the parties, without waiting for the intervention of the Organization, must seek a solution by the methods indicated in Article 33(1). Should these efforts fail, it is their duty to refer the dispute to the Council. If they disagree on the question whether the procedures of settlement have failed, the obligation to refer the dispute to the Council rests on the party or parties which contend that there has been failure.[1]
Position of the Council. On receiving from all or some of the parties to a dispute a report on the failure of the procedures indicated in Article 33(1), the Council must first decide the preliminary question whether the continuance of the dispute is " in fact " likely to endanger peace and security. The Council may have previously considered the character of the dispute under Article 34 or Article 36, and decided then that its continuance was a threat to peace. No previous decision does, however, bind the Council when proceeding under paragraph 2 of this Article ; it must re-examine its earlier findings, if any, in the light of later developments.

If the Council decides on a negative answer to the preliminary question, it must not make recommendations unless all the parties to the dispute so request under Article 38. If, however, the

---

[1] On September 29, 1948, the U.S.A., France and the United Kingdom submitted to the Security Council a detailed account of their diplomatic negotiations with the Soviet Government on the question of the *Berlin Blockade*, and contended that " the Soviet Government has taken upon itself sole responsibility for creating a situation in which further recourse to the means of settlement prescribed in Article 33 of the Charter is not, in existing circumstances, possible, and which constitutes a threat to international peace and security ". Overruling the Soviet objection that the Berlin question was within Article 107 of the Charter and outside the competence of the Organization, the Council decided to place the dispute on its agenda. On October 22, 1948, a draft resolution purporting to recommend provisional measures under Article 40, and at the same time indicating definite terms of settlement for the currency problems involved in the dispute, received nine votes in favour, but was vetoed by the Soviet Union. No further action was taken in the Council, although it retained the matter on the agenda. Eventually, the controversy was disposed of by an agreement reached on May 4, 1949, between the delegates of the Big Four to the Third Assembly.

answer to the preliminary question is positive, the Council must proceed in either of two ways :

(1) It may revert to Article 36 and instruct the parties to have recourse to specific procedures of settlement. Such a decision would imply disagreement with the contention of all or some of the parties that all suitable procedures of peaceful settlement have been tried, and that no further effort can be usefully made.

(2) It can recommend " terms of settlement ", i.e. suggest a basis on which the substance of the parties' claims and counterclaims should be disposed of.[1]

In formulating terms of settlement, the discretion of the Council is limited only by the proviso of Article 24(2), that in the discharge of its duties the Council must always act in accordance with the Purposes and Principles of the United Nations. Particularly important in this context are the references in Article 1(1) and Article 2(3) to the settlement of disputes in conformity with " justice ".[2]

Within the limits of the Purposes and Principles, however, the Council can recommend any terms which it believes to be appropriate.

ARTICLE 38

Without prejudice to the provisions of Articles 33 to 37, the Security Council may, if all the parties to any dispute so request, make recommendations to the parties with a view to a pacific settlement of the dispute.

Field of application. This Article is not applicable to " situations ", but in relation to disputes it covers a wider ground than Article 33 and Articles 35-37. All disputes are included, not only those the continuance of which is likely to endanger international peace and security.

---

[1] In the dispute between India and Pakistan on the issue of the accession of the State of *Jammu and Kashmir,* the Security Council on April 21, 1948, made detailed recommendations (1) for the restoration of peace and order, and (2) for a plebiscite to decide the issue. On January 28, 1949, the Council made specific recommendations for the settlement of the *Indonesian dispute,* including the establishment of an Interim Federal Government for Indonesia. On May 7, 1949, the delegations of the Netherlands and of the Republic of Indonesia signified to the United Nations Commission at Batavia their agreement on a number of important points at issue, including the cessation of guerilla warfare and the return of the Republican Government to Jogjakarta.

[2] The reference in Article 1(1) to international law does not limit the discretion of the Council. It applies only to legal disputes, which under Article 36(3) will, as a rule, be referred by the Council to the International Court of Justice without the Council recommending specific terms of settlement.

Submission of the parties. In disputes which involve no danger to peace, the Council has no right to intervene on its own initiative, except to the limited extent defined in Article 34. It may intervene, however, if all the parties to the dispute so request. In that case, the functions of the Council will be akin to those of an arbitral tribunal, with the important difference that, whereas arbitration awards are binding, the Council can only make recommendations. The recommendation may cover procedures of adjustment or appropriate terms of settlement, or both.

ACTION WITH RESPECT TO THREATS TO THE PEACE, BREACHES OF THE PEACE, AND ACTS OF AGGRESSION

ARTICLE 39

The Security Council shall determine the existence of any threat to the peace, breach of the peace, or act of aggression, and shall make recommendations, or decide what measures shall be taken in accordance with Articles 41 and 42 to maintain or restore international peace and security.

Discretionary powers of the Security Council. During the inter-war period, attempts were repeatedly made to establish the legal criteria of aggression.[1] None of these attempts proved to be satisfactory: and the Charter was drafted on the double assumption that (1) for practical purposes, a definition to cover every possible case of aggression was impossible, and (2) the most satisfactory way of dealing with the problem was to give the Security Council unrestricted discretion to determine whether a threat to the peace, a breach of the peace or an act of aggression had in fact occurred.

In this approach to the vital problem of sanctions lies one of the fundamental differences between the Covenant and the Charter. The League Council had no power to declare that an act of war had been committed. That was a matter to be decided by each Member for itself. Article 16 of the Covenant laid down a rudimentary definition of aggression, and required all Members to apply sanctions as soon as they were satisfied that an illegal act of war had been committed against a fellow-Member. Their duty to apply sanctions was not conditional on a previous recommendation from either the Council or the Assembly. The risk of taking the wrong decision had to be borne by the individual Member.

[1] Article 16 of the Covenant defined aggression as resort to war by a Member of the League in disregard of the provisions requiring the submission of disputes either to arbitration or judicial settlement or to inquiry by the League Council. In the Geneva Protocol of 1924 and in the Locarno Treaty of Guarantee of 1925, experiments were made with more detailed definitions.

The Charter has changed all that. No Member of the United Nations is entitled or liable to apply sanctions without previous positive decisions of the Security Council in two directions. First, subject to the " inherent " right of self-defence admitted by Article 51, Members must wait until the Council has determined the existence of a threat to the peace, a breach of the peace or an act of aggression ; secondly, they must wait until the Council has decided whether sanctions shall be taken at all, and if so, in what manner.

In both directions, the decisions of the Council are binding on all Members. This is the most important application of the principle that, in the maintenance of peace and security, the Council acts as the agent of all Members (Article 24(1)). At this one point the Charter has drawn fairly near to the conception of a " world government ".

It must be understood, however, that the Council cannot effectively use its wide discretionary powers unless there is harmony between its permanent Members. Whether an act of aggression has been committed and whether sanctions ought to be taken are questions of " substance ", which require the concurrence of all permanent Members in accordance with Article 27(3). The moment a permanent Member itself is involved in the dispute, either directly or indirectly, by being in sympathy with the case of the aggressor, the machinery must break down. As long as a conflict is still at the stage of pacific settlement (Chapter VI), a permanent Member directly involved in the dispute cannot obstruct the work of the Council; for in decisions under Chapter VI a party to a dispute must abstain from voting. That proviso to Article 27(3) does not, however, apply to decisions taken under Chapter VII. It follows that a permanent Member which has committed or is about to commit aggression, or is in league with the aggressor, can lawfully use its right of veto : it can stop the Council from finding that there has been a threat to the peace, a breach of the peace or an act of aggression. Here, precisely, lies one of the fundamental weaknesses of the Charter.

Peaceful settlement after aggression. A decision by the Council that there exists a threat to the peace, a breach of the peace or an act of aggression does not necessarily entail sanctions. The Council may still take the view that, in the circumstances, it need not do more than " make recommendations ", i.e. continue its efforts for the peaceful settlement of the dispute. There is conclusive evidence in the debates of the San Francisco Conference that the Council was not intended to take such a view except where warlike actions had only been threatened, but not yet committed. Unfortunately, that limitation of the Council's discretion has found no expression in the text of the Article ; and in any case, as long as the Council is not backed by adequate armed force, recourse to recommendations under Chapter VI must remain the easiest way of safeguarding its prestige.

Admittedly, there is a strong case for the Council to continue its efforts in the interests of an ultimate peaceful settlement although a breach of the peace or an act of aggression has actually occurred. But the prestige of the United Nations can hardly be preserved unless the continuation of these efforts is made conditional on compliance with certain " provisional measures " of the kind contemplated in Article 40. It is unfortunate that an express stipulation to this effect was not made in the text of Article 39.

Sanctions. Unless the Council determines that recommendations under Chapter VI will meet the case, it *must* bring sanctions into play. Once a threat to the peace, a breach of the peace or an act of aggression has been established, the Council cannot take the view that neither recommendations nor sanctions are necessary. Its only escape is a temporary one, i.e. a call upon the parties to comply with " provisional measures " under Article 40. Whether or not that call is obeyed, the Council must, sooner or later, dispose of the matter, either under Chapter VI or under Articles 41-42.

In the choice of sanctions the Council retains its discretion. This is another important difference from the League system. Under Article 16 of the Covenant, in the case of aggression all Members of the League were under an obligation immediately to subject the aggressor to the severance of all trade and financial relations, to prohibit all intercourse between their nationals and the nationals of the Covenant-breaking State, and to enforce against the aggressor a virtual blockade covering every kind of financial, commercial and personal intercourse between its nationals and the nationals of any other State, whether a Member of the League or not.[1] The United Nations is not bound by such hard and fast principles. The Council is free to decide whether

---

[1] Admittedly, the League soon departed from this " sledgehammer " method of economic retaliation, and already in October 1921 adopted the principle of the " progressive " application of sanctions.

to apply at once all the sanctions enumerated in Articles 41-42, or to apply them singly or in any given combination.

Transitional arrangements. As long as the special agreements contemplated in Article 43 have not come into force, the Security Council is not in a position to apply military sanctions. Under Article 106, should such measures become necessary during the period of transition, it will be the duty of the permanent members of the Security Council to consult with one another and, as occasion requires, with other Members of the Organization, with a view to such joint action as may be necessary for the maintenance of peace. The Security Council may initiate such consultations, but it has no power to require the permanent Members, let alone any other State, to take action. It follows that, pending the implementation of Article 43, the Organization is entirely dependent on the Great Powers for military force.[1]

ARTICLE 40

In order to prevent an aggravation of the situation, the Security Council may, before making the recommendations or deciding upon the measures provided for in Article 39, call upon the parties concerned to comply with such provisional measures as it deems necessary or desirable. Such provisional measures shall be without prejudice to the rights, claims or position of the parties concerned. The Security Council shall duly take account of failure to comply with such provisional measures.

The legal character of " provisional measures ". It is a normal feature of the private law of many countries that, when a person has committed, or threatens to commit, an act which may cause damage to another person or to the community, the courts may order him to refrain, pending a decision of the court on the merits of the case, from any acts likely to cause further damage. In the Anglo-American system of law such an order is called " preliminary injunction ".

The " provisional measures " mentioned in the present Article are injunctions of this kind. Their only purpose is to prevent the aggravation of a given situation ; and, in calling upon the parties to comply with them, the Security Council does not purport to

---

[1] See comment on Article 106.

decide which of them is in the right. If they comply with the injunction, they will be free to argue their case at a later stage of the proceedings.

" Provisional measures " and " sanctions " distinguished. Sanctions (Articles 41-42) are measures taken by Members of the United Nations against Members or non-members who have violated the peace, or have at least threatened to do so. Provisional measures, on the other hand, are measures which are to be carried out either by the parties directly involved in the conflict, or by States which are actively supporting them.

Types of provisional measures. The Security Council decides at its discretion what measures are necessary to meet a given situation. In the case of a mere threat of aggression, e.g. where one of the parties has ordered the mobilization of its armed forces, it may be sufficient to call upon the Government concerned to desist from further mobilization, or to withdraw its armed forces to a given distance from the frontier area. But where an invasion has already taken place, it may be necessary to insist upon a withdrawal of the invading forces to their own State territory, Again, where, following an invasion, hostilities are being waged. the Council will concentrate its efforts on obtaining a truce or a cease-fire.[1]

" The parties concerned ". The Council's call for provisional measures will be addressed, in the first place, to the Governments directly involved in the conflict. Under present conditions, Governments engaged in a conflict usually rely upon the support of one or more foreign Governments or, at least, upon the supply of war material from abroad. As a result, it may be necessary for the Council to call upon such foreign Governments to abstain from giving military and economic support. By virtue of Article 2(6) the Council may also call on States which are not Members of the Organization.[2]

Effects of failure to comply. The term " call upon " implies that Members of the Organization are under a legal obligation to

---

[1] See the resolution of the Council of May 22, 1948, calling upon " all Governments and authorities, without prejudice to the rights claims and position of the parties concerned to abstain from any hostile military action in Palestine, and to that end to issue a cease-fire order to their military and para-military forces " ; and the resolution of November 15, 1948, calling " upon the parties directly involved in the conflict in Palestine, as a further provisional measure under Article 40 of the Charter, to seek agreement forthwith, with a view to the immediate establishment of the armistice ".

[2] See the resolution of May 29, 1948, calling upon " all Governments and authorities concerned to refrain from importing or exporting war material into or to Palestine, Egypt, Iraq, Lebanon, Saudi-Arabia, Syria, Transjordan and Yemen during the cease-fire ".

comply. Failure to do so would amount to a breach of Articles 2(5) and 25: and persistent refusal to comply may lead to expulsion from the Organization (Article 6).

As far as the specific controversial issue is concerned, failure to adopt the prescribed provisional measures does not in itself prejudice the rights, claims or position of the parties, whether or not they are Members of the Organization. But the Council " shall duly take account " of the failure. When it comes to decide whether sanctions ought to be taken, or when, following the application of sanctions, it has occasion to determine appropriate terms of settlement, the Council may be influenced against the party which, by disobeying a call for provisional measures, had shown that it was lacking in good faith and in respect for its obligations under the Charter.

Suspension from rights of membership. Under Article 5 a Member against which preventive action has been taken may be suspended from the exercise of the rights and privileges of membership.

ARTICLE 41

The Security Council may decide what measures not involving the use of armed force are to be employed to give effect to its decisions, and it may call upon the Members of the United Nations to apply such measures. These may include complete or partial interruption of economic relations and of rail, sea, air, postal, telegraphic, radio and other means of communication, and the severance of diplomatic relations.

Difference from the League system. Under Article 16 of the Covenant, Members of the League were under a direct obligation to apply sanctions—but only sanctions not involving the use of armed force—immediately they were, individually, satisfied that aggression had been committed. They were not entitled to wait for a recommendation from the League Council, nor bound by a recommendation if it was given. That system of individual and automatic obligations is replaced in the Charter by a more " organic " system of enforcement. No Member of the Organization is bound — nor is it entitled, save in the case of self-defence (Article 51) — to take any enforcement measures unless called upon by the Security Council to do so.

Limits of the Council's discretion. The wording of Articles 41 and 42 may give the impression that the Security Council is entirely free to decide whether an aggressor ought to be restrained ; under both Articles the Council " *may* " (i.e. need not) call for action.

That, however, is a misconception. Articles 41 and 42 must be read in conjunction with Article 39, which makes it clear that, once the Council has determined the existence of a threat to the peace, a breach of the peace or an act of aggression, and recommendations for the maintenance or restoration of peace have proved to be unavailing, enforcement measures *must* be taken. The permissive formulation of Articles 41 and 42 means only that the Council has full discretion in the choice of specific enforcement measures, and is free to decide in which order of priority or combination they should be applied.

Non-military sanctions. The present Article deals with measures not involving the use of armed force. These fall, broadly, into two categories :

(1) *Economic sanctions.* The Charter gives no exhaustive list, but a few examples. These range from the interruption of one particular method of communication (e.g. rail services) to the complete isolation of a State through a general ban on the passage of goods and persons. These measures may be taken one by one, or gradually and progressively, or simultaneously. The choice will depend on the gravity of the situation.

(2) *Diplomatic sanctions.* These too may range from comparatively mild measures signifying little more than open disapproval (e.g. the recall of Heads of diplomatic missions) to the complete severance of diplomatic relations.

These sanctions are not necessarily less effective than military measures ; indeed, to seal off an aggressor's or would-be aggressor's sources of supply is one of the most powerful weapons. Moreover, at the present stage of the Organization's development, marked by its failure to implement Articles 43 and 45, economic sanctions are the only effective way in which the United Nations can assert its authority.

The regulation of non-military sanctions in an Article which precedes the provisions on military sanctions may lead the reader of the Charter to the conclusion that armed force must not be used unless economic and diplomatic sanctions have already proved ineffective. That is not so. The Security Council, in theory at least, is free to apply military measures without first resorting to economic or diplomatic sanctions. This follows clearly from the text of Article 42.

Liability to join in sanctions. Compliance with provisional measures under Article 40 may be demanded of Members and non-members alike. But when it comes to sanctions, the Council's call can only be addressed to Members. They alone are under a legal obligation to respond.

In practice, the situation may be different. Under Article 2(6), the Organization has power to compel non-members to act in conformity with its actions so far as these are designed to maintain peace. Sanctions applied by Members might easily be frustrated if non-members came to the assistance of the aggressor with supplies of war materials and other essentials which the aggressor can no longer obtain from Members. In such cases the Council will be justified in calling upon non-members to refrain from assistance. Failure to comply would be no breach of any legal obligation ; but it might expose the non-member to repressive measures not less strict than those applied against the aggressor himself.

Impact of economic sanctions upon Member States. See comment on Article 50.

ARTICLE 42

Should the Security Council consider that measures provided for in Article 41 would be inadequate or have proved to be inadequate, it may take such action by air, sea or land forces as may be necessary to maintain or restore international peace and security. Such action may include demonstrations, blockade and other operations by air, sea or land forces of Members of the United Nations.

Difference from the League. In case of aggression, Members of the League were under a direct and automatic obligation to apply certain sanctions not involving armed force ; they were under no obligation to apply military sanctions, not even pursuant to a specific recommendation from the League Council.

In contrast, the Charter prescribes for Members a definite obligation to join in military sanctions when called upon by the Security Council. Once the Council has decided on military action, no Member is entitled to remain neutral. That does not mean that, whenever the Council takes military action, all Members will necessarily become involved ; it is for the Council to decide which Members shall take an active part.

Who takes action ? There is a significant difference in the phraseology of Article 41 and Article 42. In the case of economic and
diplomatic sanctions, the Council may " call upon the Members "
to apply them. When it comes to military sanctions, the Council
itself " may take action ". This terminology indicates an important
difference between military and non-military measures. The latter
must be taken by the Member States themselves ; the Council
has no means of closing the frontiers of Member States or of re-
calling their ambassadors. But when military action has been
decided upon, the strategic direction of the armed forces which
Members are required to place at the Council's disposal passes
into the hands of the Military Staff Committee, which is a permanent subsidiary organ of the Council (Article 47) ; and it is for
the Council to make plans for the application of armed force
(Article 46). It is debatable whether the Council has power to
raise armed forces of its own, an international force distinct
from the national forces which Members must hold at its disposal.[1] In the view of the present writers, there is nothing in the
Charter to prevent the Council from recruiting and maintaining
an international force, and this view seems to be supported by the
wording of Article 43(1), which describes the national contingents
held at the Council's disposal as the Members' " contribution "
to the maintenance of international peace and security, but not
as the only means of maintaining it.[2]

The Council's discretionary powers. Military sanctions may be
taken not only if economic and diplomatic sanctions have proved
to be inadequate, but also if the Council considers that they would
be inadequate. If the Council has tried some economic sanctions
or some diplomatic sanctions, it need not try out the full range
before proceeding to military measures.

On the other hand — and this is a weakness of the Charter —
the Council can always stop short of military measures. If it has
failed to maintain or restore peace by recommendations for a
peaceful settlement, it *must* take either non-military or military
sanctions ; but provided it has taken non-military measures, it

---

[1] Goodrich-Hambro *op. cit.* p.163, take the view that " under the Charter as it stands,
the Security Council does not have the power to recruit and organize such a force ".

[2] In his third *Annual Report* on the work of the Organization, the Secretary-General
urged the creation of a small " United Nations Guard Force ", to be used for guard duty
with United Nations missions, in the conduct of plebiscites, in the administration of truce
terms, and also for the enforcement of provisional measures under Article 40. Although
there was determined opposition from the Soviet *bloc*, the Third Assembly, on April 29,
1949, referred the proposal to a Special Committee, with instructions to report to the
Fourth Assembly.

has discharged its responsibility under Article 39. Even though these measures may have been wholly unsuccessful, it need not go further.

The range of military sanctions. Military action by the Council need not be " shooting war " ; action may be confined to demonstrations by land, sea or air forces, or to blockade.

ARTICLE 43

1. All Members of the United Nations, in order to contribute to the maintenance of international peace and security, undertake to make available to the Security Council, on its call and in accordance with a special agreement or agreements, armed forces, assistance and facilities, including rights of passage, necessary for the purpose of maintaining international peace and security.

2. Such agreement or agreements shall govern the numbers and types of forces, their degree of readiness and general location, and the nature of the facilities and assistance to be provided.

3. The agreement or agreements shall be negotiated as soon as possible on the initiative of the Security Council. They shall be concluded between the Security Council and Members or between the Security Council and groups of Members and shall be subject to ratification by the signatory States in accordance with their respective constitutional processes.

Military sanctions : the contributions of Members. Until the time is ripe for a truly international force recruited and maintained by, and owing its loyalty exclusively to, the United Nations, the Security Council must rely on national forces placed at its disposal by Members. The Charter lays down the general principle that, by the act of joining the Organization, all Members undertake to make available armed forces, assistance and facilities, including rights of passage. The arrangements in detail are reserved for a special agreement or agreements.

Thus the United Nations system of collective security presupposes the conclusion of military agreements supplementary to the Charter. Pending these agreements, the Organization can only rely upon such joint military action as the five Great Powers (and possibly some other Members) may, under Article 106, take on its behalf. There is nothing in the Charter to compel the Great Powers to undertake such joint action ; still less would any other Member be bound to join in sanctions initiated by them.

The result is tragically clear. There is no guarantee that the Security Council will ever be able to apply, or even seriously to threaten, military sanctions. The Charter has fixed no time limit by which the special agreements must be concluded ; nor has it provided alternative machinery for determining the minimum military contributions of Members. The period of the Council's military impotence may therefore drag on indefinitely ; in fact, not one of the special agreements envisaged has so far been concluded. Politically, the reasons for this failure are clear. The assumption underlying the system was the continuing co-operation of the Great Powers ; their " contributions " under the present Article were to be the mainstay of the Organization's military strength. That assumption has proved to be fallacious. The special agreements with the Great Powers, which were to serve as the basis of and the model for agreements with other Members, have not even reached the stage of negotiation. As a logical consequence, in all matters relating to peace and security, the emphasis has shifted from collective security to self-defence and regional arrangements (Articles 51-52).

The parties to the proposed special agreements. The security system of the League rested on direct alliances between its Members ; to make the Council a party to them would have been pointless, since under the Covenant it could neither take military measures itself, nor compel Members to take them.

The system of the Charter is different. Military sanctions are to be applied by the Council itself. It follows logically that the Council should become a party to all agreements regulating the military contributions of Members. In fact, the Charter envisages the combination of a multilateral agreement between the Council and all Members, with a comprehensive network of further agreements between the Council and individual Members or groups of Members. The initiative of negotiating these agreements rests with the Council ; and the Charter requires it to negotiate them " as soon as possible ". The Council has not yet taken this initiative. It has referred the general problem of the structure and contents of these agreements to the Military Staff Committee ; and the Committee has not so far produced any agreed recommendations. Faced with this deadlock, the Council may have been politically justified in not proceeding with invitations either to individual Members or to the Members at large to join in the negotiation of special agreements. But by refraining from this initiative it has failed to discharge the duty imposed by the last paragraph of the Article. The text is mandatory ; and even though no specific time limit was imposed, the term " as soon as possible " can hardly be interpreted to allow for a passivity continuing over a period of several years. The Council's duty to take the initiative is not conditional on agreed recommendations by the Military Staff Committee, which is constitutionally a subsidiary organ with purely advisory and auxiliary functions.

Contents of special agreements. The character of the proposed agreements is technical ; they are to be concerned with

(a) the numbers and types of forces to be held at the disposal of the Council ;

(b) the "degree of readiness" of these forces, i.e. the time required for their mobilization, equipment and training in an emergency ;

(c) the " general location "[1] of the forces.

(d) the nature of military facilities, e.g., the provision of bases for land-, sea- and air-forces, rights of passage and the like ; and

(e) the nature of " assistance ".[2]

Ratification. By the ratification of the Charter the legislatures of the Member States have not delegated authority to the executive branch of their governments for the making of military agreements. These agreements are treated by the Charter as international treaties, and they will normally require ratification in accordance with the same constitutional processes as applied to the adoption of the Charter. This is yet another weakness of the Charter. By withholding ratification from any special agreement proposed under this Article, the legislature of any Member State can, in effect, render nugatory its obligation to give military assistance.

ARTICLE 44

When the Security Council has decided to use force it shall, before calling upon a Member not represented on it to provide armed forces in fulfilment of the obligations assumed under Article 43, invite that Member, if the Member so desires, to participate in the decisions of the Security Council concerning the employment of contingents of that Member's armed forces.

---

[1] An obscure term, which points on the one hand to the question how forces shall be distributed between metropolitan territories, overseas possessions, territories occupied as a result of the Second World War, bases voluntarily ceded or leased, and the high seas ; and on the other hand, to the question in what manner the responsibility for the defence of specific strategic areas shall be allocated to certain countries.

[2] This term may be taken to include all contributions (e.g. the supply of war material, exchange of information, provision of experts, etc.) not included under " forces " and "facilities ".

Purpose. This Article is designed to give Members not represented on the Security Council an opportunity to express views on the part which is to be assigned to them in the application of military sanctions. Whereas under Article 31, Members not represented on the Council may only participate, without vote, in the " discussion " of questions specially affecting their interests, under the present Article they are entitled to participate in the Council's " decisions " with the same voting rights as any non-permanent member of the Council.

The request for a hearing must come from the Member, and can only be submitted by a Government to which the Council, under Article 42, has intimated a proposal to call for its active participation in military action.

Limited scope of the Article. If the Council does not propose to employ contingents of a Member's armed forces, but merely to call for military facilities and assistance, the Member has no right to demand a hearing and a vote.

ARTICLE 45

In order to enable the United Nations to take urgent military measures, Members shall hold immediately available national air force contingents for combined international enforcement action. The strength and degree of readiness of these contingents and plans for their combined actions shall be determined, within the limits laid down in the special agreement or agreements referred to in Article 43, by the Security Council with the assistance of the Military Staff Committee.

An international air striking force. Although this idea was carefully considered at Dumbarton Oaks, the Powers were unable to agree on the setting up of an international air force composed of national contingents. They accepted the compromise solution of national air force contingents, to be held immediately available for the purposes of urgent military action.

The provisions of this Article differ from those of Article 43 in that they stipulate immediate availability. The importance of this difference should not be overestimated. Firstly, the Article does not say that each Member must hold immediately available all the air forces it may be called upon to place at the Council's disposal under Article 43. Secondly, the text makes a distinction between " immediate availability " and " degree of readiness ".

It is possible that certain contingents, although " immediately available ", will not be immediately ready for action.

Limits of the Council's discretion. The Article seems to give the Council discretion in the matter of the strength and readiness of these contingents. As, however, that discretion must be used within the limits of the special agreements referred to in Article 43, its value will depend on the contents of these agreements, none of which has so far been negotiated.

ARTICLE 46

Plans for the application of armed force shall be made by the Security Council with the assistance of the Military Staff Committee.

Strategic planning. This Article must be read in conjunction with Article 47(3). The responsibility for the strategic direction of armed forces will rest with the Military Staff Committee ; but overriding responsibility is retained by the Council for both the supervision of strategic direction and the approval of the plans for the employment of forces. This responsibility places the Council in much the same relation to the Military Staff Committee as Governments stand to their Chiefs of Staff, who have no authority other than that which is delegated to them by the Cabinet carrying the political responsibility.

ARTICLE 47

1. There shall be established a Military Staff Committee to advise and assist the Security Council on all questions relating to the Security Council's military requirements for the maintenance of international peace and security, the employment and command of forces placed at its disposal, the regulation of armaments and possible disarmament.

2. The Military Staff Committee shall consist of the Chiefs of Staff of the permanent members of the Security Council or their representatives. Any Member of the United Nations not permanently represented on the Committee shall be invited by the Committee to be associated with it when the efficient discharge of the Committee's responsibilities requires the participation of that Member in its work.

3. The Military Staff Committee shall be responsible under the Security Council for the strategic direction of any armed forces placed at the disposal of the Security Council. Questions

relating to the command of such forces shall be worked out subsequently.

4. The Military Staff Committee, with the authorization of the Security Council and after consultation with appropriate regional agencies, may establish regional sub-committees.

Composition of the Committee. The idea that the Council should be able to rely on the advice of a permanent body of military experts is not new. The League Covenant (Article 9) also provided for a permanent commission to advise on military, naval and air questions generally and, more specifically, on the regulation of national armaments. But the functions of the corresponding body in the United Nations system are more important because the Security Council has, whereas the League Council had not, authority to take military measures.

The Covenant did not define the membership of the League's permanent Military, Naval and Air Commission. The matter was left to the Council ; and, eventually, it decided that only permanent members of the Council were entitled to representation. The Charter leaves no similar discretion to the Security Council. The membership of the Military Staff Committee is fixed : it consists of the Chiefs of Staffs of the Council's permanent members, or of representatives appointed by the Chiefs of Staff. This principle was challenged by the lesser Powers at San Francisco, but the Conference accepted the view of the Sponsoring Governments that a wider committee would be too unwieldy for the purpose, and also that a committee with a constantly changing membership would have a questionable degree of efficiency. The Article leaves the door open for non-members of the Council to become associated with the work of the Committee if " the efficient discharge of the Committee's responsibilities " so requires. The condition, it will be noted, is objectively (and not, as in Article 31, subjectively) formulated ; and it may be contended that any organ of the United Nations and, indeed, any Member is entitled to press for an invitation under paragraph 2 if the Committee or the Council have failed to take the initiative.

Functions of the Committee. These are threefold :

(1) advice to the Council on all questions relating to military requirements, including the special agreements contemplated in Article 43 ;

(2) advice on the employment and command of forces, and direct responsibility for their strategic direction ;

(3) advice and assistance to the Council in the discharge of its responsibilities relating to the regulation of armaments and disarmament.

So far the Committee has only had occasion to discharge part of its responsibilities under (1). In February 1946 it was directed by the Council to examine the provisions of Article 43. On the basis of that directive, the Committee, in April 1947, submitted to the Council a Report on " General Principles Governing the Organization of the Armed Forces Made Available to the Security Council by Member Nations of the United Nations ". In June 1947, the Report was supplemented by an estimate of the overall strength and of the strength and composition of national components. Neither the Report nor the estimates were unanimous ; indeed, the views of the delegations were conflicting in the extreme, and continuing efforts to reach agreed conclusions have produced no results so far.

Regional sub-committees. Owing to the initial failure of the United Nations to establish a system of collective security backed by armed force, the emphasis has shifted gradually to arrangements for self-defence and regional security such as the Inter-American system, the Brussels Pact, the Atlantic Pact, and the network of 23 alliances between the Soviet Union and its neighbours. Viewed against this background, considerable importance attaches in principle to the regional sub-committees which may be set up by the Military Staff Committee after consultation with the appropriate regional agencies. Indeed, sub-committees of this kind would seem to be the only effective way in which regional arrangements can be properly integrated into the United Nations. At the moment, these are theoretical considerations. The Council and the Committee have no power to compel any regional agency to accept the services of a sub-committee ; and no initiative has yet been taken in that direction.

ARTICLE 48

1. The action required to carry out the decisions of the Security Council for the maintenance of international peace and security shall be taken by all the Members of the United Nations or by some of them, as the Security Council may determine.

2. Such decisions shall be carried out by the Members of the United Nations directly and through their action in the appropriate international agencies of which they are members.

Field of application. This Article applies equally to military and non-military sanctions.

Sanctions not necessarily collective. No Member State can claim, as a matter of right, exemption from participation in sanctions. On the other hand, the Security Council is under no duty so to devise sanctions that a reasonably equal burden shall be placed on all Members. Where enforcement action is to be confined to one geographical area, it would be a waste of manpower or economic resources, or both, to call for the participation of States situated thousands of miles away. Similarly, some Members are better equipped than others to undertake action of a particular kind (e.g. a naval blockade). The Council must have full discretion to decide what kind of action is required from particular Members ; and *a fortiori* to choose the Members who shall join in a particular action.

Direct and indirect action. Diplomatic and military sanctions invariably require direct action on the part of Members. The situation is different in the case of economic sanctions, as a result of the concentration of considerable economic power in the hands of functional organizations, such as the International Monetary Fund, the International Bank for Reconstruction and Development, the Universal Postal Union, the International Civil Aviation Organization and others. In many instances it may be found that, to restrain an aggressor with economic weapons, action by one or more of these international agencies is sufficient ; alternatively such action may be necessary to reinforce the immediate action of individual Members. The Security Council has no power to issue direct instructions to specialized agencies. The Charter gives it indirect influence partly through the Economic and Social Council (Article 65), and partly through the rule in paragraph 2 of the present Article, which may be so construed as to require Members to use in furtherance of the Security Council's decisions such voting rights, executive power and influence as they may possess in the appropriate specialized agencies.

ARTICLE 49

The Members of the United Nations shall join in affording mutual assistance in carrying out the measures decided upon by the Security Council.

Mutual assistance. The obligation of all Members to afford assistance to the Security Council is defined in Articles 25, 43, 45 and 48. The present Article establishes a complementary obligation, which operates not between Members and the Council but between Members and Members. In order to carry out measures required of them by the Council, individual Members may need military, economic or financial assistance from other Members. No Member State is entitled to withhold such assistance unreasonably. If the giving of it involves the Member in a disproportionately large share of the burden, recourse may be had to the procedure indicated in Article 50.

ARTICLE 50

If preventive or enforcement measures against any State are taken by the Security Council, any other State, whether a Member of the United Nations or not, which finds itself confronted with special economic problems arising from the carrying out of those measures shall have the right to consult the Security Council with regard to a solution of those problems.

Equitable sharing of the burden of sanctions. The Charter contains no guarantee that the expense of sanctions will be shared proportionately between all Members. Since, relying on its discretionary powers under Article 48, the Council may direct one single group of Members to make itself responsible for a complete set of sanctions, some machinery for the equitable distribution of the economic burden is necessary. The problem is not confined to Member States. If the Council were to enforce a naval blockade against an aggressor State, this might cause serious losses to non-members whose trade may have been brought to a standstill.

The Charter does not state that Members and non-members are entitled to compensation for their losses. Only the germ of such a principle is admitted in the provision that Members and non-members alike are entitled to " consult " the Council with regard to a solution of their economic difficulties. Whether the Council can instruct Members to make direct contributions, in the form of supplies or payments, towards the relief of another Member's economic difficulties, is doubtful ; but the " mutual assistance " principle of Article 49 seems to support a positive answer. It is even less clear whether the Council can call upon Members to make direct compensation to non-members ; for the principle of mutual assistance does not extend to outsiders.

In all probability there is no other solution than the payment of financial compensation from funds raised by the Organization, or some arrangement for action by the appropriate specialised agencies.

ARTICLE 51

Nothing in the present Charter shall impair the inherent right of individual or collective self-defence if an armed attack occurs against a Member of the United Nations, until the Security Council has taken the measures necessary to maintain international peace and security. Measures taken by Members in the exercise of this right of self-defence shall be immediately reported to the Security Council and shall not in any way affect the authority and responsibility of the Security Council under the present Charter to take at any time such action as it deems necessary in order to maintain or restore international peace and security.

Self-defence and collective security. A perfect system of collective security would exclude any resort to force, except by the international agency entrusted with the guardianship of peace. To give individual States discretionary authority to resort to arms is dangerous because it is open to abuse. Modern history is crowded with instances where aggression was committed under the cloak of self-defence.[1] Seen against this background, the overwhelming majority by which the San Francisco Conference added a self-defence clause to the Dumbarton Oaks Proposals was a measure of its lack of confidence in the perfection of the system of collective security based upon the Charter.

This lack of confidence was not unjustified. The authority of the Security Council must, in the last resort, rest on the armed forces at its command ; but the Council was to have no such forces until the conclusion, at some future date, of special agreements under Article 43. This gap in the system is not sufficiently filled by the transitional arrangements of Article 106 ; under that article the Great Powers are only entitled, but not bound, to join forces in restraining aggression.

Had not the Charter recognized the right of self-defence, individual Members would have been on the horns of a dilemma:

---

[1] The German aggression against Luxembourg and Belgium in August 1914 ; the Japanese aggression in Manchuria in 1931-2 ; the German aggression against Poland in September 1939.

while non-resistance to attack was unthinkable, resistance by armed force would have been an unlawful resort to war. The Charter's way out of this dilemma was to make self-defence lawful, and at the same time provide guarantees against its abuse. *Limitations of the right of self-defence.* Abuses of the right of self-defence were in the past facilitated by the theory that self-defence was justified in the face not only of actual, but also of threatened, aggression. The Charter does not admit self-defence against a threat. There must be an actual armed attack. That does not, however, mean that Members of the United Nations are not allowed to provide in advance for collective self-defence in case an armed attack should occur at some future date. Under Article 4 of the North Atlantic Pact of April 4, 1949, the Parties[1] agreed " to consult together whenever, in the opinion of any of them, the territorial integrity, political independence or security of any of the Parties is threatened "; and under Article 9, they have established a Council and subsidiary bodies, including a Defence Committee, to consider matters concerning the implementation of the Pact. One of the grounds on which the Soviet Union protested against the conclusion of the Pact was the contention that the mere apprehension of aggression does not warrant the making of military preparations under Article 51 of the Charter. That view, it is submitted, loses sight of the fact that Article 51 is part of a Chapter, the heading of which makes it clear that Members of the United Nations may properly take action not only with respect to breaches of the peace, but also with respect to " threats to the peace ". Whether or not an alliance is in conformity with Article 51 depends solely on the question whether the obligation of the Parties to take military and other sanctions becomes effective only in the case of an actual armed attack. Under Article 5 of the North Atlantic Pact, the obligations of the Parties are so limited, and the contention that the Pact is contrary to the Charter does not seem to be justified.

The right of self-defence does not, however, arise if the Security Council has already taken " the measures necessary to maintain international peace and security ", prior to, or immediately after the attack. But even if the Council did not act with such promptitude, self-defence must cease as soon as the Council has taken adequate measures.

[1] Belgium, Canada, Denmark, France, Iceland, Italy, Luxembourg, the Netherlands, Norway, Portugal, the United Kingdom and the United States.

The phrase "measures necessary to maintain international peace and security" imports an element of uncertainty into the system. Who is to be judge whether the Council has taken all the "necessary" measures ? At the moment of the armed attack the right to decide, it seems, rests with the State which has been attacked. Otherwise, Members might be exposed to irreparable injury.

Individual and collective self-defence. The Charter accepts the theory that the right of self-defence is inherent in every State. That theory is well-founded in international law, but is limited to States which have in fact been attacked. The Charter widens the principle in that it speaks both of individual and of collective self-defence. Many alliances for mutual defence (including the North Atlantic Pact and the Inter-American system) operate on the basis that aggression committed against one of the allies is aggression against all of them. Whether as a matter of legal principle it is justifiable to extend the "inherent" right of self-defence to attacks on third parties is questionable. But the wording of the Charter leaves no doubt that Members are free to retaliate by way of self-defence to attacks made on their allies.[1]

Authority of the Security Council. Self-defence is an emergency measure. It is designed to fill a gap in the system of collective security, caused by the temporary incapacity of the Security Council to intervene. But self-defence does not affect the authority of the Council to intervene as soon as it is ready, and this includes the right to insist on the abandonment or restriction of measures already taken under Article 51. All such measures must be immediately reported to the Council.

---

[1] On the question of the validity of treaties of alliance, see comment on Articles 52(1) and 103.

CHAPTER VIII

REGIONAL ARRANGEMENTS

ARTICLE 52

1. Nothing in the present Charter precludes the existence of regional arrangements or agencies for dealing with such matters relating to the maintenance of international peace and security as are appropriate for regional action, provided that such arrangements or agencies and their activities are consistent with the Purposes and Principles of the United Nations.

2. The Members of the United Nations entering into such arrangements or constituting such agencies shall make every effort to achieve pacific settlement of local disputes through such regional arrangements or by such regional agencies before referring them to the Security Council.

3. The Security Council shall encourage the development of pacific settlement of local disputes through such regional arrangements or by such regional agencies either on the initiative of the States concerned or by reference from the Security Council.

4. This Article in no way impairs the application of Articles 34 and 35.

What is a " regional arrangement "? Ordinarily, " region " means a limited geographical area, as distinct from a wider unit of which it forms part. At San Francisco, a proposal was made for the inclusion in the text of the Charter of a strict definition, based primarily on geographical proximity, of " regional arrangements ". That proposal was not adopted, and the Charter affords no guidance as to the precise meaning of the term. Paragraph (1) of the Article, however, seems to warrant the view that all inter-State arrangements must be considered regional if (a) they have been entered into by a group of States as distinct from the whole membership of the United Nations, (b) they relate to matters concerned with the maintenance of international peace and security, and (c) the subject-matter of the arrangement is " appropriate for regional action ", i.e., does not go beyond the parties' legitimate sphere of interest. On this construction, the 23 treaties of friendship and mutual assistance between the Soviet Union and the East European Peoples' Democracies; the Treaty of Brussels (March 17, 1948) between Great Britain, France, Belgium, the Netherlands and Luxembourg; the Treaty of Rio de Janeiro (September 2, 1948) for the Mutual Defence of the Americas; and the North Atlantic Pact (April 4, 1949) between Belgium, Canada, Denmark, France, Iceland, Italy, Luxembourg, the Netherlands, Norway, Portugal, the United Kingdom and the U.S.A. are all regional arrangements within the meaning of Article 52.

The interpretation suggested in the preceding paragraph is highly controversial. The Soviet Union, judging by the arguments used in its protests against the North Atlantic Pact, appears to contend that the adherence of non-members of the United Nations (e.g. Italy and Portugal) is incompatible with the provisions of the Charter; and further, that arrangements within the meaning of the Article must aim, in the first place, at the settlement of regional issues. Conversely, on the Western side, it has been argued that the hallmark of a regional arrangement is the assumption of responsibility for enforcement action, under the authority of the Security Council, against any party to the arrangement which may be threatening or breaking international peace. In the view of the present writers, neither of these tests is decisive, nor does the text of the Charter support the proposition that treaties directed primarily to the organization of collective self-defence under Article 51, such as the Brussels Pact and the North Atlantic Pact, do not, for that reason, qualify as regional arrangements.

The term " regional agency " presents little difficulty. It refers to the organs, — permanent or temporary, principal or subsidiary — set up under regional arrangements for the purpose of formulating policies of giving effect to them. The Consultative Council of the Brussels Pact; the Organ of Consultation, consisting of the Ministers of Foreign Affairs of the parties to the Treaty of Rio de Janeiro; and the Council and Defence Committee of the North Atlantic Pact are noteworthy examples.

" Collective " and " regional " security. In a perfect system of collective security there should be no room for separate alliances ; they tend to reduce that sense of global solidarity which is essential to the effectiveness of a collective system, and to arouse mutual suspicion and fear. It is a measure of the imperfect sense of solidarity and of the lack of mutual confidence prevailing after the two World Wars that neither the Covenant nor the Charter has excluded regional arrangements. The League system allowed and, indeed, encouraged such alliances as the Little Entente, the Balkan Entente and the Locarno Pact ; and the United Nations system has partly maintained, partly brought into being, a number of alliances, the most important of which have been mentioned. The growing tendency to regard alliances of this type as the mainstay of security has been referred to in the comment on Articles 42 and 51.

Safeguards. The draftsmen of the Charter were alive to the dangers inherent in allowing separate alliances to co-exist with a global system of security, and provided various safeguards tending to reduce the danger. These safeguards — some of which are found in this Article — may be listed as follows :

(1) Under Article 102, all regional arrangements must be registered with the Secretariat and published by it. Any party failing to comply with that obligation, which is calculated to avoid evils of secret alliances, is guilty of a definite breach of the Charter and, in addition, is precluded from invoking the treaty before any organ of the United Nations.

(2) Regional arrangements and any activities under them must be consistent with the Purposes and Principles of the United Nations. They must not aim at the settlement of conflicts by force, or be directed against the territorial integrity or political independence of any State.

The practical value of this condition must not be exaggerated. The draftsman of any treaty of alliance will take care to stress its conformity with the Purposes and Principles of the United Nations ; and in fact, all alliances concluded since the setting up of the Organization purport to have been concluded in furtherance of its objectives.

(3) Greater importance attaches to the rule in Article 103 that, in the event of a conflict between obligations under the Charter and obligations under any other agreement, the Charter shall prevail. That rule enables any party to the alliance to escape as soon as another party is about to engage in action which can no longer be said to be in accordance with the Purposes and Principles of the United Nations.

(4) As a rule, no enforcement action under any regional arrangement must be taken without express authority from the Security Council (Article 53).

(5) The arrangement must be " appropriate for regional action ", i.e. should not, in principle, deal with matters outside

the parties' legitimate sphere of interest. An alliance purporting to deal with matters of security without any geographical limitations would offend against this rule as it would usurp the functions of the Security Council.

Settlement of local disputes. Provided that regional arrangements satisfy these conditions, the Charter not only tolerates them, but encourages the parties to use them.

This Principle is expressed in two rules :

(a) The Security Council has power to refer local disputes to the appropriate regional agency.

(b) As a corollary, Members entering into regional arrangements are under an obligation to try and settle local disputes through regional agencies before referring them to the Security Council.

The proper interpretation of these rules seems to be that, where the regional arrangement does not expressly provide for the settlement of local disputes through regional agencies, the Security Council has no right to refer the matter to the regional organization. If, however, regional facilities for settlement exist, the Council is not only entitled, but expected, to insist that the parties try local methods of settlement before asking for the intervention of the Council.

A fortiori the Council is entitled (and, indeed, expected) to agree if the parties themselves initiate the reference of local disputes to regional bodies in the first place.

Overriding powers of the Security Council. The reference to Articles 34 and 35 makes it clear that, regardless of any existing regional arrangements, the Council has power to investigate any dispute or situation relevant to international peace and security, even where the character of the dispute appears to be local. Similarly, no regional arrangements can preclude Members, or (in the conditions of Article 35(2)) non-members, from bringing disputes and situations to the attention of the Security Council or the General Assembly. It would seem to follow that recommendations of the Council under Articles 36 and 38 cannot be objected to on the ground that the matter ought first to have been referred to a regional body.

ARTICLE 53

1. The Security Council shall, where appropriate, utilize such regional arrangements or agencies for enforcement action under its authority. But no enforcement action shall be taken under

regional arrangements or by regional agencies without the authorization of the Security Council, with the exception of measures against any enemy State, as defined in paragraph 2 of this Article, provided for pursuant to Article 107 or in regional arrangements directed against renewal of aggressive policy on the part of any such State, until such time as the Organization may, on request of the Governments concerned, be charged with the responsibility for preventing further aggression by such a State.

2. The term enemy State as used in paragraph 1 of this Article applies to any State which during the Second World War has been an enemy of any signatory of the present Charter.

Enforcement action upon the initiative of the Security Council. Where an actual or threatened breach of the peace is of a local character, it may be excessive to mobilize the whole machinery of the United Nations against it. In these cases, the Council may first call for enforcement action by the appropriate regional agency. The words " shall utilize ", in the first sentence of the Article, may give the impression that the Council is obliged to take such a course. That is not so. Only " where appropriate " must the Council use regional arrangements or agencies ; and a decision whether regional action is " appropriate " is entirely within its discretion.

There is nothing to preclude the Council from calling for regional action in cases which have no definite local character. Where, for instance, the degree of readiness of forces available under regional arrangements is greater than of forces at the disposal of the Security Council, it may avoid dangerous delays by calling for immediate regional action.

Excepting special agreements with the Council (and no agreement of this kind has so far been negotiated), regional agencies are not bound to respond to a call addressed to them under this Article. Nor can they be forced to act by the simple expedient of the Council invoking Article 48(2). That Article refers to " international " agencies. Although regional agencies are " international " in the sense that they involve the participation of more than one nation, it is fairly clear from the context and from the discussions at San Francisco that Article 48 is aimed at functional and not at regional bodies.

If regional agencies will not act upon a call from the Security Council, the latter must demand direct action from their members under Chapter VII of the Charter.

Regional action by consent of the Security Council. No enforcement measures must be taken under regional arrangements without either a demand, or at least an authorization, from the Council.

The exceptions to this rule will be considered in the following paragraphs.

Measures against enemy States. At the time the Charter was signed, a state of war still existed between the Allies and the Axis Powers. That situation called for specific provisions in regard to the enemy States. These provisions are embodied partly in the present Article, partly in Article 107. Taken together, they establish a special régime of security parallel to the collective security system and involve a reduction of the Security Council's authority.

This special régime was designed to be transitional ; and, in fact, Article 107 appears under the heading of " Transitional Security Arrangements ". The second sentence of the present Article belongs to the same category, though its transitional nature is not clearly expressed.

In the view of the present writers, the special security régime for enemy States must come to an end at the latest when the enemy State concerned is admitted to membership of the United Nations. There is nothing in the provisions of Chapter II (Membership) to suggest any difference in the status of original Members and of Members admitted later. Once a State is admitted, its rights and liabilities are identical with those of all other Members, regardless of its former enemy status. The continuation of any special security régime would discriminate against one group by excluding it from the safeguards inherent in the exclusive authority reserved for the Security Council in all matters of enforcement.

Definition of enemy States. The term " enemy State " applies to any State which, during the Second World War, was an enemy of any signatory of the Charter. Not all original Members were at war with all the Axis Powers. War with any one signatory of the Charter is sufficient to bring a State under the operation of the present Article and of Article 107.

Enforcement measures against enemy States. Measures may be taken without previous authorization of the Security Council under two headings :

(1) Under Article 107, in accordance with the terms of any Act of Surrender, Armistice Agreement and Peace Treaty.

(2) Under any regional arrangement directed against renewal of aggressive policy by an enemy State. It is essential that the

regional arrangement to be enforced should state openly that it is directed, either exclusively or *inter alia*, to that end. Secret clauses, being contrary to Article 102, are not protected.

Until an enemy State is admitted to membership of the United Nations, regional arrangements directed against any fresh threat from it operate without effective control by the Security Council. That does not mean that, in the absence of such regional arrangements, or if the parties to them fail to take action against fresh aggression, the Security Council is entitled to remain inactive. Its responsibility under Article 24(1) and Article 39 is comprehensive and has no geographical limitations. The final passage of the present Article means that, as long as the parties to a regional arrangement do not request the Organization to take sole responsibility for preventing aggression by a former enemy, the Council's authority is not exclusive, but concurrent with the special responsibility of the Allied Governments concerned.

ARTICLE 54

The Security Council shall at all times be kept fully informed of activities undertaken or in contemplation under regional arrangements or by regional agencies for the maintenance of international peace and security.

The obligation established by this Article rests, individually, on each Member Government which takes part in a regional arrangement or agency. The discharge of the obligation by one Member discharges the obligation of all.

The meaning of the term " activities " is somewhat obscure. It is submitted that it refers to operations for the suppression of an overt act of aggression, or for the prevention of an imminent breach of the peace. Defence plans would be quite useless if they were to be disclosed in advance.

CHAPTER IX

INTERNATIONAL ECONOMIC AND SOCIAL CO-OPERATION

ARTICLE 55

With a view to the creation of conditions of stability and well-being which are necessary for peaceful and friendly relations among nations based on respect for the principle of equal rights and self-determination of peoples, the United Nations shall promote :—

(a) higher standards of living, full employment, and conditions of economic and social progress and development ;

(b) solutions of international economic, social, health, and related problems ; and international cultural and educational co-operation ; and

(c) universal respect for, and observance of, human rights and fundamental freedoms for all without distinction as to race, sex, language, or religion.

Interdependence of the Organization's purposes. This Article reinforces what has been said or implied in paragraphs 2 and 3 of Article 1. Its purpose is not to add objectives, but to lay stress upon the interrelation of objectives previously stated. " Friendly relations among nations based on respect for the principle of equal rights and self-determination of peoples " is a quotation from Article 1(2). The point is that friendly relations among nations are dependent on conditions of stability and well-being, and that no international organization for peace can succeed unless it promotes such conditions. This recognition of the futility of any effort to preserve peace regardless of its economic and social prerequisites is not new. In the peace treaties of 1919, the Covenant of the League was followed by the Constitution of the International Labour Organization which asserted the dependence of peace on social justice. Throughout its existence the League was concerned with studies and activities in the economic and social fields. The Charter breaks no new ground, but it lifts to the level of the Organization's primary purposes certain objectives which, in the conception of the League, were ancillary.

Domestic jurisdiction. The authority of the United Nations, in relation to the objectives stated in this Article, is limited to studies and to action for their promotion. " To promote " is a word less powerful than " to maintain ", the term which defines the Organization's authority in matters of peace and security. So that the Organization should be able to maintain peace, Member States have agreed to serious inroads on national sovereignty, such as the delegation of executive powers to the Security Council and the renunciation of neutrality. No comparable concessions are made in the economic and social fields. The Organization is given neither responsibility nor power to compel the achievement of the purposes set out in paragraphs (a), (b) and (c). The responsibility and the power remain with the Member States, to be discharged and exercised through national legislative or executive action, and the making and carrying out of separate international conventions. But it is for the Organization, acting through the General Assembly and the Economic and Social Council, to keep public opinion constantly mobilized for economic and social progress ; to initiate research and studies on a scale which is beyond the resources of any one nation ; to make recommendations for individual and joint action by Members ; and particularly, to encourage co-operative action through conventions and international agencies.

The statement of objectives. The terms used in paragraphs (a), (b) and (c) require explanation on two points. First, the use of the word " international " in paragraph (b) and its absence from paragraphs (a) and (c) indicate that the Organization is entitled to scrutinize standards of living, the state of employment and the observance of human rights in each Member State individually ; and no Member can contend that recommendations on these matters are beyond the scope of the Organization. Secondly, while Article 1(3) spoke of " respect " for human rights, the present Article speaks of respect and " observance ". The Organization must see that human rights and fundamental freedoms exist not only on paper, but also in practice, and promote conventions for the international protection of these rights and freedoms.

ARTICLE 56

All Members pledge themselves to take joint and separate action in co-operation with the Organization for the achievement of the purposes set forth in Article 55.

The principle of co-operation. The weakness of the formula in this Article is illustrated by a comparison with Article 25. There, Members pledge themselves to carry out any decisions of the Security Council for the maintenance of peace and security. But the General Assembly and the Economic and Social Council, which exercise the functions of the Organization in the economic and social field, have no power to make " decisions " and compel action. They can only make recommendations. Short of making these recommendations binding, it might have been an effective way of ensuring support for the economic and social purposes of the Organization to demand from each Member *national* action " for the achievement of the purposes set forth in Article 55 " A formula of this kind was strongly urged at San Francisco, but was defeated by the anxiety to keep intact national freedom of action.

Taken singly, the three elements of the present Article (joint action, separate action, and co-operation with the Organization) are unobjectionable ; what robs them of their effectiveness is the way they are linked. If Members had undertaken " to take joint and separate action and to co-operate with the Organization ". failure to take national action for the achievement of higher standards of living and full employment, or the non-observance of human rights, would have been direct breaches of the Charter. A promise to take joint and separate action " in co-operation with the Organization " reduces the responsibility of Members to giving, separately or jointly, such support as they think fit. Even if on a stricter view the Article does not permit Members to remain inactive in the face of positive recommendations, they have no direct responsibility for the achievement of the purposes stated in Article 55. They need not act unless the Organization takes the initiative ; and Members opposed to some aspects of economic or social progress can use their influence and voting rights to resist bolder initiatives.

Ratification of conventions. The record of the first three years suggests that the General Assembly and the Economic and Social Council will invite support for international conventions rather than call for national action. It has been suggested,[1] and the present writers agree, that, once a Member Government has signed a convention sponsored by the United Nations, it is pledged to take the steps prescribed by its national constitution for the ratification of treaties, and is not free to stop at the stage of signature — which happened often during the League period.

[1] Goodrich-Hambro *op. cit.*, p.193.

ARTICLE 57

1. The various specialized agencies, established by inter-govermental agreement and having wide international responsibilities, as defined in their basic instruments, in economic, social, cultural, educational, health, and related fields, shall be brought into relationship with the United Nations in accordance with the provisions of Article 63.

2. Such agencies thus brought into relationship with the United Nations are hereinafter referred to as specialized agencies.

Co-ordination, not absorption. The United Nations claims no monopoly in international co-operation. If in the political field there were valid reasons at the time of making the Charter for tolerating regional security arrangements,[1] there were even more cogent reasons for not absorbing in the Organization all, or indeed any, of the inter-governmental agencies which had come into being before, during and since the League period. Politically, there was the difficulty that not all original Members of the Organization were members of the inter-governmental agencies ; technically, their absorption would have created almost insuperable administrative problems and required a staff of unmanageable size. Functionally there was little to gain and much to lose by rigid centralization in fields of endeavour where success depends largely on the continued co-operation of specialists in the framework of their activities in the past. Most important of all was the lesson to be drawn from the history of the League, that functional organizations in the economic and social fields can still operate successfully when the central political organization is failing. While it would be unwarranted to pretend that the tensions within the League were not reflected in, for instance, the International Labour Organization, it is notable and significant that the ILO survived the collapse of the League. The United Nations was not born in circumstances so auspicious as to justify the risk of exposing the functional agencies to those perils of dissension and obstruction which in the event have beset the central Organization. On the other hand, in the League the co-ordination of functional activities had been imperfect, and there was a strong case for investing the new organization with wide enough powers to guard against overlapping or conflicting programmes.

[1] See comment on Chapter VIII.

The Charter calls the framework of this co-ordination a " relationship " between the United Nations and the specialized agencies. " Relationship " has, in this context, a specific meaning : it is defined, individually for each case, in the agreements contemplated by Article 63.

" *Specialized agency.*" The definition of a specialized agency comprises three elements :

(1) The agency must have been established by inter-governmental agreement. Agencies established by one Government or by private organizations of a professional, social, humanitarian or cultural character are not included.[1]

(2) The agency must, by its constitution, have wide international responsibilities. This formula is rather vague, and it is a question of interpretation whether it envisages functions more ambitious than technical co-operation in specialized fields. The practice of the Organization so far suggests a negative answer. The Universal Postal Union, the International Telecommunications Union and the International Civil Aviation Organization have purely technical functions, and yet have been brought into relationship with the United Nations. On the other hand, responsibility over a wide geographical area would appear to be essential.

(3) Agencies, however specialized, are not within the definition until they have in effect been brought into relationship with the United Nations.

Functions of specialized agencies. Up to the end of 1948 eleven specialized agencies were brought into " relationship ".[2] It is beyond the scope of this commentary to deal extensively with their history, constitution and achievements and only a brief indication of their main functions can be included.

1. *International Labour Organization (ILO).*

(*a*) *Constitution :* The original constitution of the ILO came into effect on April 11, 1919 ; the present, revised constitution on September 26, 1946.

(*b*) *Functions :* The fundamental purpose of the ILO is to bring about, by continuous and concerted international effort—in which the representatives of workers and employers enjoy equal status with those of Governments—an improvement in conditions of

---

[1] For the association of non-governmental organizations with the activities of the Economic and Social Council, see Article 71.

[2] The United Nations Relief and Rehabilitation Administration (UNRRA) was not a specialized agency within the definition. Established in 1943, it was to terminate its operations by the end of 1946 in Europe, and by March 1947 in the Far East. Several of UNRRA's functions are continued by specialized agencies, notably WHO and IRO.

labour all over the world and particularly : regulation of hours of work, including the establishment of a maximum working day and week ; regulation of the labour supply ; prevention of unemployment ; provision of an adequate living wage ; protection of the worker against sickness, disease and injury arising out of his employment ; protection of children, young persons and women ; provision for old age and injury ; protection of the interests of workers when employed in countries other than their own ; recognition of the principle of equal remuneration for work of equal value ; recognition of the principle of freedom of association ; and the organization of vocational and technical education.

Under the " Philadelphia Declaration " (April-May 1944), in which the aims and purposes of the ILO were re-defined, the Organization took power to examine and consider not only matters strictly concerned with conditions of labour, but also all international, economic and financial policies and measures which are relevant to the attainment of conditions in which human beings can pursue both their material well-being and their spiritual development, "in conditions of freedom and dignity, of economic security and equal opportunity ".

2. *Food and Agriculture Organization (FAO).*

(*a*) *Constitution :* The constitution of FAO came into force on October 16, 1945.

(*b*) *Functions :* Promotion of national and international action with respect to scientific, social and economic research in the fields of nutrition, food and agriculture ; improvement of education and administration ; conservation of natural resources and the adoption of improved methods of agricultural production.

FAO furnishes technical assistance to Governments, and organizes such missions as may be needed to assist them in carrying out the recommendations of the United Nations Conference on Food and Agriculture held at Hot Springs, Virginia, in May 1943. The Organization also collects, analyses, interprets and disseminates information relating to nutrition, food and agriculture.

3. *United Nations Educational Scientific and Cultural Organization (UNESCO).*

(*a*) *Constitution :* The constitution came into force on November 4, 1946.

(*b*) *Functions :* To collaborate in the advancement of the mutual knowledge and understanding of peoples through every means of mass communication ; to give fresh impulse to popular education and the spread of culture, by assisting Members in the development of educational activities, by instituting international collaboration to advance the ideals of equality of educational opportunity, and by suggesting educational methods best suited " to prepare the children of the world for the responsibilities of freedom ".

The initial programme of work includes large-scale projects for the reconstruction and rehabilitation of educational, scientific and cultural life in war-devastated countries ; " fundamental education," in the sense of teaching the illiterates of the world —who number more than one half of the population of the globe— to read and write ; provision of a basic minimum of education everywhere ; and the promotion of international understanding through educational methods, including the exchange of teachers and students and the improvement of text-books and teaching materials.

4. *International Civil Aviation Organization (ICAO).*

(*a*) *Constitution.* The constitution came into force on April 4, 1947.

(*b*) *Functions :* To insure the safe and orderly growth of international civil aviation ; promote safety of flight and encourage the development of airways, airports and air-navigation facilities ; prevent economic waste caused by unreasonable competition ; insure that the rights of the contracting States are respected, and that each of them has a fair opportunity to operate international airlines ; and avoid discrimination between the contracting States.

5. *International Bank for Reconstruction and Development (IBRD).*

(*a*) *Constitution :* The Articles of Agreement came into force on December 27, 1945.

(*b*) *Functions :* To promote the restoration of economies destroyed or disrupted by war, and the development of productive facilities and resources in less developed countries ; to facilitate private investment by means of guarantees for, or participations in, loans ; and when private capital is not available on reasonable terms, to provide finance out of the Bank's own capital or from funds raised by it, particular attention being paid to the priority of urgent projects.

6. *International Monetary Fund (IMF).*

(*a*) *Constitution :* The Fund's Articles of Agreement came into force on December 27, 1945.

(b) *Functions :* To promote exchange stability, maintain orderly exchange arrangements and avoid competitive depreciation ; assist in the establishment of a multilateral system of payments in respect of current transactions and in the elimination of foreign exchange restrictions ; and make available to Members the Fund's resources, particularly in scarce currencies, for the purpose of correcting maladjustments in balances of payments.

7. *World Health Organization (WHO).*

(a) *Constitution :* The Constitution came into force on April 7, 1948.

(b) *Functions :* To act as the directing and co-ordinating authority in international health work ; assist Governments in strengthening health services ; maintain administrative and technical services, particularly in the fields of epidemiology and health statistics ; aid Governments in emergencies ; promote research, training and information ; and propose international conventions.

8. *International Refugee Organization (IRO).*

(a) *Constitution :* The constitution came into force on August 20, 1948.

(b) *Functions :* The repatriation, identification, care and assistance, legal and political protection of strictly defined categories of refugees and displaced persons ; and their re-settlement and re-establishment in countries able and willing to receive them.

9. *International Trade Organization (ITO).*

(a) *Constitution :* The ITO Charter, approved by the Havana Conference in March 1948, has not yet received the requisite number of ratifications.

(b) *Functions :* To promote a balanced and expanding world economy ; encourage the reduction of tariffs and the elimination of discriminating trade practices ; facilitate access to foreign markets on equal terms ; provide a forum for the settlement of trade disputes ; and develop and maintain fair trading practices.

10. *Universal Postal Union (UPU).*

(a) *Constitution :* The constitution of the Union is laid down in the Universal Postal Convention (Berne, 1874), as amended.

(b) *Functions :* To administer international conventions for the reciprocal exchange of mails in a single postal territory comprising all Member States.

11. *International Telecommunications Union (ITU).*

(a) *Constitution :* The Union derives from the International Telegraph Union (1865) and was established in 1932. Its revised constitution, adopted in 1944, came into force on January 1, 1949.

(b) *Functions :* To organize and regulate exchange of telecommunications by telegraph, telephone and radio (including the allocation of wavelengths).

Specialized agencies " in the making ". Steps have been taken to bring into relationship with the Organization, in addition to the eleven agencies indicated in the previous paragraphs, the Inter-governmental Maritime Consultative Organization (IMCO) and the World Meteorological Organization (WMO).

Other inter-governmental organizations. Efforts are being made, in order to avoid overlapping and diminish governmental expenditure, to reduce the number of inter-governmental organizations which have responsibilities similar to those of the United Nations and of the specialized agencies, in the economic, social, cultural, educational, health and related fields.[1]

ARTICLE 58

The Organization shall make recommendations for the co-ordination of the policies and activities of the specialized agencies.

Relation with Article 63. The Charter provides two ways in which the co-ordination of specialized agencies can be promoted.

The agreements between the Economic and Social Council and the specialized agencies (Article 63) provide permanent machinery for consultation, and enable the Council to exercise in some respects (e.g. the composition of the agenda) an influence which is almost executive in character. If, however, Article 63(2) were strictly interpreted, guidance from the Council under the agreements would be confined to the "activities", and not extend to the policies of specialized agencies.

The present Article is wider ; it refers to both policies and activities, and enables the Organization to make recommendations on matters which are not covered by special agreements.[2]

The co-ordinating work of the Organization is equally concerned with the improvement of machinery and the elimination

---

[1] Member States and the specialized agencies were invited by the Economic and Social Council to submit, by February 1 1949, their views regarding (a) the possible termination, absorption or integration of such organizations into the United Nations or the specialized agencies, and (b) the relationship which might be established between the organizations and the United Nations or specialized agencies ; and the Secretary-General was requested to prepare a consolidated report based on the replies received.

[2] In practice, the difference is unimportant. All matters of co-ordination are concentrated in the hands of the Administrative Committee on Co-ordination set up by the Secretary-General and the Council's own Co-ordination Committee.

of overlapping programmes. As regards machinery, constant attention is given to such problems as the rationalization of the calendar of conferences convened or sponsored by the United Nations ; a uniform policy for the distribution of documents, and for questionnaires, statistical programmes and public information. The programmes of specialized agencies are surveyed periodically in comparative reviews prepared by the Secretariat. Specific recommendations have been made on the co-ordination of programmes concerned with international commodity arrangements, migration, the world food crisis, housing, town and country planning and cartographic services.

Budgetary co-ordination. See comment on Article 17(3).

ARTICLE 59

The Organization shall, where appropriate, initiate negotiations among the States concerned for the creation of any new specialized agencies required for the accomplishment of the purposes set forth in Article 55.

Scope. The language is ambiguous. " Specialized agencies " having been defined in Article 57(2) as " agencies brought into relationship with the United Nations ", the text would admit of the construction that the negotiations shall be concerned with bringing existing organizations into relationship with the United Nations. That is not the real intent of the Article. What is meant is the promotion of new inter-governmental agencies designed to assume " wide international responsibilities " (Article 57) in fields not covered by existing organizations. The Article does not apply where such bodies can be set up as subsidiary organs of the United Nations.

New specialized agencies. Of the eleven specialized agencies listed in connection with Article 57 four were set up pursuant to recommendations by the United Nations :

(1) *UNESCO.* The foundation was laid by the Standing Conference of Allied Ministers of Education which first met in London in 1942 ; but the international conference (November 1945) which brought UNESCO into being was convened on the basis of a specific recommendation from the San Francisco Conference.

(2) *The World Health Organization.* The International Health Conference (New York, June-July 1946), at which this organization was set up, had been called by the Economic and Social Council on its own initiative.

(3) *International Refugee Organization.* This organization was launched by an Assembly Resolution of February 12, 1946, which recommended the Economic and Social Council to establish a special committee for the examination of the problem of refugees and displaced persons. On June 21, 1946, the Council recommended to the Assembly the establishment of an International Refugee Organization ; and the Assembly, on December 15, 1946, approved the constitution, the first budget and arrangements for a Preparatory Commission.

(4) *International Trade Organization.* The original proposal came from the United States Government; but it fell to the Economic and Social Council to convene the International Conference on Trade and Employment which, in March 1948, approved the Charter of the organization.

ARTICLE 60

Responsibility for the discharge of the functions of the Organization set forth in this Chapter shall be vested in the General Assembly and, under the authority of the General Assembly, in the Economic and Social Council, which shall have for this purpose the powers sets forth in Chapter X.

Primary responsibility. Concurrent responsibility is vested in the General Assembly and the Economic and Social Council. Both are principal organs, but the Article places the Council " under the authority of the Assembly ". This constitutional position reverses the formula adopted for matters of peace and security ; under Article 24 as between the General Assembly and the Security Council the " primary responsibility " is carried by the Council.

Insofar as primary responsibility for the economic and social functions of the Organization can be identified with initiative, it has devolved from the Assembly to the Economic and Social Council. During its first session, the Assembly passed important resolutions which did not originate from the Council. Notable instances were the initiative for a Universal Declaration of Human Rights ; direct appeals to Members for mitigation of the world shortage of cereals, and in support of the final stages of UNRRA's work ; and requests to the Council for the urgent study of post-UNRRA relief needs and the problem of refugees. But since the second session, the resolutions of the Assembly under Chapter IX have been largely concerned with recommendations on projects initiated by the Council ; with the reference to the Council of resolutions submitted by individual Members ; and with questions of administrative detail, e.g. the approval of agreements with, and the admission of, non-members to the specialized agencies. That most spectacular achievement of the Assembly, the Universal Declaration of Human Rights, which it " passed and proclaimed " on December 10, 1948, was largely the work of the Council, of the Human Rights Commission and of their subsidiary bodies.

These observations are not intended to reflect on the power and capacity of the Assembly to take important initiatives.[1] Recommendations on matters of economic and social policy need intensive study and careful preparation on a scale beyond the resources of a large assembly which is not in continuous session. It was natural that the major share of the work and responsibility should pass into the hands of the Council and its subsidiary organs.

Comparison with the League. Under the Covenant, the Council of the League had concurrent responsibility with the Assembly in economic and social questions. It has been suggested that, by referring these matters to a separate Council on which the Great Powers have no privileged representation, the Charter has gone a long way to avoid the danger, which was present in the League, that the economic and social work of the Organisation may be frustrated by political tensions. That suggestion is too optimistic. If the Great Powers are not legally assured of permanent representation on the Economic and Social Council, experience tends to show that they will in fact be permanently represented,[2] and that their contributions to the Council's work are highly coloured by political considerations. Real progress from the League lies in two directions : first, a specialized Council should be more efficient in the economic and social field than the Council of the League, whose attention had to be concentrated on problems of security ; secondly, the Economic and Social Council decides by simple majority, whereas the Council of the League was tied by the rule of unanimity.

---

[1] E.g. the Assembly Resolution of November 19, 1948, on Assistance to Palestine Refugees was passed without previous recommendations from the Council.
[2] See comment on Article 61.

CHAPTER X

THE ECONOMIC AND SOCIAL COUNCIL

COMPOSITION

ARTICLE 61

1. The Economic and Social Council shall consist of eighteen Members of the United Nations elected by the General Assembly.

2. Subject to the provisions of paragraph 3, six members of the Economic and Social Council shall be elected each year for a term of three years. A retiring member shall be eligible for immediate re-election.

3. At the first election, eighteen members of the Economic and Social Council shall be chosen. The term of office of six members so chosen shall expire at the end of one year, and of six other members at the end of two years, in accordance with arrangements made by the General Assembly.

4. Each member of the Economic and Social Council shall have one representative.

The position of the Great Powers. In contrast to the arrangements relating to the Security Council and the Trusteeship Council, no permanent seats are reserved for the Great Powers on the Economic and Social Council. The General Assembly has in principle greater freedom in the election of members of this Council than in the case of the non-permanent members of the Security Council. Article 23 invites consideration of such criteria as equitable geographical distribution and the Members' contribution to peace and security. There are no such criteria in the present Article. In practice, however, the effectiveness of the Council's work is dependent on the co-operation of the States of chief economic importance : and their permanent membership may be taken for granted.[1]

[1] This is illustrated by the elections held in the first three years. All five permanent members of the Security Council were elected to the Economic and Social Council in January 1946. The term of office of the U.S.A. expired at the end of that year, but the U.S.A. was immediately re-elected for a term of three years. The terms of office of the United Kingdom and the U.S.S.R. expired at the end of 1947 ; both were re-elected for a term of three years. As a result, throughout the period 1946-8, all the Great Powers were permanently represented on the Council, and it is likely that this practice will continue.

Term of office. Members of the Council are elected for three years and are eligible for immediate re-election. A system of rotation was provided by the transitional rule that, of the eighteen members first elected, six were to retire at the end of one year, and another six at the end of two years. Paragraph 3 of the Article left it for the General Assembly to determine in what manner the members retiring after one and two years shall be chosen. The First Assembly rejected the method of drawing lots, and after first electing the full membership of eighteen, proceeded by further votes to determine which of them should serve for one and two years respectively.

Representatives. As in the Security Council and the Trusteeship Council, Members are restricted to one representative in the Economic and Social Council.

FUNCTIONS AND POWERS

ARTICLE 62

1. The Economic and Social Council may make or initiate studies and reports with respect to international economic, social, cultural, educational, health, and related matters and may make recommendations with respect to any such matters to the General Assembly, to the Members of the United Nations, and to the specialized agencies concerned.

2. It may make recommendations for the purpose of promoting respect for, and observance of, human rights and fundamental freedoms for all.

3. It may prepare draft conventions for submission to the General Assembly, with respect to matters falling within its competence.

4. It may call, in accordance with the rules prescribed by the United Nations, international conferences on matters falling within its competence.

Studies and reports. The first paragraph is permissive. The Charter does not specify particular subjects on which studies and reports must be made. But an obligation to make studies incidental to carrying out the recommendations of the Assembly is implied by Article 66(1) ; and Article 68 provides the Council with subsidiary organs which, by their nature, are primarily organs concerned with studies.

In fact, as soon as the Council was formed, it launched an impressive programme of studies the main subjects of which may be summarized under the following headings :

Economic questions : employment and economic stability ; economic developments ; balances of payments ; the economic situation and prospects of Europe ; economic survey of Asia and the Far East ; economic survey of Latin America ; the world food crisis ; international commodity arrangements ; regional and world-wide problems of transport ; statistical methods, standards and training ; and safety of life at sea and in the air.

Social, humanitarian and cultural questions (other than Human Rights) : status of women (with special reference to political rights, posts in public administration, nationality, domicile, marriage and divorce, employment and educational opportunities) ; equal pay for equal work ; social welfare services (including family, youth and child welfare) ; prevention of crime and treatment of offenders ; prostitution ; traffic in women and children, and obscene publications ; migration ; housing and town and country planning ; standards of living ; narcotic drugs ; the size and structure of populations, and policies to influence them ; the interplay of demographic, economic and social factors ; the demographic aspects of migration ; refugees and displaced persons.

Recommendations. Although, as a matter of constitutional principle, the Council works " under the authority of the General Assembly " (Article 60), it is entitled to make recommendations direct to Member States and specialized agencies. The Council makes frequent use of this power, and no conflict between its recommendations and those of the General Assembly has yet arisen. Should it arise, it would follow from Article 60 that the Assembly is entitled to override the recommendations of the Council.

Human Rights. The Council's work in this field is directed to the following objectives :

(a) An " *International Bill of Human Rights* " comprising :

(i) a Universal Declaration of Human Rights (i.e. the definition of human rights and fundamental freedoms) ;

(ii) a Covenant of Human Rights (i.e. a convention or conventions giving legal effect to some or all of the rights enumerated in the Declaration) ; and

(iii) measures of implementation providing for the enforcement of the Covenant.

The first part of this programme was completed by the adoption, on December 10, 1948, by the Assembly, of the Universal Declaration. By June, 1949, the second part had also reached the stage of a provisional draft approved by the Human Rights Commission.

(b) *Freedom of information*, to be safeguarded by conventions dealing with measures to facilitate the gathering, international transmission and free publication and reception of information. In May 1949, the first of these, a Draft Convention on the International Transmission of News and the Right of Correction, was approved by the General Assembly.

(c) *Prevention of discrimination and the protection of minorities*, which involves detailed studies of the types of discrimination still practised, and of the question to which extent the so-called " Minorities Treaties " of the inter-war period are still in force.

(d) The *outlawing of " genocide "* (the extermination of a whole race) by means of an international convention. The draft Convention prepared by the Council was adopted by the General Assembly on December 9, 1948, and proposed for the adherence of Members.

Draft Conventions. Under paragraph 1 of this Article the Council may make recommendations direct to Member States, but that rule does not apply to recommendations for accession to conventions prepared by the Council. The Council must submit its draft conventions to the Assembly, and it is for the Assembly to decide whether to recommend Members to accept them.[1]

Conferences. The Council may call international conferences[2] as a matter of routine, and not only in emergencies, as some delegations suggested at San Francisco. The procedure is to be laid down in a set of " Conference Rules " approved by the General Assembly. The Assembly, at its Second Session, invited the Secretary General to prepare draft Rules, but these have not yet been adopted.

---

[1] Important conventions prepared by the Council include : the Constitution of the International Refugee Organization (adopted by Assembly Resolution of December 15, 1946) ; the Convention on the Prevention and Punishment of the Crime of Genocide (adopted by Assembly Resolution of December 9, 1948) ; and the Protocol to bring under control dangerous drugs outside the scope of the 1931 Convention (adopted by Assembly Resolution of October 8, 1948).

[2] Conferences called by the Council include : the International Health Conference (New York, June-July 1946) ; the World Statistical Congress (Washington, September 1947) ; the United Nations Conference on Trade and Employment (Havana, November 1947-March 1948) ; the United Nations Maritime Conference (Geneva, March 1948) ; the United Nations Conference on Freedom of Information (Geneva, March-April 1948) ; the United Nations Scientific Conference on the Conservation and Utilization of Resources (New York, June 1949).

ARTICLE 63

1. The Economic and Social Council may enter into agreements with any of the agencies referred to in Article 57, defining the terms on which the agency concerned shall be brought into relationship with the United Nations. Such agreements shall be subject to approval by the General Assembly.

2. It may co-ordinate the activities of the specialized agencies through consultation with and recommendations to such agencies and through recommendations to the General Assembly and to the Members of the United Nations.

Agreements. The Council's powers are permissive, not mandatory. The initiative need not in every case be taken by the Council ; it may be taken by the Assembly or by the specialized agencies themselves. The agreements, in any case, are subject to the Assembly's approval.

Although the Article does not indicate the terms of the proposed agreements, references to the specialized agencies in Articles 17(3), 58, 62, 64, 91 and 96 suggest specific points which are relevant to such agreements.

In fact, all the agreements hitherto negotiated[1] contain standard clauses dealing with the following subjects :

(1) *Reciprocal representation :* arrangements for representatives of the Organization to attend conferences and meetings of the specialized agencies ; and vice versa.

(2) *Admission of new members :* rules enabling the Economic and Social Council or the General Assembly to recommend the non-admission of States which are not Members of the United Nations.

(3) *Agenda :* arrangements for the obligatory insertion in the agenda of the Council of items proposed by specialized agencies; and vice versa.

(4) *Recommendations :* undertakings by the specialized agencies to submit to their policy-making or executive bodies all formal recommendations received from the United Nations.

(5) *Exchange of information and documents :* in particular, arrangements for the supply of regular and special reports by the specialized agencies.

(6) *Assistance to the Security Council and Trusteeship Council :* undertakings by the specialized agencies to assist the Economic

---

[1] Up to the end of 1948, agreements were concluded or negotiated with the eleven specialized agencies listed under Article 57, and with the Preparatory Committee of the Inter-governmental Maritime Consultative Organization.

and Social Council in the discharge of its obligations under Articles 65 and 91 of the Charter.

(7) *International Court of Justice :* general authority to the specialized agencies, under Article 96 of the Charter, to request the Court for advisory opinions on legal questions arising within the scope of their activities.

(8) *Personnel arrangements :* provisions for the development of common personnel standards, designed to avoid unjust differences in terms and conditions of employment.

(9) *Statistical services :* reciprocal provisions for the co-ordination and comparability of statistics.

(10) *Budgetary and financial arrangements.*

Co-ordination. The normal way in which the Council performs its co-ordinating functions is through the implementation of the agreements referred to in the first paragraph of the Article ; and particularly, through the effective use of the machinery of direct consultation. The Council also has power to make formal recommendations to the agencies and to the General Assembly ; and it may address recommendations direct to Member States.

The pivot of the working machinery is the Council's Committee on Co-ordination, which operates in close liaison with the Administrative Committee on Co-ordination set up by the Secretary-General. The Administrative Committee has several subsidiary bodies, including consultative committees on administrative questions, statistical matters and public information, the United Nations Film Board, the Inter-Library Committee, two Technical Working Groups on Fellowships and Housing, and a Regional Consultative Committee at Geneva.[1]

ARTICLE 64

1. The Economic and Social Council may take appropriate steps to obtain regular reports from the specialized agencies. It may make arrangements with the Members of the United Nations and with the specialized agencies to obtain reports on the steps taken to give effect to its own recommendations and to recommendations on matters falling within its competence made by the General Assembly.

2. It may communicate its observations on these reports to the General Assembly.

---

[1] For an indication of the direction in which co-ordination is progressing, see comment on Article 58.

These provisions are largely self-explanatory. Constant attention is given by the Council to obtaining reports which conform to uniform standards and are easily comparable. The agreements made under Article 63 contain detailed provisions for the supply of regular reports, and of periodic information on action taken pursuant to recommendations from the United Nations. Regarding action taken direct by Member Governments, the General Assembly recommended on October 31, 1947, that the Secretary-General report annually to the Economic and Social Council, and that the Council in its turn report to the General Assembly, on steps taken in various countries to give effect to recommendations of the Council and of the Assembly.

ARTICLE 65

The Economic and Social Council may furnish information to the Security Council and shall assist the Security Council upon its request.

The assistance the Security Council may demand will be largely concerned with information and technical advice, particularly on the economic side of disputes and sanctions. Whether the Security Council, in the case of purely economic disputes, can delegate its powers under Chapter VI to the Economic and Social Council must, in the view of the present writers, be answered in the negative ; the Charter speaks of " assistance " and not of the delegation of functions.

This leads to the further question whether parties to an economic dispute can refer it for settlement direct to the Economic and Social Council in cases where, a danger to peace and security not being involved, the competence of the Security Council [1] cannot be established. An attempt was made at the sixth session of the Council by Yugoslavia, which complained that Yugoslav gold entrusted to the United States Government during the war had not been returned. The Council refused to enter into the substance of that particular dispute. It did not, however, deny in general terms its competence to settle disputes ; that question of principle is still open. In the view of the present writers there is nothing in the Charter to exclude the submission of economic disputes to the Council, provided the interested parties agree, and the Council, by unanimous or majority decision, accepts the submission. As, however, the Council's present Rules of

[1] See Article 34.

Procedure contain no provisions applicable to arbitration, the procedure will have to be settled either by amendment of the general Rules or by decisions relating to individual cases.

ARTICLE 66

1. The Economic and Social Council shall perform such functions as fall within its competence in connection with the carrying out of the recommendations of the General Assembly.

2. It may, with the approval of the General Assembly, perform services at the request of Members of the United Nations and at the request of specialized agencies.

3. It shall perform such other functions as are specified elsewhere in the present Charter or as may be assigned to it by the General Assembly.

Recommendations of the General Assembly. In view of Article 60 which subordinates the Council to the authority of the Assembly, and of paragraph 3 of the present Article, the first paragraph seems to be redundant.

Special services. Individual States and also specialized agencies may from time to time find themselves in need of special assistance from the Council or its subsidiary bodies in matters of research and technical advice. The technical services of the League responded repeatedly to requests of this kind. The Economic and Social Council is also entitled to perform special services, but only with the previous approval of the Assembly.

Additional functions. By Article 60 the powers of the Council are related to those functions of the Organization which were defined in Article 55. The last paragraph of this Article enables the Assembly to assign to the Council functions which may not be specifically related to the objectives set out in Article 55, but might contribute usefully to the discharge of the Assembly's general functions. The examination of the economic aspects of disputes dealt with by the Assembly, and assistance to the Assembly in the exercise of its budgetary powers under Article 17, are examples.

VOTING

ARTICLE 67

1. Each member of the Economic and Social Council shall have one vote.

2. Decisions of the Economic and Social Council shall be made by a majority of the members present and voting.

Voting power. The Article follows the general rule that no Member of the United Nations shall have a plural vote in any of the organs. *Voting procedure*. The Council decides by a simple majority of those present and voting. The reason for the qualified majorities prescribed for the General Assembly in Article 18(2), and for the Security Council in Article 27, lies in their power to impose specific obligations upon Members. The Economic and Social Council has no such power.

PROCEDURE

ARTICLE 68

The Economic and Social Council shall set up commissions in economic and social fields and for the promotion of human rights, and such other commissions as may be required for the performance of its functions.

Subsidiary organs : This Article is akin to Articles 22 and 29, in which power was conferred upon the General Assembly and the Security Council to establish subsidiary organs. The Economic and Social Council, however, is not only entitled but obligated to set up a number of commissions.

By August 1948, the Council established a network of subsidiary organs which are officially listed under four main headings :
(*A*). *Functional Commissions and Sub-commissions.*
   1. Economic and Employment Commission
      (a) Sub-Commission on Employment and Economic Stability.
      (b) Sub-Commission on Economic Development.
   2. Transport and Communications Commission.
   3. Fiscal Commission.
   4. Statistical Commission.
      (a) Sub-Commission on Statistical Sampling.
   5. Population Commission.
   6. Social Commission.
   7. Commission on Human Rights
      (a) Sub-Commission on the Freedom of Information and of the Press
      (b) Sub-Commission on the Prevention of Discrimination and the Protection of Minorities
      (c) Drafting Committee on the Bill of Human Rights.
   8. Commission on the Status of Women.
   9. Commission on Narcotic Drugs.

(B). *Regional Economic Commissions.*
  1. Economic Commission for Europe.
  2. Economic Commission for Asia and the Far East.
  3. Economic Commission for Latin America.
(C). *United Nations International Children's Emergency Fund.*
  This Fund functions under the Social Commission of the Council, and is administered by an Executive Director under the supervision of an Executive Board on which twenty-six Member States were represented.
(D). *Committees of the Council.*
  These are partly permanent, partly *ad hoc*. The permanent committees are : (i) Agenda Committee, (ii) Committee on Negotiations with Inter-Governmental Agencies, (iii) Committee on Arrangements for Consultation with Non-Governmental Organizations, (iv) Committee on the United Nations Appeal for Children.
  Ad hoc committees have included the Interim Committee on Programmes of Meetings, the Committee on Genocide and the Committee on Procedure.
Experts. The Dumbarton Oaks Proposals suggested that all commissions of the Economic and Social Council should consist of experts. At San Francisco that requirement was deleted, as it was felt that the Council ought to have unfettered freedom in choosing the personnel of its subsidiary organs. In practice, the expert element is strongly represented on all of them.

ARTICLE 69

The Economic and Social Council shall invite any Member of the United Nations to participate, without vote, in its deliberations on any matter of particular concern to that Member.

" *Particular concern* ". The principle of this Article is identical with that of Article 31. Whether any matter before the Council is of particular concern to a Member not represented on it will be determined by the Council. If it so determines, the invitation must issue, but the Member concerned is under no obligation to attend.

ARTICLE 70

The Economic and Social Council may make arrangements for representatives of the specialized agencies to participate, without vote, in its deliberations and in those of the com-missions established by it, and for its representatives to partici-pate in the deliberations of the specialized agencies.

Arrangements of this kind have been made in all agreements concluded or negotiated with specialized agencies under Article 63.

ARTICLE 71

The Economic and Social Council may make suitable arrange-ments for consultation with non-governmental organizations which are concerned with matters within its competence. Such arrangements may be made with international organizations and, where appropriate, with national organizations after consultation with the Member of the United Nations con-cerned.

Consultative status. In the system of the League, non-govern-mental bodies had a place in many activities in the social field, e.g. the assistance of refugees, the suppression of traffic in women and children, the scientific work of the Health Organization. A link between the public and the League was provided by League of Nations Unions formed in many countries. The Unions were combined in a Federation, which at its Annual Conference passed resolutions about various concerns of the League. The resolutions were submitted to the Assembly and the Council ; but no spokes-man of the Federation could appear to sponsor them.

The Charter provides for more regular expression of non-governmental, non-official opinion. At the invitation of the U.S. Government, representatives of some 50 large voluntary or-ganizations attended the San Francisco Conference as observers and unofficial advisers to governmental delegations. The pro-visions of the Charter about human rights are in large measure due to the efforts of these observers.

The Article gives a permanent role to voluntary bodies in the work of the Economic and Social Council.

Categories. By August 1948, 69 non-governmental organizations (65 of them international) were granted consultative status. They are divided into Categories (a), (b) and (c). Under the principles of classification adopted by the Council, category (a) comprises organizations which have " a basic interest " in most of the activities of the Council, and are closely linked with the economic and social life of the areas which they represent. Nine bodies have been granted this status:

the American Federation of Labour,
the International Chamber of Commerce
the International Co-operative Alliance,
the International Federation of Agricultural Producers,
the International Federation of Christian Trade Unions,
the International Organization of Industrial Employers,
the Inter-Parliamentary Union,
the World Federation of Trade Unions, and
the World Federation of United Nations Associations.

Organizations in Category (a) may take part at all meetings of the Economic and Social Council and its commissions, submit proposals for the agenda, circulate memoranda and send representatives to speak at the public meetings of these organs. They have no access to private meetings and no vote.

Category (b) consists of bodies, mostly international,[1] which have particular competence in, and are concerned specially with, certain aspects of the activity of the Council. By August 1948, 56 bodies received this status; and a permanent committee of the Economic and Social Council constantly examines applications for its grant. Included are religious bodies of all communities, economic and professional associations, and societies for every kind of social endeavour.

Category (c) comprises organizations which are concerned with building public opinion and disseminating information. It is much smaller than the others, and includes the Rotary International, the International Federation of Secondary Teachers, the World Organization of the Teaching Profession, the International Association of Lions Clubs, and the World Alliance for International Friendship through the Churches.

Organizations in Categories (b) and (c) may send observers to public meetings of the Council and its commissions, and submit memoranda on any subject which the Council has before it. These memoranda are circularized in full if a member of the Council so requests ; otherwise they are summarized. With the permission of the Chairman, observers sent by the organizations may make oral statements before the Council and its committees.

---

[1] National organizations cannot be granted consultative status, except with the consent of the Member Government concerned.

ARTICLE 72

1. The Economic and Social Council shall adopt its own rules of procedure, including the method of selecting its President.

2. The Economic and Social Council shall meet as required in accordance with its rules, which shall include provision for the convening of meetings on the request of a majority of its members.

At its first session, the Council adopted provisionally the Rules of Procedure proposed for it by the Preparatory Commission. Later, amendments and additions were made.

Sessions. At least three regular sessions are to be held each year. Extraordinary sessions are held if requested (a) by a majority of the Council's members, (b) by the General Assembly, or (c) by the Security Council acting in pursuance of Article 41 of the Charter (economic sanctions). Extraordinary sessions may also be held if the President of the Council agrees to a request made in that behalf by the Security Council (acting outside Article 41), the Trusteeship Council, any Member of the United Nations or a specialized agency ; or if the President and the Vice-Presidents agree that an extraordinary session should be called.

Agenda. This is drawn up by the Secretary-General in consultation with the President, and must include (a) all items proposed by the Council at a previous meeting ; (b) all items proposed by any Member of the United Nations ; (c) all items proposed by the General Assembly, the Security Council, the Trusteeship Council, a specialized agency or a non-governmental organization in Category (a).[1]

Representatives. Each representative on the Council may be accompanied by such alternates and technical advisers as he requires.

Presidency. The Council elects for each calendar year a President and two Vice-Presidents.

Publicity. The meetings of the Council are public unless the Council decides otherwise.

Quorum. A majority of the members of the Council constitutes a quorum.

[1] See Article 71.

CHAPTER XI

DECLARATION REGARDING NON-SELF-GOVERNING TERRITORIES

ARTICLE 73

Members of the United Nations which have or assume responsibilities for the administration of territories whose peoples have not yet attained a full measure of self-government recognize the principle that the interests of the inhabitants of these territories are paramount, and accept as a sacred trust the obligation to promote to the utmost, within the system of international peace and security established by the present Charter, the well-being of the inhabitants of these territories, and, to this end —

(a) to ensure, with due respect for the culture of the peoples concerned, their political, economic, social, and educational advancement, their just treatment, and their protection against abuses ;

(b) to develop self-government, to take due account of the political aspirations of the peoples, and to assist them in the progressive development of their free political institutions, according to the particular circumstances of each territory and its peoples and their varying stages of advancement ;

(c) to further international peace and security ;

(d) to promote constructive measures of development, to encourage research, and to co-operate with one another and, when and where appropriate, with specialized international bodies with a view to the practical achievement of the social, economic, and scientific purposes set forth in this Article ; and

(e) to transmit regularly to the Secretary-General for information purposes, subject to such limitation as security and constitutional considerations may require, statistical and other information of a technical nature relating to economic, social, and educational conditions in the territories for which they are respectively responsible, other than those territories to which Chapters XII and XIII apply.

141

F*

The League precedent. Article 22 of the Covenant laid down the principle of a trusteeship administration ("mandate") for the former German colonies in Africa and the Pacific and for the Arab provinces of the Ottoman Empire which had been liberated from Turkey, but were regarded as not yet fit for self-determination. The Covenant declared that the rule of "peoples not yet able to stand by themselves in the strenuous conditions of the modern world" should be a sacred trust of civilization, and exercised by an experienced Power on behalf and under the supervision of the League of Nations ; that the well-being of the native inhabitants was the primary objective of their administration ; and that there must be equal opportunity for the trade and enterprise of the subjects of all Members of the League, and no preference or discrimination in favour of subjects of the Mandatory Power.

This system of a trust administration responsible to an international body was not, however, applied to the colonial possessions of the victorious nations. Article 23(b) of the Covenant did indeed lay down a general obligation for "just treatment of the native inhabitants" of all territories under control of the Members of the League ; but no machinery was set up to implement the undertaking.

As regards the territories under mandate, international supervision was effected by a Permanent Commission of the League, composed of nine (later ten) expert persons, and also by a Department of the League Secretariat. The Commission received annually a written report of the Mandatory Power about each territory ; and it conducted annually a viva voce examination of the representatives of those Powers. Any person or body in a mandated territory who had a grievance was free to petition the Commission ; and the examination of these petitions, about which the Commission could question the representative of the Mandatory Power, (but not the petitioner, who had no right of appearance), was a regular part of the Commission's scrutiny.

The minutes of the proceedings of the Commission gave a detailed account of what was being done in each mandated territory. The Commission's function was restricted to offering recommendations and advice to the Council of the League upon any matter arising from reports and petitions. In the Council itself the danger was ever-present that political considerations might override the recommendations or whittle away the advice.

In place of a single article (Article 22) in the Covenant, the

Charter contains 22 articles in three chapters dealing with non-self-governing territories. The first chapter contains a declaration concerning all such territories; the second outlines a system of trusteeship to take the place of mandates; the third defines the composition, functions and powers of the Trusteeship Council.

Scope of the Declaration.

The Declaration adopts many of the principles stated in Article 22 of the Covenant, and it makes express what was implicit there, i.e. that the interests of the inhabitants shall be paramount.[1] But the formulation is bafflingly vague in many points. What has been said about the Charter as a whole, that the " i's " are not dotted and the " t's " are not crossed, is particularly applicable to this and the following Articles.

The following points are to be noted with regard to sub-clauses (a)—(e) :

(a) The reference to " due respect for the culture of the peoples concerned ", is designed to secure regard for native traditions. This respect is the basis of the British system of " indirect rule " in the African colonies.

" Just treatment " is a phrase borrowed from Article 23 of the League Covenant, where it was used in relation to all dependent peoples and not restricted to the inhabitants of mandated areas.

" Protection against abuses " is one of the main subjects of the earliest international instruments concerned with the rule of dependent peoples ; the Berlin Act of 1885 and the Brussels Act of 1890. By those Acts the signatory States agreed to suppress slave-trade and slavery. These specific purposes were repeated in Article 22 of the Covenant ; other abuses mentioned there were traffic in arms and liquor. The Mandatory Powers were required to legislate against these abuses ; and the Administering Authorities in the United Nations system must be presumed to be under a similar obligation.[2]

(b) Self-government and not independence is made the goal. The Soviet, Chinese and several other delegations at San Francisco urged that the Charter should prescribe the " development to independence " of colonial peoples, but the Conference took the view that the word " independence " meant different things to different peoples, that its use might lead to confusion and

---

[1] The phrase about the paramountcy of native interests was contained in a White Paper issued by the British Colonial Office in 1930 with regard to the inhabitants of the Colony of Kenya.

[2] The present obligation would seem to extend also to legislation against the forced labour of natives, an abuse specifically condemned by the San Francisco Conference.

uncertainty, and that "self-government" was a more comprehensive term which did not exclude aspirations to full independence.

(c) The linking of the system of trusteeship with the system of collective security is a radical departure from the League precedent ; see comment on Article 76(c).

(d) An example of the kind of regional co-operation here contemplated is the Anglo-American Caribbean Commission, which was established during the war for advancing social and economic improvements in the West Indies. The functions of the Commission include those set out in this paragraph of the Charter ; the promotion of constructive measures of development, the encouragement of research, and co-operation of the Powers which have colonies in the West Indies. The Advisory Council of the Commission included representatives of the French and Dutch, as well as of the British and American, Governments. Another regional enterprise of this type was established during the war by Australia and New Zealand, concerning the South Pacific region. The Convention of Canberra provides for close co-operation of the two Governments in dealing with what were then territories under their mandate.

(e) The Declaration is a kind of colonial charter, laying down standards of government ; but no specific duty of accounting to the General Assembly is prescribed. The stipulation of sub-clause (e) does not go beyond the supply of information to the Secretariat ; and even this duty is hedged about with reservations concerning security and constitutional considerations.[1]

The Second Assembly (1947) appointed a special committee to examine the reports submitted in accordance with Article 73(e). The Committee drew up a questionnaire to be addressed to all States governing dependent peoples. It was left to the option of these States whether they were prepared to furnish information not only about economic, social and educational, but also about political, developments; the Secretary-General was authorised to use non-official sources of information on economic, social and educational conditions, provided that the interested Governments agreed. The Committee is composed of eight members from the countries which under the present Article are required to send information, and eight other members elected by the Assembly. At the Third Assembly a resolution was passed which invited Members to send most recent information within six

---

[1] In practice, however, the Assembly has developed a system of obtaining reports and discussing them freely.

months after the end of the administrative year, and full reports at three years' intervals.

ARTICLE 74

Members of the United Nations also agree that their policy in respect of the territories to which this Chapter applies, no less than in respect of their metropolitan areas, must be based on the general principle of good-neighbourliness, due account being taken of the interests and well-being of the rest of the world, in social, economic and commercial matters.

The words of the Article are general and indefinite. The principle of good-neighbourliness does not impose any positive obligation to maintain the open door for trade and commerce which was prescribed in Article 22 of the Covenant. It may be considered negatively to prevent discrimination ; but no system is established of accountability to any international authority for giving effect to the principle, and for seeing that the resources of dependent countries are used for the good of the world.

CHAPTER XII

INTERNATIONAL TRUSTEESHIP SYSTEM

ARTICLE 75

The United Nations shall establish under its authority an international trusteeship for the administration and supervision of such territories as may be placed thereunder by subsequent individual agreements. These territories are hereinafter referred to as trust territories.

The trusteeship system of the Charter replaces the mandate system of the League.[1] While under the Covenant the system of mandatory administration was limited to colonies and territories which had ceased to be under the sovereignty of the enemy States of the First World War, the present Article is general in its scope. It envisages a trusteeship administration for any territories which may be placed under the system by individual agreements.

ARTICLE 76

The basic objectives of the trusteeship system, in accordance with the Purposes of the United Nations laid down in Article 1 of the present Charter, shall be :—

(*a*) to further international peace and security ;

(*b*) to promote the political, economic, social and educational advancement of the inhabitants of the trust territories, and their progressive development towards self-government or independence as may be appropriate to the particular circumstances of each territory and its peoples and the freely-expressed wishes of the peoples concerned and as may be provided by the terms of each trusteeship agreement ;

(*c*) to encourage respect for human rights and for fundamental freedoms for all without distinction as to race, sex, language or religion, and to encourage recognition of the interdependence of the peoples of the world ; and

(*d*) to ensure equal treatment in social, economic and commercial matters for all Members of the United Nations and their nationals, and also equal treatment for the latter

---

[1] See comment on Article 73.

in the administration of justice, without prejudice to the attainment of the foregoing objectives and subject to the provisions of Article 80.

Basic objectives. The objectives of the trusteeship system are much more fully set out than were the principles of the system of mandates in Article 22 of the Covenant. They are, by an express provision in the introductory paragraph of the Article, linked with the overall Purposes of the United Nations (as stated in Article 1 of the Charter), which become, in this way, and with some variation of wording, applicable to territories and peoples not yet independent and therefore not eligible for membership of the Organization.

(a) The inclusion of the furtherance of international peace and security among the objectives of trusteeship marks a striking change from one of the main purposes of the system of mandates. Under Article 22 of the Covenant, the prevention of the establishment of fortifications or military or naval bases, and of military training of the natives for other than police purposes and the defence of the territory, was part of the duty of the Mandatory Power. No similar restriction is envisaged for the Administering Authorities under the Charter. In fact, the present Article prescribes that they must ensure that the trust territory shall play its part in the security system. It follows that Administering Authorities may make use of native volunteer forces, of military bases and other facilities in the trust territory, not only for purposes of local defence but also in carrying out their obligations under Chapter VII of the Charter. The reasons are obvious : the experience of the Second World War proved that it was impossible to detach the mandated territories from the emergencies of war and create a kind of international vacuum.[1]

(b) It is notable that educational advancement of the inhabitants is particularly mentioned ; it was not, under Article 22 of the Covenant, among the duties imposed on Mandatory Powers.

Whereas. in Article 73, there was no mention of " independence ",[2] in the present Article the term appears as an alternative to " self-government ". Of the two, independence seems to be the more appropriate goal for peoples which have an advanced culture. The development of self-government under the

---

[1] New Guinea, for example, which was under an Australian mandate, was in the vortex of the struggle in the Pacific. Moreover, the Japanese had long before the war fortified islands which they held under mandate, and made them bases for invasion.

[2] For the reasons of its omission, see comment on Article 73.

supervision and protection of the Administering Authority is an objective applicable to all backward peoples, like the natives of Africa and the Pacific Islands. The Article prescribes that regard must be had to the freely-expressed wishes of the peoples concerned. The trusteeship agreements (Article 77) may specify whether in the particular case development is to be towards self-government or towards independence.

(c) The reference to human rights and fundamental freedoms adds nothing to Articles 1(3) and 55(c).[1] But the mention of the " recognition of the interdependence of the peoples of the world " is new, and finds no expression in any other part of the Charter. What may have been contemplated is the encouragement of regional arrangements between States concerning territories and peoples under their administration, on the model of the Caribbean Commission and the Convention of Canberra.[2]

(d) Article 22(5) of the Covenant prescribed equal opportunities for the trade and commerce of all Members of the League. That general direction was amplified in the specific mandate arrangements for individual territories. There was no mention in the Covenant of equal treatment in the administration of justice ; that seems to have been assumed as an element of good government.

The formula of this Article is wider. " Equal treatment in social, economic and commercial matters " is more comprehensive than equal opportunities for trade and commerce. On the other hand, the proviso at the end of the clause, " without prejudice to the attainment of the foregoing objectives ", gives a latitude in regard to trade agreements, which was lacking in the system of Mandates.

The objectives to which the principle of equal treatment is subordinated include the promotion of the economic and social advancement of the inhabitants. Bilateral and preferential trade agreements between a trust territory and a particular State may well be for the benefit of the inhabitants ; but any such agreement was excluded under the terms of the Mandates for certain African territories, and for Palestine.[3]

---

[1] It is noteworthy that, for the purposes of the trusteeship system, the objective is confined to the encouragement of " respect " for these rights and freedoms, and that there is no mention, as in Article 55, of their " observance ".

[2] See comment on Article 73(d).

[3] It is noteworthy that the United States Government entered a protest against provisions in the Trusteeship Agreement for Tanganyika which would allow for preferential trade conventions and State monopolies, on the ground that such arrangements would be contrary to the freedom of international trade protected by Article 76(d).

The final proviso referring to Article 80 makes the objectives stated in this Article subject to the provisions of existing Mandates. The provisions of the Mandate were to remain in force until replaced by new trusteeship agreements.

ARTICLE 77

1. The trusteeship system shall apply to such territories in the following categories as may be placed thereunder by means of trusteeship agreements :—

(a) territories now held under mandate ;

(b) territories which may be detached from enemy States as a result of the Second World War ; and

(c) territories voluntarily placed under the system by States responsible for their administration.

2. It will be a matter for subsequent agreement as to which territories in the foregoing categories will be brought under the trusteeship system and upon what terms.

No automatic application. The trusteeship system is not imposed by the Charter on any territories. Its application is left to subsequent agreements between the States " directly concerned " (Article 79).

The three categories. The classes of territories to which the trusteeship system may be applied are broadly defined.

Category (a) comprised all territories held under mandate of the League at the time the Charter came into force. These territories included :

(i) *in Asia Minor :* Palestine and Transjordan, both under British mandate.

In the case of Transjordan, the mandate was terminated by unilateral declaration of the British Government in January 1946 : and the country became an independent State.

In the case of Palestine, pursuant to the Assembly Resolution of November 29, 1947, the mandate was brought to an end on May 15, 1948, and on the same day a new independent State, the State of Israel, was proclaimed.[1]

(ii) *in Africa :* Togoland and the Cameroons, partly under British, partly under French, mandate ; Tanganyika, under British mandate ; Ruanda-Urundi, under Belgian mandate ; and South-West Africa, under the mandate of the Union of South Africa. With the exception of South-West Africa, all

[1] In May 1949, Israel was admitted to membership of the United Nations.

these territories have now been placed under trusteeship. As regards South-West Africa, the Government of the Union of South Africa, at the first session of the General Assembly, proposed to incorporate the territory in the Union. The Assembly rejected the proposal and invited the Union Government to propose a trusteeship agreement. The Union Government did not respond to the invitation, but abandoned preparations for the incorporation of the territory, and undertook to administer it in accordance with the spirit of the mandate and submit annual reports to the United Nations. At its second session, the Assembly, without taking up a definite position to the question whether all territories previously held under mandate should be brought under trusteeship until granted self-government or independence, repeated its invitation to the Union Government to negotiate a trusteeship agreement ; and at its third session maintained this recommendation.

(iii) *in the South Pacific :* the Marianas, Caroline and Marshall Islands, under Japanese mandate ; New Guinea (Northeastern part), New Ireland, New Britain and the Solomon Islands, under Australian mandate ; Nauru, under the joint mandate of Australia, New Zealand and the United Kingdom ; and Western Samoa under the mandate of New Zealand. All these territories have now been brought under trusteeship.

Category (b) includes the former Italian colonies of Libya, Eritrea and Italian Somaliland. Under the Peace Treaty with Italy, which came into force on September 15, 1947, the final disposal of these colonies was to be determined, within a year, jointly by the Governments of France, the Soviet Union, the United Kingdom and the U.S.A. No agreement was reached, and by virtue of Annex XI to the Peace Treaty, it fell to the General Assembly to make a recommendation binding on the Four Powers.[1]

Category (c) comprises any colonial territories which the Powers responsible for their administration may agree to place under trusteeship. No action has yet been taken ; and a draft Resolution placed before the second session of the Assembly, expressing the hope that Members would propose trusteeship agreements for all or some of the territories administered by them, failed to secure the necessary majority.

[1] At the time of going to press, the matter was still under consideration.

ARTICLE 78

The trusteeship system shall not apply to territories which have become Members of the United Nations, relationship among which shall be based on respect for the principle of sovereign equality.

The Article states the obvious. Only sovereign States can become Members of the United Nations : and sovereignty and tutelage are mutually exclusive.

The reason for including the Article in the Charter lay in the ambiguous position of Syria and the Lebanon at the time of the San Francisco Conference. They attended and signed the Charter in their own right ; but France still regarded them as technically subject to her mandate from the League. Since then France has recognized the sovereign independence of these two States.

ARTICLE 79

The terms of trusteeship for each territory to be placed under the trusteeship system, including any alteration or amendment, shall be agreed upon by the States directly concerned, including the mandatory Power in the case of territories held under mandate by a Member of the United Nations, and shall be approved as provided for in Articles 83 and 85.

Parties to trusteeship agreements. Although the terms of each trusteeship agreement must be agreed upon by the States directly concerned, not all these States become parties to the formal agreement embodying the terms. The agreements purport to be made between the General Assembly or (in the case of strategic areas) the Security Council on the one hand, and the Administering Authority on the other ; and they enter into force, following formal approval by the Assembly or the Security Council, as the case may be, as soon as they are ratified by the Administering Authority.

" *Direct concern* ". The Charter, apart from stipulating that, in the case of territories formerly held under mandate, the agreement of the Mandatory Power is essential, does not say which are the States " directly concerned " with the terms of trusteeship. In regard to her mandates in Africa, Great Britain applied the term to France, Belgium and the Union of South Africa, and also consulted the U.S.A. because it had been consulted at the time the mandates were first given. In regard to the former Japanese mandates, the U.S.A. submitted the draft trusteeship agreement " for information " to all members of the Security Council, and also to New Zealand and the Philippines ; but the Security Council ruled that all those members of the Far Eastern Commission which were not represented on the Council (namely, Canada, the Netherlands, New Zealand, India and the Philippines), were not only entitled to information, but also, if they so desired, to participation in the Council's discussions on the subject.

In the case of territories detached from enemy States (Article 77(1b)), the question has not yet arisen. In view of Article 23 of the Peace Treaty with Italy, which left the question of the disposal of the Italian colonies in the first place to the Governments of the United Kingdom, the U.S.A., the Soviet Union and France, those four Powers are certainly among those " directly concerned " ; and in the case of Eritrea and Somalia, which she claims as part of her former empire, Ethiopia also has a strong claim to be so regarded.

ARTICLE 80

1. Except as may be agreed upon in individual trusteeship agreements, made under Articles 77, 79 and 81, placing each territory under the trusteeship system, and until such agreements have been concluded, nothing in this Chapter shall be construed in or of itself to alter in any manner the rights whatsoever of any States or any peoples or the terms of existing international instruments to which Members of the United Nations may respectively be parties.

2. Paragraph 1 of this Article shall not be interpreted as giving grounds for delay or postponement of the negotiation and conclusion of agreements for placing mandated and other territories under the trusteeship system as provided for in Article 77.

Conservation of status quo. The purpose of this Article was to elucidate the position of States which, at the time the Charter came into force, were administering mandated territories. It signified that, until such territories were placed under trusteeship by voluntary agreement, the Charter did not purport to interfere with existing rights and duties.

Owing to the conclusion, since the Charter came into force,

of trusteeship agreements relating to all former mandated territories except South-West Africa, the application of the Article is now confined to that one territory.[1]

ARTICLE 81

The trusteeship agreement shall in each case include the terms under which the trust territory will be administered, and designate the authority which will exercise the administration of the trust territory. Such authority, hereinafter called the administering authority, may be one or more States or the Organization itself.

Essential contents of trusteeship agreements. Ten trusteeship agreements have so far been approved :
(a) *by the General Assembly, on December* 13, 1946 : agreements relating to (1) New Guinea, (2) Ruanda-Urundi, (3) Cameroons (French), (4) Togoland (French), (5) West Samoa, (6) Tanganyika, (7) Cameroons (British), (8) Togoland (British) ;
(b) *by the General Assembly, on November* 1, 1947 : the trusteeship agreement for Nauru ;
(c) *by the Security Council on April* 2, 1947: the trusteeship agreement for the Pacific Islands, formerly under Japanese mandate.
Standard clauses. All agreements contain clauses relating to the following subjects :
(1) definition of the boundaries of the territory ;
(2) designation of the Administering Authority ;
(3) general or special undertakings concerning the promotion of the objectives set out in Article 76 ;
(4) provisions defining the rights of the Administering Authority in legislation, administration and jurisdiction ; in constituting the territory into a customs, fiscal or administrative union with adjacent territories under the control of the Administering Authority ; and in establishing naval, military and air bases ;
(5) promotion of self-governing political institutions, suited to the territory ;
(6) application to the territory of international conventions, and of recommendations from the United Nations and specialized agencies which are appropriate to the particular circumstances of the territory ;

[1] Concerning the Assembly's attitude to the question of South-West Africa, see comment on Article 77.

(7) protection of the rights and interests of the inhabitants in land and natural resources ;

(8) equal treatment in social, economic and commercial matters for all Members of the United Nations ;

(9) assurance to the inhabitants, subject only to the requirements of public order and security, of human rights and fundamental freedoms ;

(10) provisions for the reference to the International Court of Justice of disputes arising between the Administering Authority and any other Member of the United Nations.[1]

Designation of Administering Authority. Under the League each mandated territory was entrusted to a single Mandatory.[2] There was no provision in the Covenant for the League itself becoming a Mandatory.

Under the Charter, the United Nations itself may be designated as Administering Authority ; and there is an express provision, which was not in the Covenant for a territory being placed under the administration of several States (" collective trustee-ship ").

The trusteeship agreements so far concluded all provide for a single Administering Authority. Apart from the Pacific Islands, which have been transferred from the mandate of Japan to the trusteeship of the U.S.A., the former Mandatory has been in each case re-appointed as Administering Authority.

ARTICLE 82

There may be designated in any trusteeship agreement, a strategic area or areas which may include part or all of the trust territory to which the agreement applies, without prejudice to any special agreement or agreements made under Article 43.

Purpose. The Article (in common with Article 83) is a special application of Article 76(a) which establishes a link between general security and the trusteeship system. It takes account of the strategic importance of certain areas which may be placed under trusteeship, and recognizes the need for a special régime.

---

[1] There is no such provision in the Trusteeship Agreement relating to the Pacific Islands now placed under U.S. Administration.

[2] The only apparent exception was the Pacific island of Nauru, mandated to the British Empire acting through Australia, New Zealand and the United Kingdom. On the transfer of Nauru to the trusteeship system, Australia became the sole Administering Authority.

The special régime is marked by the transfer to the Security Council of the supervisory functions which are normally exercised by the General Assembly.

Relation to Article 43. The special agreements contemplated by Article 43 may contain provisions for military facilities, bases and the location of forces in dependent territories. If at a later date any of these territories is placed under trusteeship, and designated in whole or in part as a strategic area, these arrangements do not affect the validity of the earlier special agreement.

Application in practice. The only trust territories so far designated as strategic are the Pacific Islands, which have been transferred from the mandate of Japan to the administration of the U.S.A.

ARTICLE 83

1. All functions of the United Nations relating to strategic areas, including the approval of the terms of the trusteeship agreements and of their alteration or amendment, shall be exercised by the Security Council.

2. The basic objectives set forth in Article 76 shall be applicable to the people of each strategic area.

3. The Security Council shall, subject to the provisions of the trusteeship agreements and without prejudice to security considerations, avail itself of the assistance of the Trusteeship Council to perform those functions of the United Nations under the trusteeship system relating to political, economic, social and educational matters in the strategic areas.

Effect. If it is proposed, with the approval of the States directly concerned, to designate the whole or part of a trust territory as a strategic area, the trusteeship agreement, and any alteration or amendment, requires the approval of the Security Council. That gives the permanent members of the Council overriding control since, by using the veto power, any one of them can obstruct arrangements to which it may object. If the Administering Authority is itself a permanent member of the Council, it can, by its veto, frustrate any change in the original arrangements. It is a further effect of this Article that all specific functions of the General Assembly enumerated in Article 87 are, in the case of strategic areas, exercised by the Security Council.

Relation to Article 76. The Charter declares that the designation of a trust territory as strategic must not interfere with the promotion of the basic objectives set out in Article 76. It is note-worthy, however, that the trusteeship agreement relating to the Pacific Islands entrusted to the United States contains provisions which make human rights and fundamental freedoms and the equal treatment of other Members of the United Nations and their nationals " subject to the requirements of security ".

The position of the Trusteeship Council. In principle, the Adminis-tering Authority of a strategic area must avail itself of the assist-ance of the Trusteeship Council in matters of political, economic social and educational advancement. As, however, this obligation is subject to " security considerations ", the access of the Trustee-ship Council to a strategic trust territory is virtually at the dis-cretion of the Administering Authority and the Security Council.

ARTICLE 84

It shall be the duty of the administering authority to ensure that the trust territory shall play its part in the maintenance of international peace and security. To this end the administer-ing authority may make use of volunteer forces, facilities and assistance from the trust territory in carrying out the obligations towards the Security Council undertaken in this regard by the administering authority, as well as for local defence and the maintenance of law and order within the trust territory.

Reversal of the League precedent. Under Article 22 of the Covenant, the Mandatory Powers, in the case of the African and South Pacific Mandates, were not allowed to establish fortifications or military and naval bases ; and the military training of natives was only permissible for police purposes and the local defence of the mandated territory. These restrictions aimed at safeguard-ing native populations from the risk of becoming involved in the wars of the Mandatory Power.

The Charter reverses the principle. The Administering Authority is not only allowed, but under a positive duty, to ensure that the trust territory should play its part in the system of collective security. There is no restriction on the construction of fortifi-cations or military, naval and air bases. The protection of the natives is whittled down to a prohibition of their conscription into armed forces. Voluntary forces may be used not only for police duties and local defence, but also in the discharge of any military obligations the Administering Authority may assume in special agreements with the Security Council under Article 43.

ARTICLE 85

1. The functions of the United Nations with regard to trusteeship agreements for all areas not designated as strategic, including the approval of the terms of the trusteeship agreements and of their alteration or amendment, shall be exercised by the General Assembly.

2. The Trusteeship Council, operating under the authority of the General Assembly, shall assist the General Assembly in carrying out these functions.

The position of the General Assembly. Under the Covenant, the supervision of the system of Mandates was the responsibility of the Council of the League, assisted by the Permanent Mandates Commission. The League Assembly could only discuss the Report of the Council.

The Charter reverses this position and — with the exception of strategic areas — entrusts to the Assembly the primary responsibility for the discharge of the Organization's functions relating to the trusteeship system.

The position of the Trusteeship Council. Although this Article is similar in structure to Article 60, it is noteworthy that, while in the case of the economic and social functions of the United Nations concurrent responsibility is vested in the Assembly and the Economic and Social Council, the present Article states not only that the Trusteeship Council will operate " under the authority " of the Assembly, but also that its functions will be in the nature of " assistance ". In connection with Article 60 we noted that, notwithstanding the subordination of the Economic and Social Council to the Assembly, the initiative has in fact passed to the former. It is too early to say whether similar developments can be expected in the field of trusteeship.

Termination and transfer of trusteeship. The provision of this Article making the terms of trusteeship agreements and their alteration and amendment subject to the approval of the General Assembly requires no comment. But neither this Article nor any other provision of the Charter answers the question whether the General Assembly has power (1) to terminate a trusteeship on the grounds that the territory is ripe for independence ; or (2) without terminating the trusteeship, to bring to an end the trust of the Administering Authority originally appointed, e.g. on the grounds that the State concerned has ceased to be a Member, or has been suspended from membership under Article 5, or has violated the terms of the trusteeship agreement.[1]

---

[1] These questions were raised at San Francisco, but not disposed of. It was felt that the termination of trusteeship could be left to individual agreements if and when the case arose. On the question of withdrawal, the delegations of the United States and Great Britain made a formal statement expressing the view that, if the Administering Authority withdrew from the United Nations for reasons which " reflected no discredit " upon the State concerned, there was no reason why it should not continue as Administering Authority. If, however, it withdrew for other reasons or was expelled, " the resulting situation could only be judged by the General Assembly and the Security Council on its merits, in the light of all the circumstances prevailing at the time ".

CHAPTER XIII

THE TRUSTEESHIP COUNCIL

COMPOSITION

ARTICLE 86

1. The Trusteeship Council shall consist of the following Members of the United Nations :—

(*a*) those Members administering trust territories ;

(*b*) such of those Members mentioned by name in Article 23 as are not administering trust territories ; and

(*c*) as many other Members elected for three-year terms by the General Assembly as may be necessary to ensure that the total number of members of the Trusteeship Council is equally divided between those Members of the United Nations which administer trust territories and those which do not.

2. Each member of the Trusteeship Council shall designate one specially qualified person to represent it therein.

Composition. The principles on which the Trusteeship Council is organized differ radically from those which determined the composition of the Permanent Mandates Commission of the League :

(a) The Members of the Council are representatives of Governments. The members of the Commission were experts, appointed by the Council of the League on account of their special knowledge.

The expert character of the Council should be safeguarded by the second paragraph of the Article ; but within the range of " specially qualified persons ", the choice of each Government is free.

(b) The total number of Members of the Council is to be divided equally between States which administer trust territories and those which do not.[1] In the Commission, the majority of members

---

[1] On January 1, 1949, the Council was composed as follows :
Members holding office under Article 86(1*a*) :
   Australia, Belgium, France, New Zealand, U.K., U.S.A.
Members holding office under Article 86(1*b*) :
   China and the Soviet Union.
Members holding office under Article 86(1*c*) :
   Costa Rica, Iraq, Mexico and the Philippines.
   The Soviet Union did not takes its seat until the third part of the second session (April 1948).

were nationals of States which did not hold a mandate ; each of the Mandatory Powers was represented by a member, but these representatives also had to be approved by the Council.

(c) Each of the permanent members of the Security Council is entitled to a seat on the Trusteeship Council. As a result, the five Great Powers and any other Members administering trust territories are assured of permanent representation, while all other members of the Council are elected by the Assembly for three-year terms.

It follows from these arrangements that the number of members is variable, since any addition to the number of States administering trust territories necessitates an addition to the number of elected members.[1]

FUNCTIONS AND POWERS

ARTICLE 87

The General Assembly and, under its authority, the Trusteeship Council, in carrying out their functions, may :—
  (a) consider reports submitted by the administering authority ;
  (b) accept petitions and examine them in consultation with the administering authority. ;
  (c) provide for periodic visits to the respective trust territories at times agreed upon with the administering authority ; and
  (d) take these and other actions in conformity with the terms of the trusteeship agreements.

The powers granted by this Article in general terms are regulated in full detail by the Trusteeship Council's Rules of Procedure. The most important provisions are as follows :

Reports. Each Administering Authority must submit an Annual Report on the basis of a questionnaire (Article 88) formulated by the Council. When the Council examines the Report, a special representative of the Administering Authority may participate, without vote, in the discussion, without prejudice to the voting rights of the Administering Authority's regular representative on the Council.

Petitions. Petitioners may be inhabitants of Trust Territories or other parties. Petitions, apart from exceptional cases, must be

---

[1] When the trusteeship agreement for the Trust Territory of the Pacific Islands came into force on July 18, 1947, and the U.S.A. (a permanent member of the Security Council) became one of the States administering trust territories, it was necessary to elect two additional members to the Trusteeship Council.

presented in writing ; the Council may subsequently direct an oral examination. Petitions directed against judgements of competent courts of the Administering Authority, or concerning disputes with which the courts have competence to deal, are, as a rule, inadmissible. All petitions are communicated to the Administering Authority which is entitled to make written or oral observations.[1]

Visits. The Charter does not make it a duty of the Trusteeship Council to arrange for periodic visits but the Rules of Procedure have transformed the permissive into a mandatory provision[2] ; and it has been agreed that each trust territory should be visited at least once in three years. " Surprise visits " are not possible, as the Charter provides that the time of each visit must be agreed upon with the Administering Authority.

Several visits to trust territories have already been arranged, notably to Western Samoa[3] and to East Africa.[4]

ARTICLE 88

The Trusteeship Council shall formulate a questionnaire on the political, economic, social, and educational advancement of the inhabitants of each trust territory, and the administering authority for each trust territory within the competence of the General Assembly shall make an annual report to the General Assembly upon the basis of such questionnaire.

The Council is free to formulate a different questionnaire for each territory, but in practice it has made every effort to work out a " model questionnaire ", designed to introduce a degree of uniformity and comparability into the Annual Reports, of which it is to form a basis.

A provisional Questionnaire was approved at the first session of the Council. The questionnaire is subdivided into sections dealing with the general status of the territory and its inhabitants ;

[1] The Council had before it at its second session 43 petitions, all of which had been addressed to the Secretary-General directly. At its third session, the Council had before it 13 petitions, two of which had been presented to the Administering Authority concerned for transmission to the Organization.

[2] The Permanent Mandates Commission repeatedly proposed to visit mandated territories, but its proposals were invariably rejected by the Council of the League which preferred, in suitable cases, to send special missions of its own.

[3] As a result of the visit to Western Samoa (July-August 1947), the Administering Authority (New Zealand) introduced radical reforms to secure more rapid progress with self-governing institutions.

[4] Tanganyika and Ruanda-Urundi (July-August 1948). In its Report, the Mission stressed particularly the need for quicker political evolution and the reorganization of educational services.

questions of peace and security ; maintenance of law and order ; political, economic, social and educational advancement ; publications and research ; suggestions, recommendations and conclusions.

VOTING

ARTICLE 89

1. Each member of the Trusteeship Council shall have one vote.

2. Decisions of the Trusteeship Council shall be made by a majority of the members present and voting.

This Article is self-explanatory.

PROCEDURE

ARTICLE 90

1. The Trusteeship Council shall adopt its own rules of procedure, including the method of selecting its President.

2. The Trusteeship Council shall meet as required in accordance with its rules, which shall include provision for the convening of meetings on the request of a majority of its members.

The Rules of Procedure adopted on April 23, 1947, provide for two regular sessions each year. Special sessions must be held at the request of the majority of the members of the Council, or at the request of the Security Council.

The Council elects a President and a Vice-President for each year. Meetings are, in principle, public ; but the Council and its subsidiary bodies may decide that particular meetings shall be held in private.

For the procedure relating to reports, petitions and visits, see comment on Article 87.

ARTICLE 91

The Trusteeship Council shall, when appropriate, avail itself of the assistance of the Economic and Social Council and of the specialized agencies in regard to matters with which they are respectively concerned.

In practice, the representatives of the Economic and Social Council and of certain specialized agencies (particularly ILO, FAO and UNESCO), regularly attend the meetings of the Council.

CHAPTER XIV

THE INTERNATIONAL COURT OF JUSTICE

ARTICLE 92

The International Court of Justice shall be the principal judicial organ of the United Nations. It shall function in accordance with the annexed Statute, which is based upon the Statute of the Permanent Court of International Justice and forms an integral part of the present Charter.

The Court as an organ of the United Nations. The International Court is not a new institution. Under the name of the " Permanent Court of International Justice ", it had been functioning at the Hague throughout the inter-war period and in close relation with the League. The Permanent Court was not, however, an organ of the League. Its Statute did not form an integral part of the Covenant, and Members of the League were not *ipso facto* parties to the Statute. That position is now changed. The Court, under the new name of " International Court of Justice ", has become a principal organ of the United Nations ; its Statute forms an integral part of the Charter, and membership of the United Nations involves automatic adherence to the Statute of the Court.

Apart from this structural change, which lays a timely stress on the organic connection between rule of law and political order, the new Court is to all intents and purposes a continuation of the old. Its Statute follows closely that of the Permanent Court. The principles of its jurisdiction and procedure are unchanged, and even the seat at The Hague has been kept.

The Court is the " principal " judicial organ of the United Nations, but not necessarily the only one. The Organization is free to set up subsidiary judicial organs[1] ; and the jurisdiction, by virtue of existing or future treaties, of other international tribunals remains unaffected (Article 95).

No compulsory jurisdiction. In a more perfect international order it would be obligatory for all States to refer to judicial tribunals

---

[1] E.g. the proposed International Court of Human Rights.

all " justiciable " disputes, i.e. all those conflicts which revolve round legal, and not political, questions. Neither the system of the League nor that of the United Nations has reached that degree of perfection. Both were born in an atmosphere of tension and distrust, in which the constituent States were reluctant to give up their freedom of choice between the several methods (e.g. diplomatic negotiation, arbitration and judicial settlement) which are applicable to legal disputes. As a result, the reference of legal disputes to the International Court is optional. Members of the United Nations do not, by the mere fact of ratifying the Charter, undertake to submit to the Court all their legal disputes. They can do so by agreement *ad hoc*,[1] or by entering into treaties which provide that all legal disputes arising under them shall be referred to the International Court,[2] or by making a declaration under Article 36(2) of the Statute, known as the " optional clause ". Such declaration may be made unconditionally, or on condition of reciprocity on the part of several or certain States, or for a certain time and subject to specific reservations. It has the effect of recognizing as compulsory (*ipso facto* and without special agreement, but only in relation to other States accepting the same obligation) the jurisdiction of the Court in all legal disputes concerning (a) the interpretation of a treaty ; (b) any question of international law ; (c) the existence of any fact which, if established, would constitute a breach of an international obligation ; and (d) the nature or extent of the reparation to be made for the breach of an international obligation.[3]

The law applied by the Court. If the parties agree, the Court has power to decide a case *ex aequo et bono*. But failing such agreement the Court must decide according to international law, i.e. on the basis of (a) international conventions establishing rules expressly recognized by the contesting States ; (b) international custom ; (c) the general principles of law recognized by civilized nations ; and (d) judicial decisions and the teachings of the most highly qualified publicists of the various nations, as subsidiary

[1] A special agreement of this kind was made in March 1948 between the United Kingdom and Albania for the submission to the Court of the *Corfu Channel Case.*

[2] E.g. the Trusteeship Agreements approved by the General Assembly on December 13, 1946; and the Treaty of Brussels (March 17, 1948) between Belgium, France, Luxembourg, the Netherlands and the United Kingdom. The constitutions of several international organizations (ILO, UNESCO, FAO and ICAO) also contain articles providing for the compulsory reference to the Court of disputes relating to the interpretation (or to the interpretation *and* application) of the constitution.

[3] Up to June 30, 1948, declarations under Article 36 of the Statute were made by fifteen Member States ; and seventeen more Members remained bound by similar declarations made under the Statute of the Permanent Court.

means for the determination of rules of law. (*Statute*, Article 38).

The Court is not bound by its own precedents. Its decisions are final and without appeal, but have no binding force except between the parties and in respect of that particular case (*Statute*, Articles 59-60).

Composition of the Court. The Court consists of 15 judges, no two of whom may be nationals of the same State. They are elected by the General Assembly and the Security Council, each of these bodies proceeding independently of the other. An absolute majority of votes is sufficient ; the permanent members of the Security Council have no veto. The judges are elected for nine years and may be re-elected.[1]

The Court is permanently in session except during the judicial vacations. (*Statute*, Article 23).

Independence of the judges. This is safeguarded as follows :

(1) No judge may exercise any political or administrative function or engage in any other occupation of a professional nature. (*Statute*, Article 16).

(2) No judge can be dismissed by any outside authority ; he can be dismissed only by the unanimous vote of all the other judges on the grounds that he has ceased to fulfil the required conditions of his office. (*Statute*, Article 18).

(3) When engaged on the business of the Court, all judges enjoy diplomatic privileges and immunities. (*Statute*, Article 19).

On the other hand, judges of the nationality of each of the parties retain their right to sit in the case before the Court. Moreover, if the Court includes no judge of the nationality of the parties, each of these parties may proceed to choose a person to sit as judge. (*Statute*, Article 31).

Parties. Only States may be parties in cases before the Court. The access to the Court of organs of the United Nations and of specialized agencies is confined to requests for advisory opinions.[2]

ARTICLE 93

1. All Members of the United Nations are, *ipso facto*, parties to the Statute of the International Court of Justice.

2. A State which is not a Member of the United Nations may become a party to the Statute of the International Court

---

[1] However, of the judges elected at the first election, the terms of five judges expired at the end of three years, and the terms of five more expire at the end of six years. (*Statute*, Article 13).

[2] See Article 96 and comment.

of Justice on conditions to be determined in each case by the General Assembly, upon the recommendation of the Security Council.

Automatic adherence to the Statute. Under the Covenant it was possible for a State to become a Member of the League without becoming a party to the Statute of the Permanent Court. No such situation can arise in the United Nations. The Statute of the Court is now an integral part of the Charter and requires no separate ratification by Members.

The position of non-members. We have to distinguish between two groups of cases :

(1) States may wish to become parties to the Statute of the Court, but not to join the United Nations. In such cases, it is for the General Assembly to determine the conditions of admission.[1] A simple majority vote is sufficient, but the Assembly cannot approve an application without a positive recommendation from the Security Council. The vote of the Council is governed by Article 27(3).

Conditions of admission laid down in one case constitute no binding precedent for other cases.[2]

(2) It may happen that States which are not Members of the United Nations will wish to make use of the facilities of the Court without becoming parties to the Statute as a whole. Under Article 35 of the Statute, the Court is, in principle, open to such States, but only on conditions laid down by the Security Council. These conditions must take account of the provisions of any treaties that may apply to the particular case, but in no case must they have the effect of placing the parties in a position of inequality before the Court.

ARTICLE 94

1. Each Member of the United Nations undertakes to comply with the decision of the International Court of Justice in any case to which it is a party.

---

[1] Including, if required, rules for the participation of the State concerned in the election of the judges.

[2] In the case of Switzerland (which was admitted to the Statute of the Court by Assembly Resolution of December 11, 1946) the conditions were as follows : (a) acceptance of the provisions of the Statute of the Court, (b) acceptance of all obligations of a Member of the United Nations under Article 94 of the Charter, and (c) an undertaking to contribute to the expenses of the Court such equitable amount as the General Assembly will assess from time to time after consultation with the Swiss Government.

2. If any party to a case fails to perform the obligations incumbent upon it under a judgement rendered by the Court, the other party may have recourse to the Security Council, which may, if it deems necessary, make recommendations or decide upon measures to be taken to give effect to the judgement.

Obligation to comply with decisions. Since the jurisdiction of international tribunals is derived invariably from the voluntary submission of the parties (in the form of treaties, declarations or agreements *ad hoc*), it would be incompatible with the good morals of the international community if a party were allowed to go back on its submission when the decision turns out to be disappointing. This is the moral justification for the universally admitted principle of international law that the decisions of international tribunals are binding upon the parties.

If nothing more had been intended than to affirm a general principle of law, the first paragraph of this Article would be superfluous. The better interpretation seems to be that, if any Member of the United Nations fails to comply with a decision of the International Court of Justice, it infringes not only a general principle of law but also a specific obligation under the Charter. The faithful performance of all these obligations is one of the fundamental Principles, (Article 2(2)) and as such is protected by the rule in Article 6 whereby Members persistently violating the Principles of the Charter may be expelled from the Organization. *Functions of the Security Council.* In no single case decided since 1920 has any party disobeyed a judgement of the Hague Court. It remains none the less true that, if disobedience occurred at any future date, the Court as such would have no physical means of enforcement. Under the present Article, the Security Council is empowered to take such measures as may be necessary to obtain satisfaction of the Court's judgements. Two points must be noted. First, the Council can enforce a judgement not only against Members of the United Nations, but also against non-members, provided considerations of peace and security are involved. To that extent the present Article is a specific application of the rule in Article 2(6). Secondly, application for enforcement must be made by the aggrieved party and not by the Court itself. The Charter does not constitute the Council an automatically functioning enforcement agency of the Court, like sheriffs in the national systems of judicial administration.

It is within the discretion of the Council to decide whether or not enforcement action, or at least a recommendation, is necessary.

It has been suggested that the Council can only take action in the conditions of Article 39, i.e. when the situation arising from non-compliance with a judgement amounts in itself to a threat to peace. With that interpretation the present writers are unable to agree. If that had been the intent of the Charter, the second paragraph of the present Article could have been dispensed with, or would have had to include an express reference to Article 39. The proper interpretation seems to be that the powers of the Council under this Article are additional to the powers conferred in Chapter VII ; they are a specific application of the Council's general powers under Article 24. The Council is free to decide that disobedience to a judgement of the Court is a threat to the international order which underlies the system of collective security, and that there is a case for enforcing judgements even in the absence of an actual threat to peace.

ARTICLE 95

Nothing in the present Charter shall prevent Members of the United Nations from entrusting the solution of their differences to other tribunals by virtue of agreements already in existence or which may be concluded in the future.

This is a re-affirmation of the principle that the International Court of Justice has no monopoly in the settlement of legal disputes, and that Members of the Organization remain free to refer such disputes to other tribunals by treaty or *ad hoc* agreement.

ARTICLE 96

1. The General Assembly or the Security Council may request the International Court of Justice to give an advisory opinion on any legal question.
2. Other organs of the United Nations and specialized agencies, which may at any time be so authorized by the General Assembly, may also request advisory opinions of the Court on legal questions arising within the scope of their activities.

Advisory opinions. Judgement is not the only way in which the International Court can record its view of controversial issues. A judgment can only be given at the instance of States which have formulated definite claims, and, possibly, counter-claims, against each other. When a legal issue has not yet crystallized into inter-State claims, the Court can only deliver an opinion. This opinion is of an advisory nature, in contrast to judgements which finally dispose of the issue.

Who can ask for advisory opinions ? To States as such the Court cannot give advisory opinions. Only organs of the United Nations and specialized agencies acting under its authority can make a request for them.

In the case of the General Assembly and the Security Council, this privilege is absolute ; they can ask for an advisory opinion at any time and on any legal question whatsoever.[1] Other organs and the specialized agencies must first obtain express authority from the General Assembly, and can only ask for advisory opinions on legal questions arising within the scope of their activities. It is now firmly established that the General Assembly may give this authority generally, and dispense with applications relating to individual cases. Such general authority has already been given to the Economic and Social Council (Assembly Resolution of December 11, 1946) and to the Trusteeship Council, (Assemby Resolution of November 14, 1947). General authority has also been granted, by agreements concluded under Article 63, to the specialized agencies brought into relationship with the United Nations, but this authority does not cover questions concerning the mutual relationships of the agency and the United Nations or other specialized agencies.

Procedure. A request for an advisory opinion must be accompanied by all documents likely to throw light upon the question. All States which as parties to the Statute, or under special agreements, are entitled to " appear before the Court ", and such international organizations as the Court considers likely to be able to furnish information on the question, may submit written or oral statements. The advisory opinion is delivered in open court. (*Statute*, Chapter IV).

Use of advisory opinions. The purpose of advisory opinions is to offer authoritative guidance to organs of the United Nations and to specialized agencies on legal questions arising in the course of

---

[1] See Assembly Resolution of December 3, 1948, requesting an advisory opinion on certain general points of law arising from the assassination of the United Nations mediator in Palestine, Count Folke Bernadotte, and notably on the question whether, in the event of an agent of the United Nations suffering injury in the performance of his duties, the Organization as such had the capacity to bring a claim against the Government whose responsibility was involved for the damage caused (*a*) to the United Nations, (*b*) to the victim or to the persons entitled through him.

their activities. Recommendations and decisions passed on the basis of advisory opinions have the full authority of the Court behind them; and during the League régime recommendations and decisions of this kind were never challenged on legal grounds. Owing to the unfortunate refusal of the San Francisco Conference to make the Court the final arbiter of controversial interpretations of the Charter it is by no means certain that the United Nations will have the same experience.

CHAPTER XV

THE SECRETARIAT

ARTICLE 97

The Secretariat shall comprise a Secretary-General and such staff as the Organization may require. The Secretary-General shall be appointed by the General Assembly upon the recommendation of the Security Council. He shall be the chief administrative officer of the Organization.

Organization of the Secretariat. The Secretariat which, under Article 7, is a principal organ of the United Nations, comprises two elements : (1) a *Secretary-General*, whose functions are defined by the Charter and whose appointment requires the concurrence of the General Assembly and the Security Council ; and (2) the *staff* of the Secretariat, whose functions the Charter does not set out in detail, and who are appointed by the Secretary-General under regulations established by the General Assembly (Article 101(1)). The Secretary-General is the chief administrative officer of the Organization ; and, according to the Charter, it is for him to determine (subject only to the requirements set out in Article 101(2)) how the Secretariat shall be organized. In effect the structure of the Secretariat was laid down by the Assembly itself (Resolution of February 13, 1946).

Appointment of Secretary-General. The appointment is made by the General Assembly upon the recommendation of the Security Council. The recommendation is substantive and requires the concurrence of all permanent members of the Council. The General Assembly decides by the simple majority of those present and voting; for, paradoxically, the appointment of the Secretary-General is not included among the " important questions " listed in Article 18(2). The General Assembly is not bound by the Council's recommendation. If the Recommendation is rejected, the Assembly must wait for a fresh recommendation ; it cannot act on its own.

No fixed term of office is prescribed by the Charter. It is to be determined by the Council and the Assembly, whenever a fresh appointment is made.

The first Secretary-General, Mr. Trygve Lie, was appointed by unanimous resolution of the Assembly on February 1, 1946 for five years, re-appointment being open at the end of that period for a further term of five years. In the same resolution the Assembly recorded its desire that, on the retirement of a Secretary-General, no Member should offer him at least, not immediately any such governmental position as might be a source of embarrassment to other Members, in view of the wealth of confidential information that Governments communicate to the chief administrative officer of the United Nations.

The emoluments of the Secretary-General are at the discretion of the General Assembly, as part of its general budgetary powers (Article 17).[1]

Structure of the Secretariat. Under the organizational plan approved by the General Assembly on February 13, 1946, the Secretariat is divided into eight principal units (not counting the Executive Office of the Secretary-General) which are as follows :
(1) Department of Security Council Affairs,
(2) Department of Economic Affairs,
(3) Department of Social Affairs,
(4) Department of Trusteeship and Information from Non-Self-Governing Territories,
(5) Department of Public Information,
(6) Legal Department,
(7) Conference and General Services,
(8) Administrative and Financial Services.

An Assistant Secretary-General is at the head of each Department ; and each Department is subdivided into Divisions (or groups) and Sections.[2]

ARTICLE 98

The Secretary-General shall act in that capacity in all meetings of the General Assembly, of the Security Council, of the Economic and Social Council, and of the Trusteeship Council, and shall perform such other functions as are entrusted to him by these organs. The Secretary-General shall make an annual report to the General Assembly on the work of the Organization.

---

[1] On the appointment of the first Secretary-General, the Assembly voted (in addition to the use of a furnished residence) a net salary of U.S. $20,000 *per annum*, and a representation allowance of equal amount.

[2] Excluding the International Court of Justice, the Budget Estimates for the financial year 1949 provided for a total of 3,738 established posts.

Delegation of functions. Although the Charter does not say so, in practice all functions entrusted to the Secretary-General under this Article may be delegated by him to members of his staff.
Meetings of principal organs. The Secretary-General (or his deputy) must be present at all meetings of the General Assembly and the three Councils ; this duty does not extend to sittings of the International Court of Justice.
Annual Report. The Annual Report of the Secretary-General covers the whole field of the Organization's activities, but its presentation does not discharge the obligation, prescribed in Article 15 for the Security Council and other organs, to submit separate reports of their own. In practice these reports are also prepared by the appropriate Divisions of the Secretariat.

ARTICLE 99

The Secretary-General may bring to the attention of the Security Council any matter which in his opinion may threaten the maintenance of international peace and security.

Political functions of Secretary-General. In the League, the functions of the Secretary-General were, in theory at least, purely administrative. The Charter invests him with the additional power to bring to the attention of the Security Council matters which may threaten international peace and security — a privilege otherwise only granted to Governments (Article 35). Under the present Article the Secretary-General has access only to the Security Council, and not, as Governments have under Article 35, to the General Assembly also ; and he is not entitled to call the attention of the Council to infringements of the Charter which fall short of a threat to the peace.
The formulation of the Article is permissive. It is for the Secretary-General to determine at his discretion which is a proper case for the use of his exceptional powers under this Article.

ARTICLE 100

1. In the performance of their duties the Secretary-General and the staff shall not seek or receive instructions from any Government or from any other authority external to the Organization. They shall refrain from any action which might reflect on their position as international officials responsible only to the Organization.

2. Each Member of the United Nations undertakes to respect the exclusively international character of the responsibilities of the Secretary-General and the staff and not to seek to influence them in the discharge of their responsibilities.

An International Civil Service. The difficulty which this Article seeks to solve arises because, while acting as international civil servants, the Secretary-General and his staff remain citizens of national States. The solution is found partly in the privileges and immunities prescribed in Article 105(2), and partly in the liabilities imposed by the present Article (1) upon the Secretary-General and his staff, and (2) on Member Governments.

The position of the Secretariat. The Secretary-General and the staff must not seek or accept instructions from any Government or external authority. During their term of office their loyalty must be exclusively to the Organization. In fact, the Staff Regulations made under Article 101 require that, upon accepting their appointment, all members of the staff shall subscribe to an oath or declaration[1] in which they pledge themselves to discharge their functions and regulate their conduct " with the interests of the United Nations only in view ".

The prohibition of seeking or receiving instructions is not intended to isolate members of the Secretariat from all contact with their respective Governments ; the experience of the League has shown that personal liaison can be of great benefit to the Organization.

The prohibition of " action which might reflect on their position as international officials " is rather vague in the Charter, but it has been elaborated in the Staff Regulations. These provide that any member of the staff who becomes a candidate for a public office of a political character must resign from the Secretariat. In border-line cases it is for the Secretary-General to decide whether the proposed office or occupation is incompatible. Members of the staff may not accept any honour, decoration, favour, gift or fee (except for war services) from any Government or from any external authority ; and must also avoid any kind of public pronouncement which may " adversely reflect on their international position ".

The position of Governments. The restraints imposed upon Member Governments in the second paragraph of this Article are complementary to the injunction addressed to the staff. No attempt has

[1] In the case of the Secretary-General and the Assistant Secretary-General the oath or declaration is made orally at a public meeting of the General Assembly.

been made, either in the Staff Regulations or in the General Convention on Privileges and Immunities giving effect to Article 105, to define what is meant by " seeking to influence " members of the Secretariat. It would be clearly improper for any Government, directly or indirectly, to penalize a member of the Secretariat for any action or pronouncement which, but for his or her employment in the service of the United Nations, would be treasonable, disloyal, or in any other way contrary to the laws or interests of the State concerned. Members of the staff must be entirely free to discharge their duties to the United Nations, even where those duties might involve the planning or enforcement of sanctions against their own countries.

ARTICLE 101

1. The staff shall be appointed by the Secretary-General under regulations established by the General Assembly.

2. Appropriate staffs shall be permenently assigned to the Economic and Social Council, the Trusteeship Council, and, as required to other organs of the United Nations. These staffs shall form part of the Secretariat.

3. The paramount consideration in the employment of the staff and in the determination of the conditions of service shall be the necessity of securing the highest standards of efficiency, competence and integrity. Due regard shall be paid to the importance of recruiting staff on as wide a geographical basis as possible.

Staff Regulations. The fundamental rights and obligations of the staff were embodied by the Preparatory Commission in Provisional Staff Regulations, supplemented by Provisional Staff Rules dealing with questions of administrative detail. Both documents were approved by the General Assembly on February 13, 1946. The most important principles are as follows :

(1) The privileges and immunities enjoyed by members of the staff are no excuse for the non-performance of private obligations, or for any failure to observe laws and police regulations. The Secretary-General may, at his discretion, waive them in any individual case.

(2) Men and women are equally eligible for all posts, and, so far as practicable, appointments are made on a competitive basis.

(3) The normal age of retirement is 60 years; this may, in exceptional circumstances, be extended to 65 years.

(4) Proper administrative machinery must be maintained for inquiry and appeal in disciplinary cases and the termination of appointments ; the staff is entitled to participation in that machinery.

In principle, the salaries of United Nations staff are exempt from national taxation ; pending the ratification of the General Convention on Privileges and Immunities (Article 105) and in view of the reservations already made by certain States, the Secretary-General has authority (Assembly Resolution of February 13, 1946) to reimburse staff members who are required to pay taxes on their salaries and wages.

Assignment of staffs to Councils and other organs. See comment on Article 97 (Structure of the Secretariat).

Recruitment. The Charter records the desire that staff shall be recruited on as wide a geographical basis as possible. Without prejudice to the ultimate discretion of the Secretary-General, recruitment is confined to the nationals of Members, and care is taken that in this way each Member State shall have a fair share of posts in the Secretariat. For the purpose of advising the Secretary-General on methods of recruitment and staff administration an International Civil Service Advisory Board was appointed in 1948.

CHAPTER XVI

MISCELLANEOUS PROVISIONS

ARTICLE 102

1. Every treaty and every international agreement entered into by any Member of the United Nations after the present Charter comes into force shall as soon as possible be registered with the Secretariat and published by it.

2. No party to any such treaty or international agreement which has not been registered in accordance with the provisions of paragraph 1 of this Article may invoke that treaty or agreement before any organ of the United Nations.

Purpose. In President Wilson's conception one of the principal purposes of the League was to abolish secret diplomacy. This idea was expressed in Article 18 of the Covenant, which provided for the registration with the Secretariat and the publication by it[1] of every treaty or international engagement entered into by Members of the League. No treaty or engagement was to be binding until it was registered.

The Charter follows the general pattern of the provisions in the Covenant. There are, however, important differences of detail both in principle and procedure. The procedure is laid down in a set of " Regulations for the Registration and Publication of Treaties and International Agreements " approved by the General Assembly on December 14, 1946.

The generality of the obligation. The Article employs the comprehensive term " every treaty and every international agreement ", which covers every type of undertaking whatever its form, provided the parties intend to enter into a legal, as distinct from a purely moral or political, obligation.

Even unilateral engagements by one State in favour of another State seem to be included[2]; and no exception is granted for agreements of minor importance or temporary effect.

Military agreements and arrangements need not be registered if they are not intended to create legal obligations ; but the " special agreements " between Members and the Security Council

---

[1] The *Treaty Series* published by the Secretariat ran into 204 volumes and included a total of 4,822 documents.

[2] In such cases, however, the obligation to register does not arise until the State in whose favour the engagement is made has formally accepted it.

contemplated by Article 43 are obviously meant to be legally binding, and will have to be registered *ex officio*.[1]

The position of non-members. Agreements between Members and non-members must be registered and published. Agreements between non-members cannot be registered, but upon the request of any non-member State[2] will be " filed and recorded " by the Secretariat and published in the United Nations " Treaty Series ".

Agreements prior to October 24 1945. There is no obligation to register agreements entered into before the Charter came into force ; but on February 10, 1946, the General Assembly invited all Members to submit, for " filing and publication ", agreements entered into " in recent years " which had not been included in the " Treaty Series " of the League.

Procedure. (1) Treaties and agreements must be submitted for registration " as soon as possible " after they have come into force (Regulations, Article 1(2)).

(2) Each party is individually responsible for registration, but the discharge of this obligation by one party releases all other parties. Where the Organization itself is a party (e.g. under Article 43) registration takes place *ex officio*.

(3) The Secretariat publishes every month a " Statement " of the dates and titles of treaties and international agreements registered, or filed and recorded, during the preceding month. Thereafter the full text of the document, in the original language or languages followed by a translation in English and French, is published in the " Treaty Series ".

Effects of non-registration. (1) Failure to register a treaty or international agreement made after October 24, 1945, is a breach of the Charter. Persistent failure may be construed as an offence against Article 2(2) and, theoretically, may entail expulsion, under Article 6.

(2) Under the Covenant no treaty or international agreement was binding until it was registered. The Charter operates with a milder sanction. Non-registration does not affect the validity of the agreement or its enforceability before tribunals other than the International Court of Justice ; but no Member State which is a party to the agreement may invoke it before any organ of the United Nations. This disability does not, however, extend

---

[1] Regulations, Article 4.

[2] Except Spain, who has been excluded from this privilege by Assembly Resolution of February 10, 1946.

to Member States which were not parties to the agreement and had no obligation to register[1] it.

Finally, it seems that no organ of the United Nations is prevented from taking official cognizance of an agreement by reason of its non-registration. Paragraph 2 of this Article is intended to inflict a penalty on offending Members, and not to restrict the Organization in the discharge of its functions.

ARTICLE 103

In the event of a conflict between the obligations of the Members of the United Nations under the present Charter and their obligations under any other international agreement, their obligations under the present Charter shall prevail.

Purpose. This Article is designed to exclude the possibility of a Member State being impeded in carrying out its obligations or enforcing its rights[2] under the Charter by conflicting obligations which it may have accepted under other international agreements. It must not happen, for instance, that, if and when the Security Council calls upon a Member to join in military sanctions against an aggressor, the Member should be able to plead that, under a separate agreement, he had pledged assistance or neutrality to the aggressor State.

The Article applies equally to agreements between Members, and to agreements between Members and non-members.

Agreements between Members. It is a general rule of international law that a later agreement supersedes all previous agreements concluded between the same parties and dealing with the same subject. As far as agreements made before the Charter are concerned, the Article adds nothing to the general rule. Indeed, it is less strict than was the League Covenant, which expressly abrogated (Article 20) all previous obligations and understandings if they were inconsistent with its terms. The Charter does not abrogate any previous agreements ; it only says that if, in the execution of either the previous agreement or the Charter, a conflict should arise between the two sets of obligations, those laid down in the Charter must prevail.

---

[1] It would appear that non-member States which, as parties to the agreement, submitted it for " filing and recording ", are not precluded from invoking the instrument before organs of the United Nations.

[2] In 1947, Egypt contended before the Security Council that her 1936 Treaty with Great Britain, which provided for the stationing of British forces in Egypt, was contrary to the Charter's fundamental principle (Article 2(1)) declaring the sovereign equality of all Members.

Agreements made after the Charter are also covered by a general rule of international law. Parties to a multilateral agreement cannot accept obligations inconsistent with its terms except with the consent of all parties to the original agreement. Here again the Charter is less strict than Article 20 of the Covenant, by which the Members of the League gave a solemn undertaking not to enter into any engagements inconsistent with the terms of the Covenant. The present Article leaves the treaty-making power of Members intact. It is no breach of the Charter to enter into any international agreements the terms of which are inconsistent with the Charter. The test is not the conflict between terms, but the conflict which may arise in the particular circumstances of carrying them out.

Agreements with non-members. Under the Covenant, the Members of the League had to take immediate steps to procure their release from any obligations which were inconsistent with its terms. There is no such duty under the Charter. Members are bound by their agreements with non-members, but the Charter gives them dispensation — and indeed, prohibits them — from carrying out those terms of such agreements which may involve a conflict with the Charter. All organs of the United Nations, including the International Court of Justice, are bound to give effect to that dispensation, but international tribunals operating outside the Organization (e.g. an arbitral tribunal set up under the agreement concerned) are not. The Charter is a " higher law " only for the Members and organs of the United Nations ; outsiders are under no legal obligation to accept it as such.

ARTICLE 104

The Organization shall enjoy in the territory of each of its Members such legal capacity as may be necessary for the exercise of its functions and the fulfilment of its purposes.

Legal capacity. States are not bound by international law to recognize as a matter of course the legal personality of international organizations — not even of those they have joined. Whether in the national territory an international organization has capacity to acquire property, make contracts and institute legal proceedings, depends on the national law.

When a new international organization is formed, provision can be made in two ways for its legal capacity in the territory of

Member States. One method is to embody specific arrangements in the constitution of the organization. In that case, each Member is obliged to take such steps (executive action or special legislation) as may, under its own constitution, be necessary to grant the organization legal personality. The other method — and this is adopted by the Charter — is to state the principle and leave it for independent national action, or for national action regulated by international conventions, to add the details. It will be noted that the principle stated in the Article does not claim for the United Nations " full " legal capacity, as is normally enjoyed by corporations formed in accordance with the national laws of a State, but a limited capacity — such as may be necessary for the exercise of the Organization's functions and the fulfilment of its purposes.

The General Convention. In connection with this Article, the Charter did not invite (as it did in Article 105(3) with reference to privileges and immunities) the General Assembly to propose a convention. The Preparatory Commission, however, took the view that the best way of giving effect to the Article would be to include suitable provisions in the convention envisaged by Article 105. The " *Convention on the Privileges and Immunities of the United Nations* " (the so-called General Convention)[1] approved by the General Assembly on February 13, 1946 disposes of the matter in its first Article. It recognizes, without qualification or reservation, the juridical personality of the United Nations and invests it with capacity (a) to contract ; (b) to acquire and dispose of immovable and movable property ; and (c) to institute legal proceedings.[2]

The Headquarters Convention. The status of the Organization required special regulation in the U.S.A., by reason of the fact that the permanent headquarters were to be established there. These regulations are embodied in the " *Agreement between the United Nations and the United States of America regarding the Headquarters of the United Nations* " which was signed by the Secretary-General of the Organization and the U.S. Secretary of State on June 26, 1947, and formally approved by the General Assembly on October 31, 1947. The Agreement has established a

---

[1] On the state of accessions, see comment on Article 105.

[2] According to an Advisory Opinion of the International Court of Justice, delivered in April 1949, following the assassination of Count Bernadotte in the event of an agent of the United Nations suffering injury in the performance of his duties, the Organization as such has capacity to bring a claim against the Government whose responsibility is involved for the damage caused to the United Nations and to the victim or to the persons entitled through him.

special régime for a " Headquarters District " in the Borough of Manhattan, New York State. The Headquarters District is under the control and authority of the United Nations ; and the federal, state or local laws and regulations of the United States are only applicable so far as they are not inconsistent with regulations made by the Organization. The District is inviolable, and no United States personnel can enter to perform any official duties therein, except with the consent of the Secretary-General. The Organization may expel or exclude persons from the District. The United States must not impose any impediments (e.g. by the refusal of visas) to the transit to or from the District of persons travelling on United Nations business ; and the laws and regulations regarding the residence of aliens must not be applied in such manner as to interfere with persons who are staying in the District on such business. At the request of the Secretary-General, the American authorities must provide police for the preservation of law and order in the District, and for the removal of persons expelled or excluded by the United Nations. It is specifically prescribed that no form of racial or religious discrimination is permitted within the District.

ARTICLE 105

1. The Organization shall enjoy in the territory of each of its Members such privileges and immunities as are necessary for the fulfilment of its purposes.

2. Representatives of the Members of the United Nations and officials of the Organization shall similarly enjoy such privileges and immunities as are necessary for the independent exercise of their functions in connection with the Organization.

3. The General Assembly may make recommendations with a view to determining the details of the application of paragraphs 1 and 2 of this Article or may propose conventions to the Members of the United Nations for this purpose.

The position of the Organization. Under the General Convention[1] the United Nations, its property and assets enjoy immunity from every form of legal process, but the immunity can be waived. The premises of the Organization are inviolable ; so are its archives and documents. The Organization, its assets and income are exempt from all direct taxes, but not from charges for public utility services ; also from customs duties and from prohibitions

---

[1] See comment on Article 104.

and restrictions on imports and exports in respect of articles needed for official use, and any publications. The official correspondence and communications of the Organization are absolutely exempt from censorship, and may be dispatched and received by courier or in sealed bags.

The position of Members' representatives. Members of national delegations to the principal and subsidiary organs of the United Nations, and to conferences convened by it, enjoy immunity from personal arrest or detention ; from seizure of personal baggage ; from legal process of every kind in respect of words spoken or written and all acts done by them in their official capacity ; inviolability of all papers and documents ; the right to use codes and to receive papers or correspondence by courier or in sealed bags ; and generally, the privileges, immunities and facilities normally enjoyed by diplomatic envoys.

The position of United Nations staff. These enjoy immunity from legal process in respect of words spoken or written and all acts performed in their official capacity ; exemption from taxation of their salaries and emoluments, but not necessarily in their country of origin if they continue to reside therein ; immunity from national service obligations ; and immigration and repatriation facilities similar to those enjoyed by diplomatic envoys. Similar privileges and immunities are granted to experts not on the staff of the Organization who are performing missions for the United Nations.

The Organization may issue to its officials a United Nations " *laissez passer* ", which Members recognize as a valid travel document.

The position of specialized agencies. This is regulated by a separate Convention, approved by the General Assembly on November 21, 1947. It is in two parts :

(1) general provisions defining (on similar lines as the General Convention) the standard privileges and immunities applying to all specialized agencies ; and

(2) annexes, each relating to one particular agency, making such additions and amendments to the standard clauses as the particular functions of that agency require.[1]

---

[1] *Accessions.* By June 30, 1948, only twenty-five Members had ratified the General Convention, and the General Assembly, on December 8, 1948, passed a resolution urging Governments to deposit their instruments of accession at the earliest possible moment.

No accessions to the Convention on Specialized Agencies were registered before June 30, 1948, the reason being that its various annexes first required the approval, in accordance with their respective constitutional processes, of the specialized agencies themselves.

CHAPTER XVII

TRANSITIONAL SECURITY ARRANGEMENTS

ARTICLE 106

Pending the coming into force of such special agreements referred to in Article 43 as in the opinion of the Security Council enable it to begin the exercise of its responsibilities under Article 42, the parties to the Four-Nation Declaration, signed at Moscow, the 30th October 1943, and France shall, in accordance with the provisions of paragraph 5 of that Declaration, consult with one another and as occasion requires with other Members of the United Nations with a view to such joint action on behalf of the Organization as may be necessary for the purpose of maintaining international peace and security.

Need for transitional arrangements. It was clear at the San Francisco Conference that it might take considerable time before the conclusion and implementation of the special agreements envisaged in Article 43 would enable the Security Council to bring the military side of collective security into effective operation. The gap had to be bridged, and the obvious, though, as it has turned out, the least effective, method of bridging it was to give a transitional power of attorney to the five Great Powers.

This power of attorney is, in theory, revocable at the discretion of the Security Council. The mandate of the Great Powers comes to an end as soon as the Council records its opinion that it is able to begin the exercise of its responsibilities under Article 42. As, however, such a decision of the Council pre-supposes unanimity among the Great Powers, in practice any one of them can obstruct, *ad infinitum*, the termination of the transitional period.

The responsibility of the Big Five. The Article is based on the assumption that, in the face of a threat or violation of the peace, the Great Powers will act in harmony. If that assumption proves incorrect, and all the evidence suggests that it is, the responsibility of the Great Powers is empty. The formulation of the Article is mandatory, but only to that extent that the Great Powers are required to consult ; the Charter does not say what shall be the next step if the consultations end in a deadlock. If there be a deadlock, none of the Great Powers is entitled to take action alone, or jointly with others, disregarding the opposition of one or more of the remaining Great Powers; for the Charter requires " joint action," and it is clear from the context that the Great Powers must be agreed on the necessity of joint action.

Paragraph 5 of the Moscow Declaration of October 30, 1943 (which is expressly invoked by the present Article) offers no solution. It merely requires the Big Four to " consult with one another, and as occasion requires with other Members of the United Nations, with a view to joint action on behalf of the community of nations ". No authority is given for individual action in case the consultations fail.

The position of the lesser Powers. It would appear that no Member of the United Nations is entitled to refuse participation in consultations which may be initiated by the Great Powers. Members can, however, refuse to associate themselves with any joint *action* decided upon by the Great Powers if participation would involve the performance of the specific obligations envisaged in Chapter VII. These obligations pre-suppose formal decisions by the Security Council ; and cannot be imposed by decisions outside the Council. But Members must support any joint action short of sanctions that may be decided upon by the Great Powers, and refrain from giving assistance to any State against which the decision is directed. These positive and negative obligations follow from Article 2(5) of the Charter, and are not conditional on any formal decision of the Security Council.

Position of the Security Council. The transitional arrangements only operate in regard to military sanctions. They do not affect the Council's responsibilities under Chapter VI or under Articles 39-41 of Chapter VII. Even during the transitional period it is exclusively for the Security Council to determine the existence of any threat to the peace, breach of the peace or act of aggression, and to decide on provisional measures and non-military sanctions.

ARTICLE 107

Nothing in the present Charter shall invalidate or preclude action, in relation to any State which during the Second World War has been an enemy of any signatory to the present Charter, taken or authorized as a result of that war by the Governments having responsibility for such action.

Period of application. For the reasons explained in connection with Article 53, this Article is not applicable to any enemy State after its admission to membership of the United Nations.

The " Governments having responsibility for action ". The Charter does not define the phrase, but it seems clear that it does not refer to all the signatories to the Charter who may have been at war with the enemy State concerned. The proper interpretation appears to be that the Governments whose freedom of action is confirmed by the Article are those which, by virtue of any Act of Surrender, Armistice Agreement or Peace Treaty, and any supplementary instruments, e.g. the Potsdam Agreement, have taken powers to enforce their terms.

Since the action contemplated by the Article is not taken " on behalf of the Organization ", Members of the United Nations which are not directly responsible for enforcing the treaties and instruments in question do not infringe the Charter by refusing support to the " Governments having responsibility for such action ".

On the other hand, these Governments need not act themselves ; they can " authorize " other Governments to take action, and the validity of the authority does not depend upon formal approval by the Security Council.

CHAPTER XVIII

AMENDMENTS

ARTICLE 108

Amendments to the present Charter shall come into force for all Members of the United Nations when they have been adopted by a vote of two-thirds of the members of the General Assembly and ratified in accordance with their respective constitutional processes by two-thirds of the Members of the United Nations, including all the permanent members of the Security Council.

Procedure : first stage. The procedure of amendment begins with the adoption of a resolution by the General Assembly. A qualified majority of two-thirds is necessary. Whereas Article 18 expressly provides for " a two-thirds majority of the members present and voting ", the present Article speaks of " two-thirds of the Members of the General Assembly " which seems to imply the total membership of the Organization. The difference in terminology must have been intentional, and explains why amendments were not included in the list of " important questions " in Article 18(2).

Procedure : second stage. Amendments adopted by the General Assembly do not come into force until ratification by two-thirds of the total membership, including ratification by all permanent members of the Security Council. This enables any of the Great Powers to veto an amendment, regardless of the overwhelming or, indeed, unanimous support it may have received from other Members of the Organization. On the other hand, once an amendment is ratified by the requisite majority, it becomes binding on all Members, not excepting those who voted against it in the General Assembly or have withheld ratification.

This is another instance of the revaluation by the Charter of the traditional conceptions of sovereignty and equality.[1]

Withdrawal. If an amendment approved by the requisite majority in the Assembly fails to secure the necessary number of ratifications ; or if an amendment comes into force despite the opposition of one or more Members, no dissatisfied State has any

[1] See comment on Article 2(1).

other remedy than withdrawal from the Organization. Although the Charter contains no express proviso for withdrawal, the interpretation of Chapter III approved by the San Francisco Conference[1] made it clear that, in such circumstances, " it would not be the purpose of the Organization to compel a Member to remain in the Organization ".

ARTICLE 109

1. A General Conference of the Members of the United Nations for the purpose of reviewing the present Charter may be held at a date and place to be fixed by a two-thirds vote of the members of the General Assembly and by a vote of any seven members of the Security Council. Each Member of the United Nations shall have one vote in the conference.

2. Any alteration of the present Charter recommended by a two-thirds vote of the conference shall take effect when ratified in accordance with their respective constitutional processes by two-thirds of the Members of the United Nations, including all the permanent members of the Security Council.

3. If such a conference has not been held before the tenth annual session of the General Assembly following the coming into force of the present Charter, the proposal to call such a conference shall be placed on the agenda of that session of the General Assembly, and the conference shall be held if so decided by a majority vote of the members of the General Assembly and by a vote of any seven members of the Security Council.

General revision. The Charter was not born *sub specie aeternitatis.* Many of its provisions, particularly those relating to the privileged position of the Great Powers, were the result of an uneasy compromise which the delegations at San Francisco only accepted on the understanding that at some future date it would be reviewed. A comprehensive review of this kind, as distinct from piecemeal amendments, is reserved for a General Conference of Members, comparable to the constituent conference of 1945. There is no guarantee that such a Conference will ever be held ; it can only be convened if the General Assembly and the Security Council agree on the need for it.

The time element. If no General Conference has been held before the tenth annual session of the General Assembly, the agenda of

[1] See comment on Article 6.

that session must include the consideration of the case for a General Conference. The decision is made by a simple majority vote of the " members of the General Assembly " (i.e. the total membership of the Organization), and the vote of any seven members of the Security Council, the permanent members having no veto.

In all other cases, i.e. at any time before or after the tenth annual session of the Assembly, the majority required in the General Assembly is increased to two-thirds of the total membership ; but the Security Council can still decide with a vote of any seven members.

Alterations decided by the Conference. The rule is similar to that which governs amendments. Any alteration of the Charter must be approved by a two-thirds majority of the Conference, and be ratified by two-thirds of the total membership, including all permanent members of the Security Council. Any one of the permanent members can obstruct the alteration of the Charter. Members dissatisfied with the result have no remedy except withdrawal from the Organization.

CHAPTER XIX

RATIFICATION AND SIGNATURE

ARTICLE 110

1. The present Charter shall be ratified by the signatory States in accordance with their respective constitutional processes.

2. The ratifications shall be deposited with the Government of the United States of America, which shall notify all the signatory States of each deposit as well as the Secretary-General of the Organization when he has been appointed.

3. The present Charter shall come into force upon the deposit of ratifications by the Republic of China, France, the Union of Soviet Socialist Republics, the United Kingdom of Great Britain and Northern Ireland, and the United States of America, and by a majority of the other signatory States. A protocol of the ratifications deposited shall thereupon be drawn up by the Government of the United States of America which shall communicate copies thereof to all the signatory States.

4. The States signatory to the present Charter which ratify it after it has come into force will become original Members of the United Nations on the date of the deposit of their respective ratifications.

Ratification. The signing of an international treaty does not necessarily mean its final adoption by the signatory States. What further acts are necessary depends on national constitutions. In the United Kingdom ratification as such requires no legislation ; it is an executive act of His Majesty in Council, which follows automatically on the approval of the treaty by both Houses of Parliament with or without debate. In the United States all treaties (but not the so-called " executive agreements ") require the approval of the Senate by a two-thirds majority. Other countries have different procedures.

It is usual diplomatic practice to deposit ratifications(meaning, in this case, the formal documents recording the final adoption of the treaty) with the Government of a particular country, normally the country which gave hospitality to the treaty-making conference. In accordance with this practice, the Charter provided for the deposit of ratifications with the United States Government. *Entry into force.* Treaties normally specify the number of ratifications which are necessary to bring them into force. In the case of the Charter, which had fifty-one original signatories, twenty-nine ratifications were necessary : those of the Great Powers (five) and the majority (twenty-four) of the other signatories (forty-six).

These ratifications were completed by October 24, 1945; and the Charter came into force on that day. The remaining signatories completed their ratifications by December 27, 1945.

ARTICLE 111

The present Charter, of which the Chinese, French, Russian, English and Spanish Texts are equally authentic, shall remain deposited in the archives of the Government of the United States of America. Duly certified copies thereof shall be transmitted by that Government to the Governments of the other signatory States.

In faith whereof the representatives of the Governments of the United Nations have signed the present Charter.

Done at the city of San Francisco the twenty-sixth day of June, one thousand nine hundred and forty-five.

Texts. The Charter was signed in five languages. The five texts are declared to be equally authentic. This provision may yet cause difficulties in view of such discrepancies in shades of expression as are inevitable in a highly technical document. No provision is made in the Charter for the solution of difficulties should they arise ; recourse will have to be taken to the debates and papers of the San Francisco Conference.

Interpretation. Even without textual discrepancies between five equally authentic versions, a complex document like the Charter is certain to give rise to controversial interpretations. Notwithstanding that certainty, the San Francisco Conference was unable to agree, indeed, it denied the need to agree, on the manner in which controversies of this kind should be settled. The suggestion to give the International Court of Justice compulsory jurisdiction in the matter was rejected. The right of Members to refer to the Court by *ad hoc* agreement is beyond dispute ; but the experience of the first few years has shown that no such agreement can be taken for granted. Under Article 96 the General

Assembly and the Security Council (and with the authority of the Assembly, other organs and specialized agencies), may call for the Court's advisory opinion ; or, if they prefer that course, they can set up *ad hoc* committees of jurists. But though every organ is free to work out and apply its own interpretation, or accept the advisory opinion of the Court, or of an *ad hoc* committee of jurists, none of these interpretations will be binding on a Member who chooses to differ. With this possibility in mind, Committee IV/2 of the San Francisco Conference pointed to the likelihood that authoritative interpretations may have to take the form of amendments to the Charter. In view of the right of veto which any Great Power may apply to amendments, that advice may be regarded as a counsel of despair. For practical purposes the only way is to allow each organ of the United Nations not only to formulate, but also to enforce, its own interpretation of those provisions of the Charter upon which it must rely for the discharge of its functions.

THE COVENANT OF THE LEAGUE OF NATIONS

THE HIGH CONTRACTING PARTIES, in order to promote international co-operation and to achieve international peace and security by the acceptance of obligations not to resort to war, by the prescription of open, just and honourable relations between nations, by the firm establishment of the understandings of international law as the actual rule of conduct among Governments, and by the maintenance of justice and a scrupulous respect for all treaty obligations in the dealings of organized peoples with one another, agree to this Covenant of the League of Nations.

Article 1

1. The original Members of the League of Nations shall be those of the Signatories which are named in the Annex to this Covenant and also such of those other States named in the Annex as shall accede without reservation to this Covenant. Such accession shall be effected by a Declaration deposited with the Secretariat within two months of the coming into force of the Covenant. Notice thereof shall be sent to all other Members of the League.

2. Any fully self-governing State, Dominion or Colony not named in the Annex may become a Member of the League if its admission is agreed to by two-thirds of the Assembly, provided that it shall give effective guarantees of its sincere intention to observe its international obligations, and shall accept such regulations as may be prescribed by the League in regard to its military, naval and air forces and armaments.

3. Any Member of the League may, after two years' notice of its intention so to do, withdraw from the League, provided that all its international obligations and all its obligations under this Covenant shall have been fulfilled at the time of its withdrawal.

Article 2

The action of the League under this Covenant shall be effected through the instrumentality of an Assembly and of a Council, with a permanent Secretariat.

Article 3

1. The Assembly shall consist of Representatives of the Members of the League.

2. The Assembly shall meet at stated intervals and from time to time as occasion may require, at the Seat of the League or at such other place as may be decided upon.

3. The Assembly may deal at its meetings with any matter within the sphere of action of the League or affecting the peace of the world.

4. At meetings of the Assembly, each Member of the League shall have one vote, and may have not more than three Representatives.

Article 4

1. The Council shall consist of Representatives of the Principal Allied and Associated Powers, together with Representatives of four other Members of the League. These four Members of the League shall be selected by the Assembly from time to time in its discretion. Until the appointment of the Representatives of the four Members of the League first selected by the Assembly, Representatives of Belgium, Brazil, Spain and Greece shall be members of the Council.

2. With the approval of the majority of the Assembly, the Council may name additional Members of the League whose Representatives shall always be members of the Council ; the Council with like approval may increase the number of Members of the League to be selected by the Assembly for representation on the Council. The Assembly shall fix by a two-thirds majority the rules dealing with the election of the non-permanent Members of the Council, and particularly such regulations as relate to their term of office and the conditions of re-eligibility.

3. The Council shall meet from time to time as occasion may require, and at least once a year, at the Seat of the League, or at such other place as may be decided upon.

4. The Council may deal at its meetings with any matter within the sphere of action of the League or affecting the peace of the world.

5. Any Member of the League not represented on the Council shall be invited to send a Representative to sit as a member at any meeting of the Council during the consideration of matters specially affecting the interests of that Member of the League.

6. At meetings of the Council each Member of the League represented on the Council shall have one vote, and may have not more than one Representative.

Article 5

1. Except where otherwise expressly provided in this Covenant or by the terms of the present Treaty, decisions at any meeting of the Assembly or of the Council shall require the agreement of all the Members of the League represented at the meeting.

2. All matters of procedure at meetings of the Assembly or of the Council, including the appointment of Committees to investigate particular matters, shall be regulated by the Assembly or by the Council, and may be decided by a majority of the Members of the League represented at the meeting.

3. The first meeting of the Assembly and the first meeting of the Council shall be summoned by the President of the United States of America.

Article 6

1. The permanent Secretariat shall be established at the Seat of the League. The Secretariat shall comprise a Secretary-General and such secretaries and staff as may be required.

2. The first Secretary-General shall be the person named in the Annex; thereafter the Secretary-General shall be appointed by the Council with the approval of the majority of the Assembly.

3. The secretaries and staff of the Secretariat shall be appointed by the Secretary-General with the approval of the Council.

4. The Secretary-General shall act in that capacity at all meetings of the Assembly and of the Council.

5. The expenses of the League shall be borne by the Members of the League in the proportion decided by the Assembly.

Article 7

1. The Seat of the League is established at Geneva.

2. The Council may at any time decide that the Seat of the League shall be established elsewhere.

3. All positions under or in connection with the League, including the Secretariat, shall be open equally to men and women.

4. Representatives of the Members of the League and officials of the League when engaged on the business of the League shall enjoy diplomatic privileges and immunities.

5. The buildings and other property occupied by the League or its officials or by Representatives attending its meetings shall be inviolable.

Article 8

1. The Members of the League recognize that the maintenance of peace requires the reduction of national armaments to the lowest point consistent with national safety and the enforcement by common action of international obligations.

2. The Council, taking account of the geographical situation and circumstances of each State, shall formulate plans for such reduction for the consideration and action of the several Governments.

3. Such plans shall be subject to reconsideration and revision at least every ten years.

4. After these plans shall have been adopted by the several Governments, the limits of armaments therein fixed shall not be exceeded without the concurrence of the Council.

5. The Members of the League agree that the manufacture by private enterprise of munitions and implements of war is open to grave objections. The Council shall advise how the evil effects attendant upon such manufacture can be prevented, due regard being had to the necessities of those Members of the League which are not able to manufacture the munitions and implements of war necessary for their safety.

6. The Members of the League undertake to interchange full and frank information as to the scale of their armaments, their military, naval and air programmes and the condition of such of their industries as are adaptable to war-like purposes.

Article 9

A permanent Commission shall be constituted to advise the Council on the execution of the provisions of Articles 1 and 8 and on military, naval and air questions generally.

Article 10

The Members of the League undertake to respect and preserve as against external aggression the territorial integrity and existing political independence of all Members of the League. In case of any such aggression or in case of any threat or danger of such aggression the Council shall advise upon the means by which this obligation shall be fulfilled.

Article 11

1. Any war or threat of war, whether immediately affecting any of the Members of the League or not, is hereby declared a matter of concern to the whole League, and the League shall take any action that may be deemed wise and effectual to safeguard the peace of nations. In case any such emergency should arise the Secretary-General shall on the request of any Member of the League forthwith summon a meeting of the Council.
2. It is also declared to be the friendly right of each Member of the League to bring to the attention of the Assembly or of the Council any circumstance whatever affecting international relations which threatens to disturb international peace or the good understanding between nations upon which peace depends.

Article 12

1. The Members of the League agree that if there should arise between them any dispute likely to lead to a rupture, they will submit the matter either to arbitration or judicial settlement or to inquiry by the Council, and they agree in no case to resort to war until three months after the award by the arbitrators or the judicial decision or the report by the Council.
2. In any case under this Article the award of the arbitrators or the judicial decision shall be made within a reasonable time, and the report of the Council shall be made within six months after the submission of the dispute.

Article 13

1. The Members of the League agree that whenever any dispute shall arise between them which they recognize to be suitable for submission to arbitration or judicial settlement and which cannot be satisfactorily settled by diplomacy, they will submit the whole subject-matter to arbitration or judicial settlement.
2. Disputes as to the interpretation of a treaty, as to any question of international law, as to the existence of any fact which if established would constitute a breach of any international obligation, or as to the extent and nature of the reparation to be made for any such breach, are declared to be among those which are generally suitable for submission to arbitration or judicial settlement.
3. For the consideration of any such dispute, the court to which the case is referred shall be the Permanent Court of International Justice, established in accordance with Article 14, or any tribunal agreed on by the parties to the dispute or stipulated in any convention existing between them.
4. The Members of the League agree that they will carry out in full good faith any award or decision that may be rendered and that they will not resort to war against a Member of the League which complies therewith. In the event of any failure to carry out such an award or decision, the Council shall propose what steps should be taken to give effect thereto.

Article 14

The Council shall formulate and submit to the Members of the League for adoption plans for the establishment of a Permanent Court of International Justice. The Court shall be competent to hear and determine any dispute of an international character which the parties thereto submit to it. The Court may also give an advisory opinion upon any dispute or question referred to it by the Council or by the Assembly.

Article 15

1. If there should arise between Members of the League any dispute likely to lead to a rupture, which is not submitted to arbitration or judicial settlement in accordance with Article 13, the Members of the League agree that they will submit the matter to the Council. Any party to the dispute may effect such submission by giving notice of the existence of the dispute to the Secretary-General, who will make all necessary arrangements for a full investigation and consideration thereof.

2. For this purpose the parties to the dispute will communicate to the Secretary-General, as promptly as possible, statements of their case with all the relevant facts and papers, and the Council may forthwith direct the publication thereof.

3. The Council shall endeavour to effect a settlement of the dispute, and if such efforts are successful, a statement shall be made public giving such facts and explanations regarding the dispute and the terms of settlement thereof as the Council may deem appropriate.

4. If the dispute is not thus settled, the Council, either unanimously or by a majority vote, shall make and publish a report containing a statement of the facts of the dispute and the recommendations which are deemed just and proper in regard thereto.

5. Any Member of the League represented on the Council may make public a statement of the facts of the dispute and of its conclusions regarding the same.

6. If a report by the Council is unanimously agreed to by the members thereof other than the Representatives of one or more of the parties to the dispute, the Members of the League agree that they will not go to war with any party to the dispute which complies with the recommendations of the report.

7. If the Council fails to reach a report which is unanimously agreed to by the members thereof, other than the Representatives of one or more of the parties to the dispute, the Members of the League reserve to themselves the right to take such action as they shall consider necessary for the maintenance of right and justice.

8. If the dispute between the parties is claimed by one of them, and is found by the Council to arise out of a matter which by international law is solely within the domestic jurisdiction of that party, the Council shall so report, and shall make no recommendation as to its settlement.

9. The Council may in any case under this Article refer the dispute to the Assembly. The dispute shall be so referred at the request of either party to the dispute, provided that such request be made within fourteen days after the submission of the dispute to the Council.

10. In any case referred to the Assembly, all the provisions of this Article and of Article 12 relating to the action and powers of the Council shall apply to the action and powers of the Assembly, provided that a report made by the Assembly, if concurred in by the Representatives of those Members of the League represented on the Council and of a majority of the other Members of the League, exclusive in each case of the Representatives of the parties to the dispute, shall have the same force as a report by the Council concurred in by all the members thereof other than the Representatives of one or more of the parties to the dispute.

Article 16

1. Should any Member of the League resort to war in disregard of its covenants under Articles 12, 13 or 15, it shall *ipso facto* be deemed to have committed an act of war against all other Members of the League, which hereby undertake immediately to subject it to the severance of all trade or financial relations, the prohibition of all intercourse between their nationals and the nationals of the covenant-breaking State, and the prevention of all financial, commercial or personal intercourse between the nationals of the covenant-breaking State and the nationals of any other State, whether a Member of the League or not.

2. It shall be the duty of the Council in such case to recommend to the several Governments concerned what effective military, naval or air force the Members of the League shall severally contribute to the armed forces to be used to protect the covenants of the League.

3. The Members of the League agree, further, that they will mutually support one another in the financial and economic measures which are taken under this article, in order to minimize the loss and inconvenience resulting from the above measures, and that they will mutually support one another in resisting any special measures aimed at one of their number by the covenant-breaking State, and that they will take the necessary steps to

afford passage through their territory to the forces of any of the Members of the League which are co-operating to protect the covenants of the League.

4. Any Member of the League which has violated any covenant of the League may be declared to be no longer a Member of the League by a vote of the Council concurred in by the Representatives of all the other Members of the League represented thereon.

Article 17

1. In the event of a dispute between a Member of the League and a State which is not a Member of the League, or between States not Members of the League, the State or States not Members of the League shall be invited to accept the obligations of membership in the League for the purposes of such dispute, upon such conditions as the Council may deem just. If such invitation is accepted, the provisions of Articles 12 to 16 inclusive shall be applied with such modifications as may be deemed necessary by the Council.

2. Upon such invitation being given the Council shall immediately institute an inquiry into the circumstances of the dispute and recommend such action as may seem best and most effectual in the circumstances.

3. If a State so invited shall refuse to accept the obligations of membership in the League for the purposes of such dispute, and shall resort to war against a Member of the League, the provisons of Article 16 shall be applicable as against the State taking such action.

4. If both parties to the dispute when so invited refuse to accept the obligations of membership in the League for the purposes of such dispute, the Council may take such measures and make such recommendations as will prevent hostilities and will result in the settlement of the dispute.

Article 18

Every treaty or international engagement entered into hereafter by any Member of the League shall be forthwith registered with the Secretariat and shall as soon as possible be published by it. No such treaty or international engagement shall be binding until so registered.

Article 19

The Assembly may from time to time advise the reconsideration by Members of the League of treaties which have become inapplicable and the consideration of international conditions whose continuance might endanger the peace of the world.

Article 20

1. The Members of the League severally agree that this Covenant is accepted as abrogating all obligations or understandings *inter se* which are inconsistent with the terms thereof, and solemnly undertake that they will not hereafter enter into any engagements inconsistent with the terms thereof.

2. In case any Member of the League shall, before becoming a Member of the League, have undertaken any obligations inconsistent with the terms of this Covenant, it shall be the duty of such Member to take immediate steps to procure its release from such obligations.

Article 21

Nothing in this Covenant shall be deemed to affect the validity of international engagements, such as treaties of arbitration or regional understandings like the Monroe Doctrine, for securing the maintenance of peace.

Article 22

1. To those colonies and territories which as a consequence of the late war have ceased to be under the sovereignty of the States which formerly governed them and which are inhabited by peoples not yet able to stand by themselves under the strenuous conditions of the modern world, there should be applied the principle that the well-being and development of such peoples form a sacred trust of civilization and that securities for the performance of this trust should be embodied in this Covenant.

2. The best method of giving practical effect to this principle is that the tutelage of such peoples should be entrusted to advanced nations who by reason of their resources, their experience or their geographical position can best undertake this responsibility, and who are willing to accept it, and that this tutelage should be exercised by them as Mandatories on behalf of the League.

3. The character of the mandate must differ according to the stage of the development of the people, the geographical situation of the territory, its economic conditions and other similar circumstances.

4. Certain communities formerly belonging to the Turkish Empire have reached a stage of development where their existence as independent nations can be provisionally recognized subject to the rendering of administrative advice and assistance by a Mandatory until such time as they are able to stand alone. The wishes of these communities must be a principal consideration in the selection of the Mandatory.

5. Other peoples, especially those of Central Africa, are at such a stage that the Mandatory must be responsible for the administration of the territory under conditions which will guarantee freedom of conscience and religion, subject only to the maintenance of public order and morals, the prohibition of abuses such as the slave trade, the arms traffic and the liquor traffic, and the prevention of the establishment of fortifications or military and naval bases and of military training of the natives for other than police purposes and the defence of territory, and will also secure equal opportunities for the trade and commerce of other Members of the League.

6. There are territories, such as South-West Africa and certain of the South Pacific Islands, which, owing to the sparseness of their population, or their small size, or their remoteness from the centres of civilization, or their geographical contiguity to the territory of the Mandatory, and other circumstances, can be best administered under the laws of the Mandatory as integral portions of its territory, subject to the safeguards above mentioned in the interests of the indigenous population.

7. In every case of mandate, the Mandatory shall render to the Council an annual report in reference to the territory committed to its charge.

8. The degree of authority, control, or administration to be exercised by the Mandatory shall, if not previously agreed upon by the Members of the League, be explicitly defined in each case by the Council.

9. A permanent Commission shall be constituted to receive and examine the annual reports of the Mandatories and to advise the Council on all matters relating to the observance of the mandates.

Article 23

Subject to an in accordance with the provisions of international conventions existing or hereafter to be agreed upon, the Members of the League :

(a) will endeavour to secure and maintain fair and humane conditions of labour for men, women, and children, both in their own countries and in all countries to which their commercial and industrial relations extend, and for that purpose will establish and maintain the necessary international organizations ;

(b) undertake to secure just treatment of the native inhabitants of territories under their control ;

(c) will entrust the League with the general supervision over the execution of agreements with regard to the traffic in women and children, and the traffic in opium and other dangerous drugs ;

(d) will entrust the League with the general supervision of the trade in arms and ammunition with the countries in which the control of this traffic is necessary in the common interest ;

(e) will make provision to secure and maintain freedom of communications and of transit and equitable treatment for the commerce of all Members of the League. In this connexion, the special necessities of the regions devastated during the war of 1914-1918 shall be borne in mind ;

(f) will endeavour to take steps in matters of international concern for the prevention and control of disease.

Article 24

1. There shall be placed under the direction of the League all international bureaux already established by general treaties if the parties to such treaties consent. All such international bureaux and all commissions for the regulation of matters of international interest hereafter constituted shall be placed under the direction of the League.

2. In all matters of international interest which are regulated by general conventions but which are not placed under the control of international bureaux or commissions, the Secretariat of the League shall, subject to the consent of the Council and if desired by the parties, collect and distribute all relevant information and shall render any other assistance which may be necessary or desirable.

3. The Council may include as part of the expenses of the Secretariat the expenses of any bureau or commission which is placed under the direction of the League.

Article 25

The Members of the League agree to encourage and promote the establishment and co-operation of duly authorized voluntary national Red Cross organizations havin. as purposes the improvement of health, the prevention of disease and the mitigation of suffering throughout the world.

Article 26

1. Amendments to this Covenant will take effect when ratified by the Members of the League whose Representatives compose the Council and by a majority of the Members of the League whose Representatives compose the Assembly.

2. No such amendment shall bind any Member of the League which signifies its dissent therefrom, but in that case it shall cease to be a Member of the League.

CHARTER OF THE UNITED NATIONS

WE, THE PEOPLES OF THE UNITED NATIONS, DETERMINED to save succeeding generations from the scourge of war, which twice in our lifetime has brought untold sorrow to mankind, and to reaffirm faith in fundamental human rights, in the dignity and worth of the human person, in the equal rights of men and women and of nations large and small, and to establish conditions under which justice and respect for the obligations arising from treaties and other sources of international law can be maintained, and to promote social progress and better standards of life in larger freedom,
AND FOR THESE ENDS to practise tolerance and live together in peace with one another as good neighbours, and to unite our strength to maintain international peace and security, and to ensure, by the acceptance of principles and the institution of methods, that armed force shall not be used, save in the common interest, and to employ international machinery for the promotion of the economic and social advancement of all peoples,
HAVE RESOLVED TO COMBINE OUR EFFORTS TO ACCOMPLISH THESE AIMS.
Accordingly, our respective Governments, through representatives assembled in the city of San Francisco, who have exhibited their full powers found to be in good and due form, have agreed to the present Charter of the United Nations and do hereby establish an international organization to be known as the United Nations.

CHAPTER I

PURPOSES AND PRINCIPLES

Article 1

The Purposes of the United Nations are :
1. To maintain international peace and security, and to that end : to take effective collective measures for the prevention and removal of threats to the peace, and for the suppression of acts of aggression or other breaches of the peace, and to bring about by peaceful means, and in conformity with the principles of justice and international law, adjustment or settlement of international disputes or situations which might lead to a breach of the peace ;
2. To develop friendly relations among nations based on respect for the principle of equal rights and self-determination of peoples, and to take other appropriate measures to strengthen universal peace ;
3. To achieve international co-operation in solving international problems of an economic, social, cultural, or humanitarian character, and in promoting and encouraging respect for human rights and for fundamental freedoms for all without distinction as to race, sex, language, or religion ; and
4. To be a centre for harmonizing the actions of nations in the attainment of these common ends.

Article 2

The Organization and its Members, in pursuit of the Purposes stated in Article 1, shall act in accordance with the following Principles :
1. The Organization is based on the principle of the sovereign equality of all its Members.
2. All Members, in order to ensure to all of them the rights and benefits resulting from membership, shall fulfil in good faith the obligations assumed by them in accordance with the present Charter.
3. All Members shall settle their international disputes by peaceful means in such a manner that international peace and security, and justice, are not endangered.

4. All Members shall refrain in their international relations from the threat or use of force against the territorial integrity or political independence of any State, or in any other manner inconsistent with the Purposes of the United Nations.

5. All Members shall give the United Nations every assistance in any action it takes in accordance with the present Charter, and shall refrain from giving assistance to any State against which the United Nations is taking preventive or enforcement action.

6. The Organization shall ensure that States which are not Members of the United Nations act in accordance with these Principles so far as may be necessary for the maintenance of international peace and security.

7. Nothing contained in the present Charter shall authorize the United Nations to intervene in matters which are essentially within the domestic jurisdiction of any State or shall require the Members to submit such matters to settlement under the present Charter ; but this principle shall not prejudice the application of enforcement measures under Chapter VII.

CHAPTER II

MEMBERSHIP

Article 3

The original Members of the United Nations shall be the States which, having participated in the United Nations Conference on International Organization at San Francisco, or having previously signed the Declaration by United Nations of 1st January, 1942, sign the present Charter and ratify it in accordance with Article 110.

Article 4

1. Membership in the United Nations is open to all other peace-loving States which accept the obligations contained in the present Charter and, in the judgement of the Organization, are able and willing to carry out these obligations.

2. The admission of any such State to membership in the United Nations will be effected by a decision of the General Assembly upon the recommendation of the Security Council.

Article 5

A Member of the United Nations against which preventive or enforcement action has been taken by the Security Council may be suspended from the exercise of the rights and privileges of membership by the General Assembly upon the recommendation of the Security Council. The exercise of these rights and privileges may be restored by the Security Council.

Article 6

A Member of the United Nations which has persistently violated the Principles contained in the present Charter may be expelled from the Organization by the General Assembly upon the recommendation of the Security Council.

CHAPTER III

ORGANS

Article 7

1. There are established as the principal organs of the United Nations : a General Assembly, a Security Council, an Economic and Social Council, a Trusteeship Council, an International Court of Justice, and a Secretariat.

2. Such subsidiary organs as may be found necessary may be established in accordance with the present Charter.

Article 8

The United Nations shall place no restrictions on the eligibility of men and women to participate in any capacity and under conditions of equality in its principal and subsidiary organs.

CHAPTER IV

THE GENERAL ASSEMBLY

Composition

Article 9

1. The General Assembly shall consist of all the Members of the United Nations.
2. Each Member shall have not more than five representatives in the General Assembly.

Functions and Powers   *Article* 10

The General Assembly may discuss any questions or any matters within the scope of the present Charter or relating to the powers and functions of any organs provided for in the present Charter, and, except as provided in Article 12, may make recommendations to the Members of the United Nations or to the Security Council or to both on any such questions or matters.

Article 11

1. The General Assembly may consider the general principles of co-operation in the maintenance of international peace and security, including the principles governing disarmament and the regulation of armaments, and may make recommendations with regard to such principles to the Members or to the Security Council or to both.
2. The General Assembly may discuss any questions relating to the maintenance of international peace and security brought before it by any Member of the United Nations, or by the Security Council, or by a State which is not a Member of the United Nations in accordance with Article 35, paragraph 2, and, except as provided in Article 12, may make recommendations with regard to any such questions to the State or States concerned or to the Security Council or to both. Any such question on which action is necessary shall be referred to the Security Council by the General Assembly either before or after discussion.
3. The General Assembly may call the attention of the Security Council to situations which are likely to endanger international peace and security.
4. The powers of the General Assembly set forth in this Article shall not limit the general scope of Article 10.

Article 12

1. While the Security Council is exercising in respect of any dispute or situation the functions assigned to it in the present Charter, the General Assembly shall not make any recommendation with regard to that dispute or situation unless the Security Council so requests.
2. The Secretary-General, with the consent of the Security Council, shall notify the General Assembly at each session of any matters relative to the maintenance of international peace and security which are being dealt with by the Security Council, and shall similarly notify the General Assembly, or the Members of the United Nations if the General Assembly is not in session, immediately the Security Council ceases to deal with such matters.

Article 13

1. The General Assembly shall initiate studies and make recommendations for the purpose of —
(a) promoting international co-operation in the political field and encouraging the progressive development of international law and its codification ;
(b) promoting international co-operation in the economic, social, cultural, educational and health fields, and assisting in the realization of human rights and fundamental freedoms for all without distinction as to race, sex, language or religion.
2. The further responsibilities, functions and powers of the General Assembly with respect to matters mentioned in paragraph 1(b) above are set forth in Chapters IX and X.

Article 14

Subject to the provisions of Article 12, the General Assembly may recommend measures for the peaceful adjustment of any situation, regardless of origin, which it deems likely to impair the general welfare or friendly relations among nations, including situations resulting from a violation of the provisions of the present Charter setting forth the Purposes and Principles of the United Nations.

Article 15

1. The General Assembly shall receive and consider annual and special reports from the Security Council ; these reports shall include an account of the measures that the Security Council has decided upon or taken to maintain international peace and security.

2. The General Assembly shall receive and consider reports from the other organs of the United Nations.

Article 16

The General Assembly shall perform such functions with respect to the international trusteeship system as are assigned to it under Chapters XII and XIII, including the approval of the trusteeship agreements for areas not designated as strategic.

Article 17

1. The General Assembly shall consider and approve the budget of the Organization.

2. The expenses of the Organization shall be borne by the Members as apportioned by the General Assembly.

3. The General Assembly shall consider and approve any financial and budgetary arrangements with specialized agencies referred to in Article 57 and shall examine the administrative budgets of such specialized agencies with a view to making recommendations to the agencies concerned.

Voting

Article 18

1. Each Member of the General Assembly shall have one vote.

2. Decisions of the General Assembly on important questions shall be made by a two-thirds majority of the members present and voting. These questions shall include : recommendations with respect to the maintenance of international peace and security, the election of the non-permanent members of the Security Council, the election of the members of the Economic and Social Council, the election of members of the Trusteeship Council in accordance with paragraph 1(c) of Article 86, the admission of new Members to the United Nations, the suspension of the rights and privileges of membership, the expulsion of Members, questions relating to the operation of the trusteeship system, and budgetary questions.

3. Decisions on other questions, including the determination of additional categories of questions to be decided by a two-thirds majority, shall be made by a majority of the members present and voting.

Article 19

A Member of the United Nations which is in arrears in the payment of its financial contributions to the Organization shall have no vote in the General Assembly if the amount of its arrears equals or exceeds the amount of the contributions due from it for the preceding two full years. The General Assembly may, nevertheless, permit such a Member to vote if it is satisfied that the failure to pay is due to conditions beyond the control of the Member.

Procedure

Article 20

The General Assembly shall meet in regular annual sessions and in such special sessions as occasion may require. Special sessions shall be convoked by the Secretary-General at the request of the Security Council or of a majority of the Members of the United Nations.

Article 21

The General Assembly shall adopt its own rules of procedure. It shall elect its President for each session.

Article 22

The General Assembly may establish such subsidiary organs as it deems necessary for the performance of its functions.

CHAPTER V

THE SECURITY COUNCIL

Composition

Article 23

1. The Security Council shall consist of eleven Members of the United Nations. The Republic of China, France, the Union of Soviet Socialist Republics, the United Kingdom of Great Britain and Northern Ireland, and the United States of America shall be permanent members of the Security Council. The General Assembly shall elect six other Members of the United Nations to be non-permanent members of the Security Council, due regard being specially paid, in the first instance to the contribution of Members of the United Nations to the maintenance of international peace and security and to the other purposes of the Organization, and also to equitable geographical distribution.

2. The non-permanent members of the Security Council shall be elected for a term of two years. In the first election of the non-permanent members, however, three shall be chosen for a term of one year. A retiring member shall not be eligible for immediate re-election.

3. Each member of the Security Council shall have one representative.

Functions and Powers

Article 24

1. In order to ensure prompt and effective action by the United Nations, its Members confer on the Security Council primary responsibility for the maintenance of international peace and security, and agree that in carrying out its duties under this responsibility the Security Council acts on their behalf.

2. In discharging these duties the Security Council shall act in accordance with the Purposes and Principles of the United Nations. The specific powers granted to the Security Council for the discharge of these duties are laid down in Chapters VI, VII, VIII, and XII.

3. The Security Council shall submit annual and, when necessary, special reports to the General Assembly for its consideration.

Article 25

The Members of the United Nations agree to accept and carry out the decisions of the Security Council in accordance with the present Charter.

Article 26

In order to promote the establishment and maintenance of international peace and security with the least diversion for armaments of the world's human and economic resources, the Security Council shall be responsible for formulating, with the assistance of the Military Staff Committee referred to in Article 47, plans to be submitted to the Members of the United Nations for the establishment of a system for the regulation of armaments.

Voting

Article 27

1. Each member of the Security Council shall have one vote.

2. Decisions of the Security Council on procedural matters shall be made by an affirmative vote of seven members.

3. Decisions of the Security Council on all other matters shall be made by an affirmative vote of seven members including the concurring votes of the permanent members ; provided that, in decisions under Chapter VI, and under paragraph 3 of Article 52, a party to a dispute shall abstain from voting.

Procedure

Article 28

1. The Security Council shall be so organized as to be able to function continuously. Each member of the Security Council shall for this purpose be represented at all times at the seat of the Organization.

2. The Security Council shall hold periodic meetings at which each of its members may, if it so desires, be represented by a member of the Government or by some other specially designated representative.

3. The Security Council may hold meetings at such places other than the seat of the Organization as in its judgement will best facilitate its work.

Article 29

The Security Council may establish such subsidiary organs as it deems necessary for the performance of its functions.

Article 30

The Security Council shall adopt its own rules of procedure, including the method of selecting its President.

Article 31

Any Member of the United Nations which is not a member of the Security Council may participate, without vote, in the discussion of any question brought before the Security Council whenever the latter considers that the interests of that Member are specially affected.

Article 32

Any Member of the United Nations which is not a member of the Security Council or any State which is not a Member of the United Nations, if it is a party to a dispute under consideration by the Security Council, shall be invited to participate, without vote, in the discussion relating to the dispute. The Security Council shall lay down such conditions as it deems just for the participation of a State which is not a Member of the United Nations.

CHAPTER VI

PACIFIC SETTLEMENT OF DISPUTES

Article 33

1. The parties to any dispute, the continuance of which is likely to endanger the maintenance of international peace and security, shall, first of all, seek a solution by negotiation, enquiry, mediation, conciliation, arbitration, judicial settlement, resort to regional agencies or arrangements, or other peaceful means of their own choice.

2. The Security Council shall, when it deems necessary, call upon the parties to settle their dispute by such means.

Article 34

The Security Council may investigate any dispute, or any situation which might lead to international friction or give rise to a dispute, in order to determine whether the continuance of the dispute or situation is likely to endanger the maintenance of international peace and security.

Article 35

1. Any Member of the United Nations may bring any dispute, or any situation of the nature referred to in Article 34, to the attention of the Security Council or of the General Assembly.

2. A State which is not a Member of the United Nations may bring to the attention of the Security Council or of the General Assembly any dispute to which it is a party if it accepts in advance, for the purposes of the dispute, the obligations of pacific settlement provided in the present Charter.

3. The proceedings of the General Assembly in respect of matters brought to its attention under this Article will be subject to the provisions of Articles 11 and 12.

Article 36

1. The Security Council may, at any stage of a dispute of the nature referred to in Article 33 or of a situation of like nature, recommend appropriate procedures or methods of adjustment.

2. The Security Council should take into consideration any procedures for the settlement of the dispute which have already been adopted by the parties.

3. In making recommendations under this Article the Security Council should also take into consideration that legal disputes should as a general rule be referred by the parties to the International Court of Justice in accordance with the provisions of the Statute of the Court.

Article 37

1. Should the parties to a dispute of the nature referred to in Article 33 fail to settle it by the means indicated in that Article, they shall refer it to the Security Council.

2. If the Security Council deems that the continuance of the dispute is in fact likely to endanger the maintenance of international peace and security, it shall decide whether to take action under Article 36 or to recommend such terms of settlement as it may consider appropriate.

Article 38

Without prejudice to the provisions of Articles 33 to 37, the Security Council may, if all the parties to any dispute so request, make recommendations to the parties with a view to a pacific settlement of the dispute.

CHAPTER VII

ACTION WITH RESPECT TO THREATS TO THE PEACE, BREACHES OF THE PEACE, AND ACTS OF AGGRESSION

Article 39

The Security Council shall determine the existence of any threat to the peace, breach of the peace, or act of aggression, and shall make recommendations, or decide what measures shall be taken in accordance with Articles 41 and 42 to maintain or restore international peace and security.

Article 40

In order to prevent an aggravation of the situation, the Security Council may, before making the recommendations or deciding upon the measures provided for in Article 39, call upon the parties concerned to comply with such provisional measures as it deems necessary or desirable. Such provisional measures shall be without prejudice to the rights, claims or position of the parties concerned. The Security Council shall duly take account of failure to comply with such provisional measures.

Article 41

The Security Council may decide what measures not involving the use of armed force are to be employed to give effect to its decisions, and it may call upon the Members of the United Nations to apply such measures. These may include complete or partial interruption of economic relations and of rail, sea, air, postal, telegraphic, radio and other means of communication, and the severance of diplomatic relations.

Article 42

Should the Security Council consider that measures provided for in Article 41 would be inadequate or have proved to be inadequate, it may take such action by air, sea or land forces as may be necessary to maintain or restore international peace and security. Such action may include demonstrations, blockade and other operations by air, sea or land forces of Members of the United Nations.

Article 43

1. All Members of the United Nations, in order to contribute to the maintenance of international peace and security, undertake to make available to the Security Council, on its call and in accordance with a special agreement or agreements, armed forces, assistance and facilities, including rights of passage, necessary for the purpose of maintaining international peace and security.

2. Such agreement or agreements shall govern the numbers and types of forces, their degree of readiness and general location, and the nature of the facilities and assistance to be provided.

3. The agreement or agreements shall be negotiated as soon as possible on the initiative of the Security Council. They shall be concluded between the Security Council and Members or between the Security Council and groups of Members and shall be subject to ratification by the signatory States in accordance with their respective constitutional processes.

Article 44

When the Security Council has decided to use force it shall, before calling upon a Member not represented on it to provide armed forces in fulfilment of the obligations assumed under Article 43, invite that Member, if the Member so desires, to participate in the decisions of the Security Council concerning the employment of contingents of that Member's armed forces.

Article 45

In order to enable the United Nations to take urgent military measures, Members shall hold immediately available national air force contingents for combined international enforcement action. The strength and degree of readiness of these contingents and plans for their combined action shall be determined, within the limits laid down in the special agreement or agreements referred to in Article 43, by the Security Council with the assistance of the Military Staff Committee.

Article 46

Plans for the application of armed force shall be made by the Security Council with the assistance of the Military Staff Committee.

Article 47

1. There shall be established a Military Staff Committee to advise and assist the Security Council on all questions relating to the Security Council's military requirements for the maintenance of international peace and security, the employment and command of forces placed at its disposal, the regulation of armaments, and possible disarmament.
2. The Military Staff Committee shall consist of the Chiefs of Staff of the permanent members of the Security Council or their representatives. Any Member of the United Nations not permanently represented on the Committee shall be invited by the Committee to be associated with it when the efficient discharge of the Committee's responsibilities requires the participation of that Member in its work.
3. The Military Staff Committee shall be responsible under the Security Council for the strategic direction of any armed forces placed at the disposal of the Security Council. Questions relating to the command of such forces shall be worked out subsequently.
4. The Military Staff Committee, with the authorization of the Security Council and after consultation with appropriate regional agencies, may establish regional sub-committees.

Article 48

1. The action required to carry out the decisions of the Security Council for the maintenance of international peace and security shall be taken by all the Members of the United Nations or by some of them, as the Security Council may determine.
2. Such decisions shall be carried out by the Members of the United Nations directly and through their action in the appropriate international agencies of which they are members.

Article 49

The Members of the United Nations shall join in affording mutual assistance in carrying out the measures decided upon by the Security Council.

Article 50

If preventive or enforcement measures against any State are taken by the Security Council, any other State, whether a Member of the United Nations or not, which finds itself confronted with special economic problems arising from the carrying out of those measures shall have the right to consult the Security Council with regard to a solution of those problems.

Article 51

Nothing in the present Charter shall impair the inherent right of individual or collective self-defence if an armed attack occurs against a Member of the United Nations, until the Security Council has taken the measures necessary to maintain international peace and security. Measures taken by Members in the exercise of this right of self-defence shall be immediately reported to the Security Council and shall not in any way affect the authority and responsibility of the Security Council under the present Charter to take at any time such action as it deems necessary in order to maintain or restore international peace and security.

REGIONAL ARRANGEMENTS

Article 52

1. Nothing in the present Charter precludes the existence of regional arrangements or agencies for dealing with such matters relating to the maintenance of international peace and security as are appropriate for regional action, provided that such arrangements or agencies and their activities are consistent with the Purposes and Principles of the United Nations.

2. The Members of the United Nations entering into such arrangements or constituting such agencies shall make every effort to achieve pacific settlement of local disputes through such regional arrangements or by such regional agencies before referring them to the Security Council.

3. The Security Council shall encourage the development of pacific settlement of local disputes through such regional arrangements or by such regional agencies either on the initiative of the States concerned or by references from the Security Council.

4. This Article in no way impairs the application of Articles 34 and 35.

Article 53

1. The Security Council shall, where appropriate, utilize such regional arrangements or agencies for enforcement action under its authority. But no enforcement action shall be taken under regional arrangements or by regional agencies without the authorization of the Security Council, with the exception of measures against an enemy State, as defined in paragraph 2 of this Article, provided for pursuant to Article 107 or in regional arrangements directed against renewal of aggressive policy on the part of any such State, until such time as the Organization may, on request of the Governments concerned, be charged with the responsibility for preventing further aggression by such a State.

2. The term "enemy State" as used in paragraph 1 of this Article applies to any State which during the Second World War has been an enemy of any signatory of the present Charter.

Article 54

The Security Council shall at all times be kept fully informed of activities undertaken or in contemplation under regional arrangements or by regional agencies for the maintenance of international peace and security.

CHAPTER IX

INTERNATIONAL ECONOMIC AND SOCIAL CO-OPERATION

Article 55

With a view to the creation of conditions of stability and well-being which are necessary for peaceful and friendly relations among nations based on respect for the principle of equal rights and self-determination of peoples, the United Nations shall promote —

(*a*) higher standards of living, full employment, and conditions of economic and social progress and development ;

(*b*) solutions of international economic, social, health, and related problems ; and international cultural and educational co-operation ; and

(*c*) universal respect for, and observance of, human rights and fundamental freedoms for all without distinction as to race, sex, language, or religion.

Article 56

All Members pledge themselves to take joint and separate action in co-operation with the Organization for the achievement of the purposes set forth in Article 55.

Article 57

1. The various specialized agencies, established by inter governmental agreement and having wide international responsibilities, as defined in their basic instruments, in economic, social, cultural, educational, health, and related fields, shall be brought into relationship with the United Nations in accordance with the provisions of Article 63.
2. Such agencies thus brought into relationship with the United Nations are hereinafter referred to as specialized agencies.

Article 58

The Organization shall make recommendations for the co-ordination of the policies and activities of the specialized agencies.

Article 59

The Organization shall, where appropriate, initiate negotiations among the States concerned for the creation of any new specialized agencies required for the accomplishment of the purposes set forth in Article 55.

Article 60

Responsibility for the discharge of the functions of the Organization set forth in this Chapter shall be vested in the General Assembly and, under the authority of the General Assembly, in the Economic and Social Council, which shall have for this purpose the powers set forth in Chapter X.

CHAPTER X

THE ECONOMIC AND SOCIAL COUNCIL

Composition

Article 61

1. The Economic and Social Council shall consist of eighteen Members of the United Nations elected by the General Assembly.
2. Subject to the provisions of paragraph 3, six members of the Economic and Social Council shall be elected each year for a term of three years. A retiring member shall be eligible for immediate re-election.
3. At the first election, eighteen members of the Economic and Social Council shall be chosen. The term of office of six members so chosen shall expire at the end of one year, and of six other members at the end of two years, in accordance with arrangements made by the General Assembly.
4. Each member of the Economic and Social Council shall have one representative.

Functions and Powers

Article 62

1. The Economic and Social Council may make or initiate studies and reports with respect to international economic, social, cultural, educational, health, and related matters and may make recommendations with respect to any such matters to the General Assembly, to the Members of the United Nations, and to the specialized agencies concerned.
2. It may make recommendations for the purpose of promoting respect for, and observance of, human rights and fundamental freedoms for all.
3. It may prepare draft conventions for submission to the General Assembly, with respect to matters falling within its competence.
4. It may call, in accordance with the rules prescribed by the United Nations, international conferences on matters falling within its competence.

Article 63

1. The Economic and Social Council may enter into agreements with any of the agencies referred to in Article 57, defining the terms on which the agency concerned shall be brought into relationship with the United Nations. Such agreements shall be subject to approval by the General Assembly.

2. It may co-ordinate the activities of the specialized agencies through consultation with and recommendations to such agencies and through recommendations to the General Assembly and to the Members of the United Nations.

Article 64

1. The Economic and Social Council may take appropriate steps to obtain regular reports from the specialized agencies. It may make arrangements with the Members of the United Nations and with the specialized agencies to obtain reports on the steps taken to give effect to its own recommendations and to recommendations on matters falling within its competence made by the General Assembly.

2. It may communicate its observations on these reports to the General Assembly.

Article 65

The Economic and Social Council may furnish information to the Security Council and shall assist the Security Council upon its request.

Article 66

1. The Economic and Social Council shall perform such functions as fall within its competence in connection with the carrying out of the recommendations of the General Assembly.

2. It may, with the approval of the General Assembly, perform services at the request of Members of the United Nations and at the request of specialized agencies.

3. It shall perform such other functions as are specified elsewhere in the present Charter or as may be assigned to it by the General Assembly.

Voting

Article 67

1. Each Member of the Economic and Social Council shall have one vote.

2. Decisions of the Economic and Social Council shall be made by a majority of the members present and voting.

Procedure

Article 68

The Economic and Social Council shall set up commissions in economic and social fields and for the promotion of human rights, and such other commissions as may be required for the performance of its functions.

Article 69

The Economic and Social Council shall invite any Member of the United Nations to participate, without vote, in its deliberations on any matter of particular concern to that Member.

Article 70

The Economic and Social Council may make arrangements for representatives of the specialized agencies to participate, without vote, in its deliberations and in those of the commissions established by it, and for its representatives to participate in the deliberations of the specialized agencies.

Article 71

The Economic and Social Council may make suitable arrangements for consultation with non-governmental organizations which are concerned with matters within its competence. Such arrangements may be made with international organizations and, where appropriate, with national organizations after consultation with the Member of the United Nations concerned.

Article 72

1. The Economic and Social Council shall adopt its own rules of procedure, including the method of selecting its President.

2. The Economic and Social Council shall meet as required in accordance with its rules, which shall include provision for the convening of meetings on the request of a majority of its members.

CHAPTER XI

DECLARATION REGARDING NON-SELF-GOVERNING TERRITORIES

Article 73

Members of the United Nations which have or assume responsibilities for the administration of territories whose peoples have not yet attained a full measure of self-government recognize the principle that the interests of the inhabitants of these territories are paramount, and accept as a sacred trust the obligation to promote to the utmost, within the system of international peace and security established by the present Charter, the well-being of the inhabitants of these territories, and, to this end —

(a) to ensure, with due respect for the culture of the peoples concerned, their political, economic, social, and educational advancement, their just treatment, and their protection against abuses ;

(b) to develop self-government, to take due account of the political aspirations of the peoples, and to assist them in the progressive development in their free political institutions, according to the particular circumstances of each territory and its peoples and their varying stages of advancement ;

(c) to further international peace and security ;

(d) to promote constructive measures of development, to encourage research, and to co-operate with one another and, when and where appropriate, with specialized international bodies with a view to the practical achievement of the social, economic, and scientific purposes set forth in this Article ; and

(e) to transmit regularly to the Secretary-General for information purposes, subject to such limitation as security and constitutional considerations may require, statistical and other information of a technical nature relating to economic, social, and educational conditions in the territories for which they are respectively responsible other than those territories to which Chapters XII and XIII apply.

Article 74

Members of the United Nations also agree that their policy in respect of the territories to which this Chapter applies, no less than in respect of their metropolitan areas, must be based on the general principle of good-neighbourliness, due account being taken of the interests and well-being of the rest of the world, in social, economic, and commercial matters.

CHAPTER XII

INTERNATIONAL TRUSTEESHIP SYSTEM

Article 75

The United Nations shall establish under its authority an international trusteeship system for the administration and supervision of such territories as may be placed thereunder by subsequent individual agreements. These territories are hereinafter referred to as trust territories.

Article 76

The basic objectives of the trusteeship system, in accordance with the Purposes of the United Nations laid down in Article 1 of the present Charter, shall be —

(a) to further international peace and security ;

(b) to promote the political, economic, social and educational advancement of the inhabitants of the trust territories, and their progressive development towards self-government or independence as may be appropriate to the particular circumstances of each territory and its peoples and the freely expressed wishes of the peoples concerned and as may be provided by the terms of each trusteeship agreement ;

(c) to encourage respect for human rights and for fundamental freedoms for all without distinction as to race, sex, language or religion, and to encourage recognition of the interdependence of the peoples of the world ; and

(d) to ensure equal treatment in social, economic and commercial matters for all Members of the United Nations and their nationals, and also equal treatment for the latter in the administration of justice, without prejudice to the attainment of the foregoing objectives and subject to the provisions of Article 80.

Article 77

1. The trusteeship system shall apply to such territories in the following categories as may be placed thereunder by means of trusteeship agreements —

(a) territories now held under mandate ;

(b) territories which may be detached from enemy States as a result of the Second World War ; and

(c) territories voluntarily placed under the system by States responsible for their administration.

2. It will be a matter for subsequent agreement as to which territories in the foregoing categories will be brought under the trusteeship system and upon what terms.

Article 78

The trusteeship system shall not apply to territories which have become Members of the United Nations, relationship among which shall be based on respect for the principle of sovereign equality.

Article 79

The terms of trusteeship for each territory to be placed under the trusteeship system, including any alteration or amendment, shall be agreed upon by the States directly concerned, including the mandatory Power in the case of territories held under mandate by a Member of the United Nations, and shall be approved as provided for in Articles 83 and 85.

Article 80

1. Except as may be agreed upon in individual trusteeship agreements, made under Articles 77, 79 and 81, placing each territory under the trusteeship system, and until such agreements have been concluded, nothing in this Chapter shall be construed in or of itself to alter in any manner the rights whatsoever of any States or any peoples or the terms of existing international instruments to which Members of the United Nations may respectively be parties.

2. Paragraph 1 of this Article shall not be interpreted as giving grounds for delay or postponement of the negotiation and conclusion of agreements for placing mandated and other territories under the trusteeship system as provided for in Article 77.

Article 81

The trusteeship agreement shall in each case include the terms under which the trust territory will be administered and designate the authority which will exercise the administration of the trust territory. Such authority, hereinafter called the administering authority, may be one or more States or the Organizations itself.

Article 82

There may be designated, in any trusteeship agreement, a strategic area or areas which may include part or all of the trust territory to which the agreement applies, without prejudice to any special agreement or agreements made under Article 43.

Article 83

1. All functions of the United Nations relating to strategic areas, including the approval of the terms of the trusteeship agreements and of their alteration or amendment, shall be exercised by the Security Council.

2. The basic objectives set forth in Article 76 shall be applicable to the people of each strategic area.

3. The Security Council shall, subject to the provisions of the trusteeship agreements and without prejudice to security considerations, avail itself of the assistance of the Trusteeship Council to perform those functions of the United Nations under the trusteeship system relating to political, economic, social and educational matters in the strategic areas.

Article 84

It shall be the duty of the administering authority to ensure that the trust territory shall play its part in the maintenance of international peace and security. To this end the administering authority may make use of volunteer forces, facilities and assistance from the trust territory in carrying out the obligations towards the Security Council undertaken in this regard by the administering authority, as well as for local defence and the maintenance of law and order within the trust territory.

Article 85

1. The functions of the United Nations with regard to trusteeship agreements for all areas not designated as strategic, including the approval of the terms of the trusteeship agreements and of their alteration or amendment, shall be exercised by the General Assembly.

2. The Trusteeship Council, operating under the authority of the General Assembly, shall assist the General Assembly in carrying out these functions.

CHAPTER XIII

THE TRUSTEESHIP COUNCIL

Composition

Article 86

1. The Trusteeship Council shall consist of the following Members of the United Nations —

(a) those Members administering trust territories ;

(b) such of those Members mentioned by name in Article 23 as are not administering trust territories ; and

(c) as many other Members elected for three-year terms by the General Assembly as may be necessary to ensure that the total number of members of the Trusteeship Council is equally divided between those Members of the United Nations which administer trust territories and those which do not.

2. Each member of the Trusteeship Council shall designate one specially qualified person to represent it therein.

Functions and Powers   Article 87

The General Assembly and, under its authority, the Trusteeship Council, in carrying out their functions, may —

(a) consider reports submitted by the administering authority ;

(b) accept petitions and examine them in consultation with the administering authority ;

(c) provide for periodic visits to the respective trust territories at times agreed upon with the administering authority ; and

(d) take these and other actions in conformity with the terms of the trusteeship agreements.

Article 88

The Trusteeship Council shall formulate a questionnaire on the political, economic, social, and educational advancement of the inhabitants of each trust territory, and the administering authority for each trust territory within the competence of the General Assembly shall make an annual report to the General Assembly upon the basis of such questionnaire.

Voting

Article 89

1. Each member of the Trusteeship Council shall have one vote.

2. Decisions of the Trusteeship Council shall be made by a majority of the members present and voting.

Procedure

Article 90

1. The Trusteeship Council shall adopt its own rules of procedure, including the method of selecting its President.

2. The Trusteeship Council shall meet as required in accordance with its rules, which shall include provision for the convening of meetings on the request of a majority of its members.

Article 91

The Trusteeship Council shall, when appropriate, avail itself of the assistance of the Economic and Social Council and of the specialized agencies in regard to matters with which they are respectively concerned.

CHAPTER XIV

THE INTERNATIONAL COURT OF JUSTICE

Article 92

The International Court of Justice shall be the principal judicial organ of the United Nations. It shall function in accordance with the annexed Statute, which is based upon the Statute of the Permanent Court of International Justice and forms an integral part of the present Charter.

Article 93

1. All Members of the United Nations are, *ipso facto*, parties to the Statute of the International Court of Justice.

2. A State which is not a Member of the United Nations may become a party to the Statute of the International Court of Justice on conditions to be determined in each case by the General Assembly upon the recommendation of the Security Council.

Article 94

1. Each Member of the United Nations undertakes to comply with the decision of the International Court of Justice in any case to which it is a party.

2. If any party to a case fails to perform the obligations incumbent upon it under a judgement rendered by the Court, the other party may have recourse to the Security Council, which may, if it deems necessary, make recommendations or decide upon measures to be taken to give effect to the judgement.

Article 95

Nothing in the present Charter shall prevent Members of the United Nations from entrusting the solution of their differences to other tribunals by virtue of agreements already in existence or which may be concluded in the future.

Article 96

1. The General Assembly or the Security Council may request the International Court of Justice to give an advisory opinion on any legal question.

2. Other organs of the United Nations and specialized agencies, which may at any time be so authorized by the General Assembly, may also request advisory opinions of the Court on legal questions arising within the scope of their activities.

CHAPTER XV

THE SECRETARIAT

Article 97

The Secretariat shall comprise a Secretary-General and such staff as the Organization may require. The Secretary-General shall be appointed by the General Assembly upon the recommendation of the Security Council. He shall be the chief administrative officer of the Organization.

Article 98

The Secretary-General shall act in that capacity in all meetings of the General Assembly, of the Security Council, of the Economic and Social Council, and of the Trusteeship Council, and shall perform such other functions as are entrusted to him by these organs. The Secretary-General shall make an annual report to the General Assembly on the work of the Organization.

Article 99

The Secretary-General may bring to the attention of the Security Council any matter which in his opinion may threaten the maintenance of international peace and security.

Article 100

1. In the performance of their duties the Secretary-General and the staff shall not seek or receive instructions from any Government or from any other authority external to the Organization. They shall refrain from any action which might reflect on their position as international officials responsible only to the Organization.

2. Each Member of the United Nations undertakes to respect the exclusively international character of the responsibilities of the Secretary-General and the staff and not to seek to influence them in the discharge of their responsibilities.

Article 101

1. The staff shall be appointed by the Secretary-General under regulations established by the General Assembly.

2. Appropriate staffs shall be permanently assigned to the Economic and Social Council, the Trusteeship Council, and, as required, to other organs of the United Nations. These staffs shall form a part of the Secretariat.

3. The paramount consideration in the employment of the staff and in the determination of the conditions of service shall be the necessity of securing the highest standards of efficiency, competence, and integrity. Due regard shall be paid to the importance of recruiting the staff on as wide a geographical basis as possible.

CHAPTER XVI

MISCELLANEOUS PROVISIONS

Article 102

1. Every treaty and every international agreement entered into by any Member of the United Nations after the present Charter comes into force shall as soon as possible be registered with the Secretariat and published by it.

2. No party to any such treaty or international agreement which has not been registered in accordance with the provisions of paragraph 1 of this Article may invoke that treaty or agreement before any organ of the United Nations.

Article 103

In the event of a conflict between the obligations of the Members of the United Nations under the present Charter and their obligations under any other international agreement, their obligations under the present Charter shall prevail.

Article 104

The Organization shall enjoy in the territory of each of its Members such legal capacity as may be necessary for the exercise of its functions and the fulfilment of its purposes.

Article 105

1. The Organization shall enjoy in the territory of each of its Members such privileges and immunities as are necessary for the fulfilment of its purposes.

2. Representatives of the Members of the United Nations and officials of the Organization shall similarly enjoy such privileges and immunities as are necessary for the independent exercise of their functions in connection with the Organization.

3. The General Assembly may make recommendations with a view to determining the details of the application of paragraphs 1 and 2 of this Article or may propose conventions to the Members of the United Nations for this purpose.

CHAPTER XVII

TRANSITIONAL SECURITY ARRANGEMENTS

Article 106

Pending the coming into force of such special agreements referred to in Article 43 as in the opinion of the Security Council enable it to begin the exercise of its responsibilities under Article 42, the parties to the Four-Nation Declaration, signed at Moscow, 30th October 1943, and France shall, in accordance with the provisions of paragraph 5 of that Declaration, consult with one another and as occasion requires with other Members of the United Nations with a view to such joint action on behalf of the Organization as may be necessary for the purpose of maintaining international peace and security.

Article 107

Nothing in the present Charter shall invalidate or preclude action, in relation to any State which during the Second World War has been an enemy of any signatory to the present Charter, taken or authorized as a result of that war by the Governments having responsibility for such action.

CHAPTER XVIII

AMENDMENTS

Article 108

Amendments to the present Charter shall come into force for all Members of the United Nations when they have been adopted by a vote of two-thirds of the members of the General Assembly and ratified in accordance with their respective constitutional processes by two-thirds of the Members of the United Nations, including all the permanent members of the Security Council.

Article 109

1. A General Conference of the Members of the United Nations for the purpose of reviewing the present Charter may be held at a date and place to be fixed by a two-thirds vote of the members of the General Assembly and by a vote of any seven members of the Security Council. Each Member of the United Nations shall have one vote in the conference.

2. Any alteration of the present Charter recommended by a two-thirds vote of the conference shall take effect when ratified in accordance with their respective constitutional processes by two-thirds of the Members of the United Nations, including all the permanent members of the Security Council.

3. If such a conference has not been held before the tenth annual session of the General Assembly following the coming into force of the present Charter, the proposal to call such a conference shall be placed on the agenda of that session of the General Assembly, and the conference shall be held if so decided by a majority vote of the members of the General Assembly and by a vote of any seven members of the Security Council.

CHAPTER XIX

RATIFICATION AND SIGNATURE

Article 110

1. The present Charter shall be ratified by the signatory States in accordance with their respective constitutional processes.

2. The ratifications shall be deposited with the Government of the United States of America, which shall notify all the signatory States of each deposit as well as the Secretary-General of the Organization when he has been appointed.

3. The present Charter shall come into force upon the deposit of ratifications by the Republic of China, France, the Union of Soviet Socialist Republics, the United Kingdom of Great Britain and Northern Ireland, and the United States of America, and by a majority of the other signatory States. A protocol of the ratifications deposited shall thereupon be drawn up by the Government of the United States of America which shall communicate copies thereof to all the signatory States.

4. The States signatory to the present Charter which ratify it after it has come into force will become original Members of the United Nations on the date of the deposit of their respective ratifications.

Article 111

The present Charter, of which the Chinese, French, Russian, English and Spanish texts are equally authentic, shall remain deposited in the archives of the Government of the United States of America. Duly certified copies thereof shall be transmitted by that Government to the Governments of the other signatory States.

IN FAITH WHEREOF the representatives of the Governments of the United Nations have signed the present Charter.

DONE at the city of San Francisco the twenty-sixth day of June, one thousand nine hundred and forty-five.

China
Union of Soviet Socialist Republics
United Kingdom
United States of America
France
Argentina
Australia
Belgium
Bolivia
Brazil
Byelorussian Soviet Socialist Republic
Canada
Chile
Colombia
Costa Rica
Cuba
Czechoslovakia
Denmark
Dominican Republic
Ecuador
Egypt
El Salvador
Ethiopia
Greece
Guatemala
Haiti
Honduras
India
Iran
Iraq
Lebanon
Liberia
Luxembourg
Mexico
Netherlands
New Zealand
Nicaragua
Norway
Panama
Paraguay
Peru
Philippine Commonwealth
Poland
Saudi Arabia
Syria
Turkey
Ukrainian Soviet Socialist Republic
Union of South Africa
Uruguay
Venezuela
Yugoslavia

STATUTE OF
THE INTERNATIONAL COURT OF JUSTICE

Article 1

THE INTERNATIONAL COURT OF JUSTICE established by the Charter of the United Nations as the principal judicial organ of the United Nations shall be constituted and shall function in accordance with the provisions of the present Statute.

CHAPTER I

ORGANIZATION OF THE COURT

Article 2

The Court shall be composed of a body of independent judges, elected regardless of their nationality from among persons of high moral character, who possess the qualifications required in their respective countries for appointment to the highest judicial offices, or are jurisconsults of recognized competence in international law.

Article 3

1. The Court shall consist of fifteen members, no two of whom may be nationals of the same State.

2. A person who for the purposes of membership in the Court could be regarded as a national of more than one State shall be deemed to be a national of the one in which he ordinarily exercises civil and political rights.

Article 4

1. The members of the Court shall be elected by the General Assembly and by the Security Council from a list of persons nominated by the national groups in the Permanent Court of Arbitration, in accordance with the following provisions.

2. In the case of Members of the United Nations not represented in the Permanent Court of Arbitration, candidates shall be nominated by national groups appointed for this purpose by their Governments under the same conditions as those prescribed for members of the Permanent Court of Arbitration by Article 44 of the Convention of The Hague of 1907 for the pacific settlement of international disputes.

3. The conditions under which a State which is a party to the present Statute but is not a Member of the United Nations may participate in electing the members of the Court shall, in the absence of a special agreement, be laid down by the General Assembly upon recommendation of the Security Council.

Article 5

1. At least three months before the date of the election, the Secretary-General of the United Nations shall address a written request to the members of the Permanent Court of Arbitration belonging to the States which are parties to the present Statute, and to the members of the national groups appointed under Article 4, paragraph 2, inviting them to undertake, within a given time, by national groups, the nomination of persons in a position to accept the duties of a member of the Court.

2. No group may nominate more than four persons, not more than two of whom shall be of their own nationality. In no case may the number of candidates nominated by a group be more than double the number of seats to be filled.

Article 6

Before making these nominations, each national group is recommended to consult its highest court of justice, its legal faculties and schools of law, and its national academies and national sections of international academies devoted to the study of law.

Article 7

1. The Secretary-General shall prepare a list in alphabetical order of all the persons thus nominated. Save as provided in Article 12, paragraph 2, these shall be the only persons eligible.

2. The Secretary-General shall submit this list to the General Assembly and to the Security Council.

Article 8

The General Assembly and the Security Council shall proceed independently of one another to elect the members of the Court.

Article 9

At every election, the electors shall bear in mind not only that the persons to be elected should individually possess the qualifications required, but also that in the body as a whole the representation of the main forms of civilization and of the principal legal systems of the world should be assured.

Article 10

1. Those candidates who obtain an absolute majority of votes in the General Assembly and in the Security Council shall be considered as elected.

2. Any vote of the Security Council, whether for the election of judges or for the appointment of members of the conference envisaged in Article 12, shall be taken without any distinction between permanent and non-permanent members of the Security Council.

3. In the event of more than one national of the same State obtaining an absolute majority of the votes both of the General Assembly and of the Security Council, the eldest of these only shall be considered as elected.

Article 11

If, after the first meeting held for the purpose of the election, one or more seats remain to be filled, a second and, if necessary, a third meeting shall take place.

Article 12

1. If, after the third meeting, one or more seats still remain unfilled, a joint conference consisting of six members, three appointed by the General Assembly and three by the Security Council, may be formed at any time at the request of either the General Assembly or the Security Council, for the purpose of choosing by the vote of an absolute majority one name for each seat still vacant, to submit to the General Assembly and the Security Council for their respective acceptance.

2. If the joint conference is unanimously agreed upon any person who fulfils the required conditions, he may be included in its list, even though he was not included in the list of nominations referred to in Article 7.

3. If the joint conference is satisfied that it will not be successful in procuring an election, those members of the Court who have already been elected shall, within a period to be fixed by the Security Council, proceed to fill the vacant seats by selection from among those candidates who have obtained votes either in the General Assembly or in the Security Council.

4. In the event of an equality of votes among the judges, the eldest judge shall have a casting vote.

Article 13

1. The members of the Court shall be elected for nine years and may be re-elected ; provided, however, that, of the judges elected at the first election, the terms of five judges shall expire at the end of three years, and the terms of five more judges shall expire at the end of six years.

2. The judges whose terms are to expire at the end of the above-mentioned initial periods of three and six years shall be chosen by lot to be drawn by the Secretary-General immediately after the first election has been completed.

3. The members of the Court shall continue to discharge their duties until their places have been filled. Though replaced, they shall finish any cases which they may have begun.

4. In the case of the resignation of a member of the Court, the resignation shall be addressed to the President of the Court for transmission to the Secretary-General. The last notification makes the place vacant.

Article 14

Vacancies shall be filled by the same method as that laid down for the first election, subject to the following provision : the Secretary-General shall, within one month of the occurrence of the vacancy, proceed to issue the invitations provided for in Article 5, and the date of the election shall be fixed by the Security Council.

Article 15

A member of the Court elected to replace a member whose term of office has not expired shall hold office for the remainder of his predecessor's term.

Article 16

1. No member of the Court may exercise any political or administrative function, or engage in any other occupation of a professional nature.
2. Any doubt on this point shall be settled by the decision of the Court.

Article 17

1. No member of the Court may act as agent, counsel, or advocate in any case.
2. No member may participate in the decision of any case in which he has previously taken part as agent, counsel, or advocate for one of the parties, or as a member of a national or international court, or of a commission of inquiry, or in any other capacity.
3. Any doubt on this point shall be settled by the decision of the Court.

Article 18

1. No member of the Court can be dismissed unless, in the unanimous opinion of the other members, he has ceased to fulfil the required conditions.
2. Formal notification thereof shall be made to the Secretary-General by the Registrar.
3. This notification makes the place vacant.

Article 19

The members of the Court, when engaged on the business of the Court, shall enjoy diplomatic privileges and immunities.

Article 20

Every member of the Court shall, before taking up his duties, make a solemn declaration in open court that he will exercise his powers impartially and conscientiously.

Article 21

1. The Court shall elect its President and Vice-President for three years ; they may be re-elected.
2. The Court shall appoint its Registrar and may provide for the appointment of such other officers as may be necessary.

Article 22

1. The seat of the Court shall be established at The Hague. This, however, shall not prevent the Court from sitting and exercising its functions elsewhere whenever the Court considers it desirable.
2. The President and the Registrar shall reside at the seat of the Court.

Article 23

1. The Court shall remain permanently in session, except during the judicial vacations, the dates and duration of which shall be fixed by the Court.
2. Members of the Court are entitled to periodic leave, the dates and duration of which shall be fixed by the Court, having in mind the distance between The Hague and the home of each judge.
3. Members of the Court shall be bound, unless they are on leave or prevented from attending by illness or other serious reasons duly explained to the President, to hold themselves permanently at the disposal of the Court.

Article 24

1. If, for some special reason, a member of the Court considers that he should not take part in the decision of a particular case, he shall so inform the President.

2. If the President considers that for some special reason one of the members of the Court should not sit in a particular case, he shall give him notice accordingly.

3. If in any such case the member of the Court and the President disagree, the matter shall be settled by the decision of the Court.

Article 25

1. The full Court shall sit except when it is expressly provided otherwise in the present Statute.

2. Subject to the condition that the number of judges available to constitute the Court is not thereby reduced below eleven, the Rules of the Court may provide for allowing one or more judges, according to circumstances and in rotation, to be dispensed from sitting.

3. A quorum of nine judges shall suffice to constitute the Court.

Article 26

1. The Court may from time to time form one or more chambers, composed of three or more judges as the Court may determine, for dealing with particular categories of cases ; for example, labour cases and cases relating to transit and communications.

2. The Court may at any time form a chamber for dealing with a particular case. The number of judges to constitute such a chamber shall be determined by the Court with the approval of the parties.

3. Cases shall be heard and determined by the chambers provided for in this Article if the parties so request.

Article 27

A judgement given by any of the chambers provided for in Articles 26 and 29 shall be considered as rendered by the Court.

Article 28

The chambers provided for in Articles 26 and 29 may, with the consent of the parties, sit and exercise their functions elsewhere than at The Hague.

Article 29

With a view to the speedy despatch of business, the Court shall form annually a chamber composed of five judges which, at the request of the parties, may hear and determine cases by summary procedure. In addition, two judges shall be selected for the purpose of replacing judges who find it impossible to sit.

Article 30

1. The Court shall frame rules for carrying out its functions. In particular, it shall lay down rules of procedure.

2. The Rules of the Court may provide for assessors to sit with the Court or with any of its chambers, without the right to vote.

Article 31

1. Judges of the nationality of each of the parties shall retain their right to sit in the case before the Court.

2. If the Court includes upon the Bench a judge of the nationality of one of the parties, any other party may choose a person to sit as judge. Such person shall be chosen preferably from among those persons who have been nominated as candidates as provided in Articles 4 and 5.

3. If the Court includes upon the Bench no judge of the nationality of the parties, each of these parties may proceed to choose a judge as provided in paragraph 2 of this Article.

4. The provisions of this Article shall apply to the case of Articles 26 and 29. In such cases, the President shall request one or, if necessary, two of the members of the Court forming the chamber to give place to the members of the Court of the nationality of the parties concerned, and, failing such, or if they are unable to be present, to the judges specially chosen by the parties.

5. Should there be several parties in the same interest, they shall, for the purpose of the preceding provisions, be reckoned as one party only. Any doubt upon this point shall be settled by the decision of the Court.

6. Judges chosen as laid down in paragraphs 2, 3 and 4 of this Article shall fulfil the conditions required by Articles 2, 17 (paragraph 2), 20, and 24 of the present Statute. They shall take part in the decision on terms of complete equality with their colleagues.

Article 32

1. Each member of the Court shall receive an annual salary.

2. The President shall receive a special annual allowance.

3. The Vice-President shall receive a special allowance for every day on which he acts as President.

4. The judges chosen under Article 31, other than members of the Court, shall receive compensation for each day on which they exercise their functions.

5. These salaries, allowances, and compensation shall be fixed by the General Assembly. They may not be decreased during the term of office.

6. The salary of the Registrar shall be fixed by the General Assembly on the proposal of the Court.

7. Regulations made by the General Assembly shall fix the conditions under which retirement pensions may be given to members of the Court and to the Registrar, and the conditions under which members of the Court and the Registrar shall have their travelling expenses refunded.

8. The above salaries, allowances, and compensation shall be free of all taxation.

Article 33

The expenses of the Court shall be borne by the United Nations in such a manner as shall be decided by the General Assembly.

CHAPTER II

COMPETENCE OF THE COURT

Article 34

1. Only States may be parties in cases before the Court.

2. The Court, subject to and in conformity with its Rules, may request of public international organizations information relevant to cases before it, and shall receive such information presented by such organizations on their own initiative.

3. Whenever the construction of the constituent instrument of a public international organization or of an international convention adopted thereunder is in question in a case before the Court, the Registrar shall so notify the public international organization concerned and shall communicate to it copies of all the written proceedings.

Article 35

1. The Court shall be open to the States parties to the present Statute.

2. The conditions under which the Court shall be open to other States shall, subject to the special provisions contained in treaties in force, be laid down by the Security Council, but in no case shall such conditions place the parties in a position of inequality before the Court.

3. When a State which is not a Member of the United Nations is a party to a case, the Court shall fix the amount which that party is to contribute towards the expenses of the Court. This provision shall not apply if such State is bearing a share of the expenses of the Court.

Article 36

1. The jurisdiction of the Court comprises all cases which the parties refer to it and all matters specially provided for in the Charter of the United Nations or in treaties and conventions in force.

2. The States parties to the present Statute may at any time declare that they recognize as compulsory, *ipso facto* and without special agreement, in relation to any other State accepting the same obligation, the jurisdiction of the Court in all legal disputes concerning —

(a) the interpretation of a treaty ;

(b) any question of international law ;

(c) the existence of any fact which, if established, would constitute a breach of an international obligation ;

(d) the nature or extent of the reparation to be made for the breach of an international obligation.

3. The declarations referred to above may be made unconditionally or on condition of reciprocity on the part of several or certain States, or for a certain time.

4. Such declarations shall be deposited with the Secretary-General of the United Nations, who shall transmit copies thereof to the parties to the Statute and to the Registrar of the Court.

5. Declarations made under Article 36 of the Statute of the Permanent Court of International Justice and which are still in force shall be deemed, as between the parties to the present Statute, to be acceptances of the compulsory jurisdiction of the International Court of Justice for the period which they still have to run and in accordance with their terms.

6. In the event of a dispute as to whether the Court has jurisdiction, the matter shall be settled by the decision of the Court.

Article 37

Whenever a treaty or convention in force provides for reference of a matter to a tribunal to have been instituted by the League of Nations, or to the Permanent Court of International Justice, the matter shall, as between the parties to the present Statute, be referred to the International Court of Justice.

Article 38

1. The Court, whose function is to decide in accordance with international law such disputes as are submitted to it, shall apply —

(a) international conventions, whether general or particular, establishing rules expressly recognized by the contesting States ;

(b) international custom, as evidence of a general practice accepted as law ;

(c) the general principles of law recognized by civilized nations ;

(d) subject to the provisions of Article 59, judicial decisions and the teachings of the most highly qualified publicists of the various nations, as subsidiary means for the determination of rules of law.

2. This provision shall not prejudice the power of the Court to decide a case *ex aequo et bono*, if the parties agree thereto.

CHAPTER III

PROCEDURE

Article 39

1. The official languages of the Court shall be French and English. If the parties agree that the case shall be conducted in French, the judgement shall be delivered in French. If the parties agree that the case shall be conducted in English, the judgement shall be delivered in English.

2. In the absence of an agreement as to which language shall be employed, each party may, in the pleadings, use the language which it prefers ; the decision of the Court shall be given in French and English. In this case the Court shall at the same time determine which of the two texts shall be considered as authoritative.

3. The Court shall, at the request of any party, authorize a language other than French or English to be used by that party.

Article 40

1. Cases are brought before the Court, as the case may be, either by the notification of the special agreement or by a written application addressed to the Registrar. In either case the subject of the dispute and the parties shall be indicated.

2. The Registrar shall forthwith communicate the application to all concerned.

3. He shall also notify the Members of the United Nations through the Secretary-General, and also any other States entitled to appear before the Court.

Article 41

1. The Court shall have the power to indicate, if it considers that circumstances so require, any provisional measures which ought to be taken to preserve the respective rights of either party.

2. Pending the final decision, notice of the measures suggested shall forthwith be given to the parties and to the Security Council.

Article 42

1. The parties shall be represented by agents.

2. They may have the assistance of counsel or advocates before the Court.

3. The agents, counsel and advocates of parties before the Court shall enjoy the privileges and immunities necessary to the independent exercise of their duties.

Article 43

1. The procedure shall consist of two parts : written and oral.

2. The written proceedings shall consist of the communication to the Court and to the parties of memorials, counter-memorials and, if necessary, replies ; also all papers and documents in support.

3. These communications shall be made through the Registrar, in the order and within the time fixed by the Court.

4. A certified copy of every document produced by one party shall be communicated to the other party.

5. The oral proceedings shall consist of the hearing by the Court of witnesses, experts, agents, counsel, and advocates.

Article 44

1. For the service of all notices upon persons other than the agents, counsel, and advocates, the Court shall apply direct to the Government of the State upon whose territory the notice has to be served.

2. The same provision shall apply whenever steps are to be taken to procure evidence on the spot.

Article 45

The hearing shall be under the control of the President or, if he is unable to preside, of the Vice-President ; if neither is able to preside, the senior judge present shall preside.

Article 46

The hearing in Court shall be public, unless the Court shall decide otherwise, or unless the parties demand that the public be not admitted.

Article 47

1. Minutes shall be made at each hearing and signed by the Registrar and the President.

2. These minutes alone shall be authentic.

Article 48

The Court shall make orders for the conduct of the case, shall decide the form and time in which each party must conclude its arguments, and make all arrangements connected with the taking of evidence.

Article 49

The Court may, even before the hearing begins, call upon the agents to produce any document or to supply any explanations. Formal note shall be taken of any refusal.

Article 50

The Court may, at any time, entrust any individual, body, bureau, commission, or other organization that it may select, with the task of carrying out an inquiry or giving an expert opinion.

Article 51

During the hearing any relevant questions are to be put to the witnesses and experts under the conditions laid down by the Court in the rules of procedure referred to in Article 30.

Article 52

After the Court has received the proofs and evidence within the time specified for the purpose, it may refuse to accept any further oral or written evidence that one party may desire to present unless the other side consents.

Article 53

1. Whenever one of the parties does not appear before the Court, or fails to defend its case, the other party may call upon the Court to decide in favour of its claim.
2. The Court must, before doing so, satisfy itself, not only that it has jurisdiction in accordance with Articles 36 and 37, but also that the claim is well founded in fact and law.

Article 54

1. When, subject to the control of the Court, the agents, counsel, and advocates have completed their presentation of the case, the President shall declare the hearing closed.
2. The Court shall withdraw to consider the judgement.
3. The deliberations of the Court shall take place in private and remain secret.

Article 55

1. All questions shall be decided by a majority of the judges present.
2. In the event of an equality of votes, the President or the judge who acts in his place shall have a casting vote.

Article 56

1. The judgement shall state the reasons on which it is based.
2. It shall contain the names of the judges who have taken part in the decision.

Article 57

If the judgement does not represent in whole or in part the unanimous opinion of the judges, any judge shall be entitled to deliver a separate opinion.

Article 58

The judgement shall be signed by the President and by the Registrar. It shall be read in open court, due notice having been given to the agents.

Article 59

The decision of the Court has no binding force except between the parties and in respect of that particular case.

Article 60

The judgement is final and without appeal. In the event of dispute as to the meaning or scope of the judgement, the Court shall construe it upon the request of any party.

Article 61

1. An application for revision of a judgement may be made only when it is based upon the discovery of some fact of such a nature as to be a decisive factor, which fact was, when the judgement was given, unknown to the Court and also to the party claiming revision, always provided that such ignorance was not due to negligence.
2. The proceedings for revision shall be opened by a judgement of the Court expressly recording the existence of the new fact, recognizing that it has such a character as to lay the case open to revision, and declaring the application admissible on this ground.
3. The Court may require previous compliance with the terms of the judgement before it admits proceedings in revision.
4. The application for revision must be made at latest within six months of the discovery of the new fact.
5. No application for revision may be made after the lapse of ten years from the date of the judgement.

Article 62

1. Should a State consider that it has an interest of a legal nature which may be affected by the decision in the case, it may submit a request to the Court to be permitted to intervene.

2. It shall be for the Court to decide upon this request.

Article 63

1. Whenever the construction of a convention to which States other than those concerned in the case are parties is in question, the Registrar shall notify all such States forthwith.

2. Every State so notified has the right to intervene in the proceedings ; but if it uses this right, the construction given by the judgement will be equally binding upon it.

Article 64

Unless otherwise decided by the Court, each party shall bear its own costs.

CHAPTER IV

ADVISORY OPINIONS

Article 65

1. The Court may give an advisory opinion on any legal question at the request of whatever body may be authorized by or in accordance with the Charter of the United Nations to make such a request.

2. Questions upon which the advisory opinion of the Court is asked shall be laid before the Court by means of a written request containing an exact statement of the question upon which an opinion is required, and accompanied by all documents likely to throw light upon the question.

Article 66

1. The Registrar shall forthwith give notice of the request for an advisory opinion to all States entitled to appear before the Court.

2. The Registrar shall also, by means of a special and direct communication, notify any State entitled to appear before the Court or international organization considered by the Court, or, should it not be sitting, by the President, as likely to be able to furnish information on the question, that the Court will be prepared to receive, within a time limit to be fixed by the President, written statements, or to hear, at a public sitting to be held for the purpose, oral statements relating to the question.

3. Should any such State entitled to appear before the Court have failed to receive the special communication referred to in paragraph 2 of this Article, such State may express a desire to submit a written statement or to be heard ; and the Court will decide.

4. States and organizations having presented written or oral statements or both shall be permitted to comment on the statements made by other States or organizations in the form, to the extent, and within the time limits which the Court, or, should it not be sitting, the President, shall decide in each particular case. Accordingly, the Registrar shall in due time communicate any such written statements to States and organizations having submitted similar statements.

Article 67

The Court shall deliver its advisory opinions in open court, notice having been given to the Secretary-General and to the representatives of Members of the United Nations, of other States and of international organizations immediately concerned.

Article 68

In the exercise of its advisory functions the Court shall further be guided by the provisions of the present Statute which apply in contentious cases to the extent to which it recognizes them to be applicable.

CHAPTER V

AMENDMENT

Article 69

Amendments to the present Statute shall be effected by the same procedure as is provided by the Charter of the United Nations for amendments to that Charter, subject however to any provisions which the General Assembly upon recommendation of the Security Council may adopt concerning the participation of States which are parties to the present Statute but are not Members of the United Nations.

Article 70

The Court shall have power to propose such amendments to the present Statute as it may deem necessary, through written communications to the Secretary-General, for consideration in conformity with the provisions of Article 69.

SHORT BIBLIOGRAPHY

Atomic Energy, Its International Implications. Chatham House Study Group. London, Royal Institute of International Affairs, 1948.

Bentwich, Norman. *From Geneva to San Francisco. An Account of the International Organization of the New Order*. London, Victor Gollancz Ltd., 1946.

Brierly, J. L. *The Covenant and the Charter*. London, Cambridge University Press, 1947.

Burton, Margaret E. *The Assembly of the League of Nations*. Chicago, University of Chicago Press, 1941.

Conwell-Evans, T. P. *The League Council in Action*. London, Oxford University Press, 1939.

Davis, Harriet Eager, ed. *Pioneers in World Order: An American Appraisal of the League of Nations*. New York, Columbia University Press, 1944.

Evatt, H. V. *The United Nations*. Cambridge, Mass., Harvard University Press, 1948.

Finer, Herman. *The United Nations Social and Economic Council*. Boston, World Peace Foundation, 1946.

Gathorne-Hardy, Geoffrey M. *A Short History of International Affairs, 1920 to 1939*. Third revised edition to the outbreak of war. London, Royal Institute of International Affairs, 1942.

Goodrich, L. M. *and* Hambro, E. *Charter of the United Nations: Commentary and Documents*. Boston, World Peace Foundation, 1946.

Great Britain. Foreign Office. *Commentary on the Charter of the United Nations*. London, H.M.S.O., 1945.

Hawtrey, R. S. *Bretton Woods: For Better or Worse*. London, Longmans, 1946.

Hill, Martin. *The Economic and Financial Organization of the League of Nations, A Survey of Twentyfive Years' Experience*. Washington, Carnegie Endowment for International Peace, 1945.

Huxley, Julian. *U.N.E.S.C.O.: Its Purpose and Its Philosophy*. Washington, Public Affairs Press, 1947.

Hudson, Manley O. *The Permanent Court of International Justice, 1920-1942: A Treatise*. New York, Macmillan, 1943.

International Sanctions. Report by a group of members of the Royal Institute of International Affairs. London, Oxford University Press, 1938.

The International Secretariat of the Future: Lessons from Experience of a Group of Former Officials of the League of Nations. London, Royal Institute of International Affairs, 1944.

Jenks, C. Wilfred. *The Headquarters of International Institutions: A Study of their Location and Status*. London, Royal Institute of International Affairs, 1945.

229

I

Kelsen, Hans. *Law and Peace in International Relations*. Cambridge, Harvard University Press, 1942.

Kelsen, Hans. *Peace Through Law*. Chapel Hill, University of North Carolina Press, 1944.

Koo, Wellington, Jr. *Voting Procedures in International Political Organizations*. New York, Columbia University Press, 1947.

Kopelmanas, Lazare. *L'Organisation des Nations Unies*. I: *L'Organisation constitutionelle des Nations Unies*. Paris, Sirey, 1947.

League of Nations. *The League Hands Over*. London, Allen & Unwin, 1946.

Lauterpacht, Hersch. *An International Bill of the Rights of Man*. New York, Columbia University Press, 1945.

Masters, Ruth D. *Handbook of International Organisations in the Americas*. New York, Carnegie Endowment for International Peace, 1945.

Mitrany, David. *A Working Peace System: An Argument for the Functional Development of International Organization*. 4th edition. London, National Peace Council, 1946.

Moore, Bernard. *The United Nations Second Assembly, New York* 1947. London, United Nations Association, 1948.

Morgenthau, Hans T., ed. *Peace, Security and the United Nations*. Chicago, University of Chicago Press, 1946.

Murray, Gilbert. *From the League to U.N.* London, Oxford University Press, 1948.

Oppenheim, L. *International Law*. (6th edition, ed. Lauterpacht, H.) London, Longmans, 1947.

Patterson, E. M. ed. " *Making the United Nations Work*," The American Academy of Political and Social Science, *The Annals*, CCXLVI (July, 1946).

Potter, Pitman B. *An Introduction to the Study of International Organization*. New York, Appleton (5th ed. rev.), 1948.

Price, John. *The International Labour Movement*. Issued under the auspices of the Royal Institute of International Affairs. New York and Toronto, Oxford University Press, 1945.

Purves, Chester. *The Internal Administration of an International Secretariat: Some Notes Based on the Experience of the League of Nations*. London, Royal Institute of International Affairs, 1946.

Ranshofen-Wertheimer, Egon F. *The International Secretariat: A Great Experiment in International Administration*. Washington, Carnegie Endowment for International Peace, 1945.

Royal Institute of International Affairs. *United Nations Documents, 1941-1945*. London, 1946.

Schücking, W. and Wehberg, H. *Die Satzung des Völkerbundes*. Berlin, F. Vahlen, 1931. (3rd ed.).

The United States and Non-Self-Governing Territories. Washington, Department of State Publication 2812, United States—United Nations Information Series 18, 1947.

Webster, Sir Charles. " The United Nations Reviewed," *International Conciliation*, No. 443 (September 1948).

White, Freda. *United Nations, the First Assembly, London, 1946.* London, United Nations Association, 1946.

Yearbook of the United Nations, 1946-47. Lake Success, Department of Public Information, 1947.

Zimmern, Alfred. *The League of Nations and the Rule of Law, 1918-1935.* London, Macmillan, 1939.

INDEX

ABBREVIATIONS : ECOSOC, Economic and Social Council; FAO, Food and Agriculture Organization; GA, General Assembly; ICAO, International Civil Aviation Organization; ILO, International Labour Organization; IMCO, Intergovernmental Maritime Consultative Organization; IRO, International Refugee Organization; ITO, International Trade Organization; ITU, International Telecommunications Union; SC, Security Council; TC, Trusteeship Council; UN, United Nations; UNESCO, United Nations Educational, Scientific and Cultural Organization; UNO, United Nations Organization; UNRRA, United Nations Relief and Rehabilitation Administration; UPU, Universal Postal Union; WHO, World Health Organization; WMO, World Meteorological Organization.

For Product Safety Concerns and Information please contact our EU
representative GPSR@taylorandfrancis.com
Taylor & Francis Verlag GmbH, Kaufingerstraße 24, 80331 München, Germany

9 7 8 1 0 3 2 7 6 1 6 7 1